Hidden Self-Harm

of related interest

Self-Mutilation and Art Therapy
Violent Creation
Diana Milia
ISBN 1 85302 683 2

Arts Therapies and Clients with Eating Disorders
Fragile Board
Edited by Ditty Dokter
ISBN 1 85302 256 X

In and Out of Anorexia
The Story of the Client, the Therapist
and the Process of Recovery
Tammie Ronen and Ayelet
ISBN 1 85302 990 4

Anorexics on Anorexia
Edited by Rosemary Shelley
ISBN 1 85302 471 6

A Systemic Treatment of Bulimia Nervosa
Women in Transition
Carole Kayrooz
ISBN 1 85302 918 1

Next Steps in Parenting the Child Who Hurts
Tykes and Teens
Caroline Archer
Adoption UK
ISBN 1 85302 802 9

Hidden Self-Harm

Narratives from Psychotherapy

Maggie Turp

Jessica Kingsley Publishers
London and Philadelphia

The author and the publisher gratefully acknowledge permission from the following journals to reprint passages of previously published material.
Chapter 2: 'The Many Faces of Self-Harm' in *Psychodynamic Practice, 8, 2, 2002*; Chapter 8: 'Acting, feeling and thinking: psychoanalytic psychotherapy with Tracey' in *European Journal of Psychotherapy, Counselling and Health, 5, 3, 2002*.
The above journals are published by Routledge, Taylor and Francis Ltd;
http://www.tandf.co.uk/journals/routledge/13642537.html

First published in the United Kingdom in 2003
by Jessica Kingsley Publishers Ltd
116 Pentonville Road
London N1 9JB, England
and
325 Chestnut Street
Philadelphia, PA 19106, USA
www.jkp.com

Library of Congress Cataloging-in-Publication Data
Turp, Maggie
  Hidden self-harm : narratives from psychotherapy / Maggie Turp.
    p. cm.
  Includes bibliographical references and index.
  ISBN 1-85302-901-7 (pbk : alk. paper)
  1. Self mutilation--Case studies. 2. Self-injurous behaviour--Case studies. 3. Psychotherapy--Case studies. I. Title.

RC552.S4 T87 2003
616.85'82--dc21   2002072697

British Library Cataloguing in Publication Data
A CIP catalogue record for this book is available from the British Library

ISBN 1 85302 901 7

Printed and Bound in Great Britain by
Athenaeum Press, Gateshead, Tyne and Wear

Contents

Acknowledgements 6

Dedication 7

1. Introduction 9

2. What Do We Mean by 'Self-Harm'? 23

3. The Capacity for Self-Care: Observations of Esther 39

4. Bodily Integrity and Psychic Skin: Observations of Esther 53

5. Themes and Theoretical Frameworks 67

6. Trauma and Dramatic Repetition: Working with Lorraine 79

7. The Skin in Question: Working with Ellen May 97

8. Acting, Feeling and Thinking: Working with Tracey 119

9. A Body in Pieces: Working with Peter 143

10. Self-Harm by Omission: Working with Kate 167

11. Reflections on Case Study Themes 187

12. The Self-Harming Individual and 'The System' 209

Bibliography 225

Subject Index 235

Author Index 237

Acknowledgements

My thanks go first to the clients and to the observed infants and their families, without whom no book would have been possible, and to the CASSEL Centre in the London Borough of Lewisham. The clinical and observation work described took place over a period of more than ten years and involved several supervisors. Many thanks to Ian Brown, Alexander Fanning, Janet Fitzsimmons, Jennifer Marsh, Asha Phillips and Val Richards for their encouragement and support.

Other colleagues have been informally involved in the book, through conversations and ideas sparked by conversations. I will single out for special mention Julia Buckroyd, Roz Carroll, Nicola Diamond, Miera Likierman, Del Loewenthal, Ann May, Jane Ryan and Cathy Seigal. My thanks go also to members of my 'psychosomatic issues' supervision groups – I have learned at least as much from them as they have learned from me. Correspondence with Anne Crump, a counsellor and member of the National Self-Harm Network, gave me the idea for the title *Hidden Self-Harm* and I thank her for her thoughtful comments.

Jane Sufian, Senior Information and Policy Adviser at 'First Key', read the whole of the book in draft and helped particularly with the sections on 'looked-after' children. Conversations with Nicola Hope, who worked for many years as a sister in accident and emergency, and Keith Sewell, a counsellor with a background in mental health nursing, helped me to gain insight into a nursing perspective on self-harm. My husband, Phil Leask, played the part of 'intelligent lay reader' and made many helpful suggestions.

I thank you all for your friendship and your enthusiasm for the project.

For the clients, with gratitude and respect

'The truth is rarely pure and never simple'

— Oscar Wilde

1

Introduction

For many people, the term 'self-harm' conjures up an image of violent self-cutting, self-scalding or overdosing. These 'high visibility' manifestations of self-harm are those most often highlighted in the literature, both popular and professional. In this book, I suggest that this characterisation of self-harm is too narrow in its scope. It seems to me that self-harming tendencies find expression in many different ways, ranging from the highly dramatic to the virtually invisible. A wide variety of self-injurious or health-impairing behaviours can perhaps be best understood if we think in terms of broadly similar underlying states of mind. In the chapters that follow, the reader is invited to consider this proposition through his or her imaginative interaction with a series of detailed case study examples.

I wish to suggest also that we all know something of the states of mind in question, through our personal acquaintance with entirely normal behaviours which I refer to as 'cashas' – an acronym for *c*ulturally *a*cceptable *s*elf-*h*arming *a*cts or activitie*s*. Some 'cashas' have a specific role and meaning, serving as a rite of passage or signifying identification with a particular tribe. Such rituals are not limited to geographically remote parts of the world; scarifying, tattooing and body piercing, for example, are highly valued signatures of group belonging in some British and American youth sub-cultures. 'Cashas' can also be associated with religious practices, as for example with self-flagellation or pilgrimages that involve covering long distances over stony ground, barefoot or on bended knee. Favazza's work (1989a, 1989b) offers extensive and fascinating accounts of such phenomena.

The 'cashas' that are of most interest in relation to the question of the relationship between normal, flawed self-care and actual self-harm fall into a third category. They consist of everyday, low-key actions and behaviours, which are nevertheless associated with injury or ill-health. Smoking offers an obvious example. Its physically harmful consequences are well documented but (except possibly in California) smoking is not generally seen as an example of self-harm. In a similar vein, chronic overwork is a major source of 'stress' and is known to be a factor in many mental and physical health problems. The Japanese, perhaps taking matters to their logical conclusion, have coined a new term, '*karoshi*':

> Talk about a bad day at work. Nobuo Miuro was simply getting on with his job, when he keeled over and died. It had been a busy few weeks for the interiors fitter from Tokyo; he was struggling to get a new restaurant ready for its launch and had been putting in a fair bit of overtime. The day before he collapsed he had worked from 11am until 4.30am the next morning, but had managed to snatch a few hours' sleep before starting again. But when Miuro, 47, tried to pick up his hammer and nails again, he suddenly took ill. He died a week later. Last week a coroner returned a verdict of 'karoshi': death by overwork. (Addley and Barton in *The Guardian*, 13 March 2001)

Large numbers of civil lawsuits have apparently now been filed in Japan by relatives of those believed or found by the coroner to have died from *karoshi*. Nevertheless, in the United Kingdom as well as in Japan, over-working remains culturally acceptable. One might even say that it is widely encouraged.

The 'continuum model' of self-harm and self-care, set out and discussed in Chapter 2, brings into view an area of experience that lies between, and so connects, the 'abnormal' phenomenon of self-harm and the 'normal' phenomenon of the 'casha'. My suggestion is that internal dramas that fuel behaviour conventionally recognised as self-harm are broadly similar to those that underpin 'cashas'. There is a difference but it is a difference of intensity rather than one of kind. In other words, *the difference resides in the level of desperation and emotional distress involved.*

It was with these thoughts in mind that I responded to a recent call by NICE (National Institute for Clinical Excellence) for suggestions and evidence relevant to the question of services for individuals who self-harm. I argued in favour of the establishment of an early intervention unit, to provide a clinical service for people who were beginning to be concerned about the intensity of their self-destructive thinking or behaviour and to serve as an educational resource for the practitioners in many different professions whose work brings them into contact with self-harming behaviour. As things stand, the term 'self-harm' is widely associated with florid and dramatic behaviour and carries a certain stigma. Individuals are unlikely to seek help at an early stage, while it is still possible for them to keep their self-harm hidden. Disclosure eventually becomes inevitable but by this time self-harm has become an entrenched coping strategy, and therapeutic intervention, while by no means impossible, is that much more difficult. An early intervention unit could begin to address some of these issues.

As a psychotherapist based in the community, I work from time to time with clients who harm themselves, by which I mean that their behaviour on the one hand leads to injury or ill-health, and on the other goes beyond the limits of cultural acceptability. Much of the behaviour I encounter lies close to the border area between 'cashas' and self-harm proper. In contrast to the florid and dramatic examples more frequently referred to, it has a low-key or 'hidden' quality. This kind of low-key self-harm is seldom described. In the literature, as in life, it is not in the limelight. It seems to me that the focus on high visibility self-harm results in the loss of a valuable opportunity, the opportunity to enter into the client's frame of reference. While we may be unwilling or unable to enter imaginatively into the world of a client who is engaged in violent and repetitive self-cutting or self-scalding, the task is less daunting when the self-harm in question is low-key and hence closer to behaviour that we already recognise and acknowledge as part of our own repertoire.

In some cases, the self-harm described in the book falls within conventionally recognised parameters, involving episodes of self-cutting or self-hitting and in one case a very serious eating disorder. In other cases, the self-harm in question is hidden and falls outside conventionally recognised parameters. Partly for this reason, it passes unnoticed, or is noticed but not seen for what it is. Some individuals are themselves blind to the self-injurious or health-damaging nature of their actions. Others recognise that they are harming themselves but keep this knowledge to themselves, fearing, not unreasonably, that disclosure may meet with an unsympathetic response.

Over ten years of practice as a social worker and a further fifteen years as a psychotherapist, I have learned to appreciate the multifaceted and subtly shaded nature of self-harming behaviour. I know that 'high visibility' self-harm – whether witnessed or recounted – is the cause of a great deal of shock and dismay. Maintaining a compassionate and ethical stance in the face of disturbing and distressing behaviour is not easy and the particular issues raised merit ongoing discussion. At the same time, we will wish to ensure that our thinking about self-harm is based on the consideration of a representative range of examples. It is a matter of concern therefore that there is so little reference in the literature to hidden self-harm, although it is a part of the day-to-day experience of many counsellors, psychotherapists, social workers, youth workers, nurses and practitioners in other professions.

Sarah's story

The following vignette offers a first example of the kind of scenario I have in mind. I have called the client in question 'Sarah'.

> About three months into our work together, Sarah tells me about a period of her life, shortly after she finished university, when she became very depressed and retreated from the world. She did not seek work and became more and more isolated as, one by one, her friends left the university town. She made no contact with her family, who lived over a hundred miles away.
>
> In therapy, Sarah describes various symptoms she experienced at that time – a buzzing in her head, a feeling of being cut off and unreal and an all-encompassing 'mental blankness'. She tells me that she also developed very bad eczema. We talk about this and share an understanding that this symptom represented some kind of eruption into the outside world of a disturbed inner state. There is a tense silence as Sarah struggles to tell me the next part of her story. Then she describes how she neglected her eczema to the point where she developed secondary infections and her body was covered in sores. It became

difficult to move around. Dressing and undressing were acutely painful, as her clothes repeatedly adhered to her weeping skin.

I feel dismayed when Sarah tells me that she remained in this state for more than six months. Finally, at Christmas, she went home to her family. Her mother became aware of the state of her skin and 'marched her off' to the local doctor. The doctor was profoundly shocked and shouted at Sarah in the surgery. Subsequently, he apologised, adding that it was the worst case of eczema and skin infection he had ever seen.

I ask Sarah what help she was offered and she tells me that the doctor prescribed antibiotics and steroid creams. There was no suggestion of counselling or any other kind of psychological help.

I undertook some preliminary research for the book, which will be described in more detail in Chapter 2. As part of this research, the vignette of 'Sarah' was presented to a gathering of seventy practitioners at a conference at the University of Hertfordshire (2001). All but three of them expressed the view that what was described was a clear case of self-harm.

Theory and practice

All kinds of practitioners – nurses, social workers, doctors, teachers and youth workers as well as counsellors and psychotherapists – are familiar with this kind of low-visibility self-harm. I would go as far as to say that for many practitioners working in the community, 'high visibility' examples of self-harm are only the tip of the iceberg. Perhaps (as with an iceberg) 10 per cent of the phenomenon of self-harm is clearly visible, another 20 per cent is 'low visibility' – submerged but vaguely discernible – and the remaining 70 per cent is entirely hidden from view. Sometimes a change of circumstances leads to a degree of thawing as when, in the context of a good therapeutic relationship, the client begins to let go of frozen defences. Then that which was entirely hidden may move closer to the surface, where its contours can begin to be traced and explored.

Once we bring hidden self-harm into the equation, we find that, in many cases, widely familiar theories are of limited relevance. For example, the theory of secondary gain, which suggests that self-harm is primarily a bid for love and attention (Feldman 1988), seems irrelevant in a case like Sarah's, where the difficulty has remained undisclosed for such a very long time. The gradual nature of Sarah's self-harm conflicts with the idea that self-harm indicates a 'disorder of impulse control' (Pattison and Kahan 1983) or a 'multi-impulsive personality disorder' (Lacey and Evans 1986). Having worked with Sarah for two years, I can state with confidence that she was not suffering from a 'borderline personality disorder' (Walsh and Rosen 1988). Welldon (1988) has drawn attention to the element of perverse pleasure often associated with self-harm. In Sarah's case, however, there was little evidence of this autoerotic element. Sarah's self-harm was not linked to childhood sexual abuse (Wise 1989) or to adult experiences of rape or trauma (Greenspan and Samuel 1989).

In introducing their work on children's literature, Michael and Margaret Rustin write: 'Our method is to provide a number of detailed readings of stories, not an encyclopaedic review or general history' (Rustin and Rustin 2001, p.1).

My own method is similar, although the 'stories' in question are real-life rather than fictional accounts. My aim is to describe and reflect on individual encounters and individual narratives. While I will endeavour to identify such themes as suggest themselves, it is not my intention to put forward a new 'meta-narrative' or to attempt to decide between the various competing theories already in existence. The theories referred to above – and the list I have given is far from complete – may be relevant in certain cases of self-harm but it is clear that none of them applies across the board. At best, they provide a backdrop, a context for our one-to-one encounters with individual clients. At worst, they create the illusion that every case will fit into one of the existing scenarios.

With these thoughts in mind I have chosen to devote a considerable amount of space to sequences of dialogue, as they come into being between client and psychotherapist at particular moments in time. Given the vagaries of memory and the inevitability of narrative smoothing, I do not claim to be presenting the 'real thing' in an unadulterated form. I have, however, endeavoured to ensure that theory is brought into play in a sensitive and respectful way.

Psychoanalytic understandings

I have long thought that a holistic perspective on the human subject is in the true spirit of psychoanalytic thinking. As practitioners, we rely on our experience of being with the whole person – feeling, thinking, always embodied, always in relationship – to help us in the search for meaning that is the essence of the psychoanalytic endeavour. Together with the client, we seek out ways of making sense of initially incomprehensible eruptions of thought, feeling and action. We rely on our awareness of our own physical responses, as well as on intellectual effort, as we tune in to unconscious aspects of client communications. Past experiences find active expression in the therapeutic relationship, shaping the client's experience of the present and colouring his or her expectations of the future.

The therapeutic encounters described in the book take place in the context of weekly or twice-weekly psychoanalytic psychotherapy or psychodynamic counselling. A search for the meaning behind the distress, rather than an exclusive concern with the symptom, is a hallmark of all psychoanalytic practice. More specifically, the body of theory called into play in this book derives from a contemporary 'object relations' approach. Bollas writes about relations between 'internal objects' in terms of what it means to be oneself, to be a 'character':

> To be a character is to gain a history of internal objects, inner presences that are the trace of our encounters, but not intelligible, or even clearly knowable: just intense ghosts who do not populate the machine but inhabit the human mind. (Bollas 1993, p.59)

Gardner offers a description of an object relations approach, which she then links to the subject of self-harm:

> It means that both our real experiences of and our fantasies about parental and other figures (objects) are internalised, and become embedded in the way we cope with life. These inner objects pattern our psyches and influence other relationships and the way we behave. In that sense self-harm can be seen as a system of signs marking statements about the self, and past relationships and previous experiences. (Gardner 2001, p.4)

My aim is to render object relations theory accessible to as wide range of readers as possible, given that counselling and psychotherapy are by no means the only useful resources for people who harm themselves. Lay helpers and many different professional practitioners also have an interest in reflecting on the sense of self-harm. Object relations theory offers a valuable way of thinking about what is going on. It sets out a general understanding of the dynamics in play in the internal world of the human subject, while at the same time respecting the uniqueness of each individual and his or her experience.

One of the many strengths of a psychoanalytic perspective is its continuing insistence on the *mixed nature* of the human individual, on the existence within each of us of dark and destructive tendencies. Such tendencies are understood to exist side by side and in a finely balanced tension with those aspects of ourselves that are generous and creative. To contain and begin to make sense of the turmoil and distress that ensues when the balance is lost and destructive tendencies break through in action and reaction, we need a language in which to speak of very difficult states of mind. The language of the 'innocent victim' can be unhelpful. We are often of more use to those who come to us in distress if we enable them to recognise and reflect on feelings that are hard to own – feelings of rage, envy, shame or even numb indifference. Psychoanalysis has the advantage of offering a language specifically adapted to this task, a series of narratives that offer a framework for thinking about how such states of mind come into being and an understanding of the conscious and unconscious ways in which they can be expressed, managed and mitigated.

Such states of mind do not, of course, arise without cause but are the consequence of trauma of one kind or another. The verb 'to traumatise' comes from a Greek root and means literally 'to pierce'. Winnicott (1896–1971) emphasised that events that pierce, that break through the individual's capacity to negotiate and make sense of what is happening, are not limited to episodes of obvious abuse, whether sexual, physical or emotional. The piercing effect of a thousand small pinpricks can be as traumatic as that of a few major, more obvious, cuts and blows. Major impingements and/or accumulated minor impingements engender in the infant or child states of 'unthinkable anxiety' (Winnicott 1962a) or 'nameless dread' (Bion 1962). Young and Gibb (1998) refer also to a pervasive sense of grievance that can be part of the aftermath of trauma, something that is relevant to several of the clients described in the case study chapters.

Evidence emerging from the field of neuroscience offers an alternative narrative of the effects of trauma, describing measurable changes in chemical and electrical activity in the brain and ultimately in brain structure. This evidence is complementary to object relations thinking, attesting to the brain-altering effects of chronically raised levels of arousal (Pert 1990). Neuroscience research also supports the suggestion that trauma can result from the absence of what should be present, as well as from the presence of what should be absent. The situation of Romanian orphans, who suffered extreme deprivation, offers a chilling illustration of the case in point. PET brain scans of orphan children reveal areas of the frontal-occipital lobes where neurological activity is negligible. One of the physiological mechanisms in play involves the effects of opiates. These substances are produced in abundance when an 'attuned' parent interacts with an infant. The opiates facilitate the formation of neural networks. In their absence, networks are not properly formed and brain cells die (Schore 1994, 2001).

These findings are broadly in line with the day-to-day experience of child psychotherapists, social workers and fostercarers involved with neglected, abused or otherwise traumatised children. In some cases, it appears that the neurological damage is irreversible, a heart-breaking situation for adoptive parents who invest heavily of themselves, only to find that the child concerned cannot make a normal emotional attachment. Unless something can be done, the child who cannot make a primary attachment is likely to become the adult who cannot make intimate relationships and who is socially maladroit, or even antisocial:

> Attachment in infancy has the primary evolutionary function of generating a mind capable of inferring things about other people's minds, their thoughts, ideas, motivations, and intentions... Awareness of others' thoughts and feelings is necessary to ensure social collaboration. (Fonagy 2001, p.427)

The subjective experience of emotion – whether rage, fear, envy, joy or excitement – is primarily body based – it is not for nothing that we speak of being 'heartbroken' or 'bone weary'. Recognising and differentiating between different feeling states is partly a question of good somatic awareness, of good access to 'gut feelings'. In psychotherapy, much time is devoted to thinking about the client's emotions and the perceived and imagined emotions of others. When things go well, we witness a number of parallel developments. Somatic awareness improves, emotional states become more accessible and clearly differentiated and the client becomes more able to think about, and makes sense of, his or her feelings.

The question of self-care

Clinical experience and research into the difficulties experienced by 'looked-after' children (Saunders and Broad 1997; Stein, Sufian and Hazlehurst 2001) combine to suggest that inadequate maternal care is linked to an impaired capacity for self-care and a higher risk of self-harm. I have included extracts from infant observation material in the book in an effort to develop a clearer understanding of the normal evolution of a capacity for self-care. By attending closely to the building blocks of 'good enough' self-care, I hope to refine my own and the reader's understanding of the kinds of deficits in maternal care that leave certain individuals particularly vulnerable to self-harming tendencies.

I am aware that the issue of health enhancement, including self-care, is somewhat problematic. We are frequently exhorted to 'take better care of ourselves', perhaps by taking vitamins, substituting butter for margarine (or margarine for butter, depending on the latest guidance), cutting down on alcohol or embarking on a programme of exercise. In this way, we are urged to subscribe to the idea of perfectibility, to 'the myth of perfect health' (Adam Phillips 1999; Turp 2001). The tenor of these communications calls to mind Foucault's description (1970, 1984) of the invisible forms of social and political control that, in contemporary Western society, have largely replaced control through physical restraint:

> [Foucault] treats the space of the body as the irreducible element in our social scheme of things, for it is upon that space that the forces of

repression, socialization, disciplining, and punishing are inflicted. (Harvey 1989, p.213)

Foucault suggests that the concept of health has itself become 'disciplinary'. We are driven by an unstated ideal of perfection and urged towards constant self-criticism and self-surveillance. The way in which medicine is practised and the language of medicine are highly influential factors, setting the parameters within which most of us think about health and illness. Against this background, it becomes difficult to discuss the subject of care and self-care without appearing to subscribe to the view that we should constantly try harder to maintain and improve our own and our children's mental and physical health, as if we were engaged in some kind of 'project':

> Whether it is to be perfected, sculpted, deprived, obsessed over, injured, ignored, neglected or narcissistically worshipped, the body tends increasingly to be regarded as *other than* the self. Attention is lavished on physical appearance while physicality as experienced from within fades from consciousness. Although the body is clearly both a palpable and visible object existing in external space *and* the home of our being, experienced from within, the latter cognisance seems fragile and tends to slip away. (Turp 2001, p.27)

What I have in mind when I speak of 'self-care' is not, in fact, the objectified body but the body as 'the home of our being' and the quality of something described by Winnicott as 'the psyche indwelling in the soma' (Winnicott 1960b, p.45). In other words, my concern is not with the body perceived as if from the outside looking in but with the lived body, experienced from within. The difference between the two was emphasised for me recently, when I watched a tennis match where all the players were in wheelchairs. The skill and enjoyment demonstrated by the players made it clear that a paraplegic person, whose body is by conventional standards neither perfect nor perfectible, is fully capable of experiencing a good quality of indwelling, a body-based feeling of ease and 'at-homeness'.

Winnicott was a great champion of the idea of the 'good enough' mother. In normal circumstances, the mother[1] intuitively senses her infant's needs. Winnicott emphasised that good enough care is not achieved by following advice from 'experts' but by tuning in to a 'gut feeling' for the infant's needs and state of mind. Similarly, one's own self-care is best guided by 'gut feelings', supported by a sense of being deserving of care. As noted above, access to these feelings depends on a reasonably good level of somatic awareness and this can be an area of difficulty for people who harm themselves. Many of the people who come to us for help have learned to *reduce* their level of somatic awareness in order to set a distance between themselves and the things that are happening to them. Cutting off or 'dissociating', in the sense of feeling 'this is not really happening' or 'I am not really here' or 'I am not the person to whom this is happening', is at times a necessary and appropriate survival strategy.

Culturally accepted self-harming acts/activities ('cashas')

As noted above, a salient feature of self-harm, especially hidden self-harm, is its close affinity with courses of action or inaction that are familiar and indeed entirely 'normal'. Most readers will recognise in the client accounts intimations of their own states of mind. Perhaps they will be reminded of times when they have neglected themselves because they felt low and 'couldn't be bothered' or when they took risks because they were angry and 'didn't care'. Or perhaps they will be reminded of their own tendency to 'carry on regardless' until physical symptoms become apparent and remind them that they are human beings and not machines.

In introducing the idea of the 'casha' and examining points of connection between 'normal' and 'abnormal' self-harming behaviour, the book offers an unusual framework for thinking about self-harm, one that I hope the reader will find refreshing and illuminating. Self-harm is viewed

---

1   Much of Winnicott's work was written in the 1950s and 1960s. Since then, many of us have come to understand that 'mothering' is also carried out by others who have an intimate relationship with the child, including at times fathers, same-sex partners and other close relatives and friends.

in the context of ordinary behaviour, rather than as a circumscribed difficulty or disorder. Actions are considered with reference to their cultural and sub-cultural underpinnings and a number of prevailing stereotypes and assumptions are called into question. These ideas are made explicit in early chapters and continue as an underlying theme in the presentation and discussion of the case examples.

The clients are the heroes and heroines of the various tales. Sorely wounded and in the midst of flight, they have stopped, turned and begun to address the damage. They have brought themselves, sometimes kicking and screaming, into the consulting room to face their internal demons. These are no mean acts of courage. In the wake of the experience, some clients have felt happy for me to publish detailed accounts of the work undertaken. These accounts are lessons in themselves, more instructive in many ways than any amount of theorising. In presenting them here, I am able to offer a particular perspective on self-harm, one where a phenomenological approach that gives full weight to the testimony of people who harm themselves is integrated with contemporary psychoanalytic thinking. Some of the ideas introduced in *Psychosomatic Health: The Body and the Word* (Turp 2001) are in evidence again here, set in the specific context of self-harming behaviour.

My hope is to leave the reader better equipped for the task of remaining thoughtful and compassionate in interactions with any person – whether a client, a student, a work colleague, a friend or a family or self-help group member – who finds himself or herself in the grip of self-harming tendencies.

Outline of the book

Chapter 2 continues the exploration of the phenomenon of self-harm by considering the question: 'What do we mean by self-harm?' It begins with a description of preliminary research, on the basis of which the case study examples were chosen, and continues with a broader discussion of themes that emerged during the course of research.

In Chapters 3 and 4, the question of self-care is explored. Extracts from infant observations undertaken on a weekly basis in a 'normal' family are presented and discussed. This work serves a dual purpose. On the one hand, it establishes a base-line from which to consider the lapses in and deviations from self-care described in the case studies. On the other, it serves to sensitise the reader to the subtle and delicate nature of physical inter-relatedness.

The book continues with five accounts of therapeutic work with clients, introduced in Chapter 5 and presented in Chapters 6 to 10. Chapter 6 revolves around 'Lorraine', who has taken a number of overdoses and whose current behaviour includes occasional episodes of self-cutting. Chapter 7 concerns a client, 'Ellen May', who suffers from anorexia and bulimia. Parallels between eating disorders and other kinds of self-harm are discussed in the context of this particular case study. These two examples serve as a bridge between familiar 'high visibility' examples of self-harm on the one hand and 'hidden' examples of self-harm on the other.

Chapter 8 describes work with 'Tracey', whose intermittent episodes of self-hitting are disclosed for the first time during the period of psycho-therapy. This account is followed by descriptions of work with two clients whose self-harm is more fundamentally hidden and is identified and named only when the therapeutic work is well under way. They are 'Peter' (Chapter 9), who suffers from unexplained physical eruptions, who sustains a number of apparently 'invited' accidents and who uses drugs and alcohol to excess, and 'Kate' (Chapter 10), who fails to attend to warning signs of repetitive strain injury, an oversight that has very serious consequences. The ratio of clients – four females to one male – reflects my impression of the general situation on the ground. Self-harm is not exclusively a female issue, as is sometimes implied, but it remains the case, at least in contemporary Western society, that women are more likely to turn their aggression towards themselves, while men are more likely to turn it towards others.

Chapter 11 offers space for consideration of some of the common themes that can be identified in the clinical material and for reflection on theoretical issues and 'matters arising'. The book concludes with Chapter 12, 'The Self-Harming Individual and "The System"'. In this final chapter, I consider the particular challenges faced by practitioners who work with clients who self-harm and offer some thoughts on the vital questions of practitioner support and service provision.

2

What Do We Mean by 'Self-Harm'?

I still hurt myself in lots of ways, really. Worrying, blaming myself for things, doing too much, not letting myself sleep – they're just as bad for me. ('Woman A' in Arnold 1995, p.8)

In much of the literature and in many people's minds, the term 'self-harm' is reserved for obvious acts of self-directed violence, in particular repetitive self-cutting, self-burning and overdosing. 'Woman A' proposes a different version of events. She includes under the umbrella of self-harm 'worrying' and 'doing too much' – behaviour that most of us would see as falling well within the normal range. A question arises as to where a line might most usefully be drawn between the lapses and failures of self-care characteristic of 'normal' behaviour and actual self-harm. Writing a book on self-harm brought me face to face with this particular question. Having chosen to include examples of 'hidden' self-harm, I needed a means of deciding what to count in and what to count out. Enlisting the assistance of fellow practitioners, I undertook some preliminary research, which is described below.

The specific aim of the research was to assist with the selection of clinical examples for inclusion in the book. I decided to include only examples where 70 per cent or more of practitioners felt, after reading and discussing the relevant clinical vignette, that the behaviour in question qualified as self-harm. In addition, through presenting alternative models of self-harming behaviour and introducing the concept of the 'casha' – a culturally accepted self-harming act/activity – I aimed to open up in a general way the question: 'What do we mean by self-harm?' My expectation, which in the event was fully met, was of receiving feedback from the audience that would prove useful to the development of a better understanding of the subject of self-harm as a whole.

Clinical examples from group supervision

The first phase of the research involved the generation of clinical examples for consideration. Some clinical examples were readily available, being taken from my own work. This was the case with 'Sarah', described in the Introduction, and with the clinical examples involving 'Ellen May', 'Peter' and 'Kate', presented later in the book. I did not feel it necessary to include vignettes of work with 'Lorraine' and 'Tracey' in the research, as the behaviour in question (self-cutting and self-hitting) fell clearly within the parameters of what is usually thought of as self-harm.

I did not want to rely solely on examples from my own work and sought to generate clinical vignettes derived from the work of other practitioners. Over the years, I have supervised counsellors and psychotherapists, some of them students, in a number of group settings. As the book began to take shape in my mind, I asked several such groups to participate in the preliminary phase of the research by discussing the question: 'What do we mean by self-harm?' They generously agreed. The following narrative was compiled, using a version of grounded theory methodology (Glaser and Strauss 1967), from material that emerged over the course of three supervision sessions, each of which involved between four and eight participants.

> One group member begins by saying: 'So far, I haven't had anyone come to me who harms herself.' I see a couple of others nod and murmur in assent. I comment that, while this may turn out to be the case, I wonder if we may discover that they have, after all, come across self-harming behaviour of one kind or another.
>
> There is a thoughtful silence, then Sheila, a general practice counsellor, begins to speak: 'I'm thinking about Ruth, a woman I'm seeing for twelve sessions at the surgery. She has a baby, about ten months old I think. And she's nineteen, though to look at her you would take her for even younger. I've seen her four times and I really don't think she's coping. She looks terrible – so pale and thin, with huge dark circles under her eyes. And yester-

day it was quite cold out, but she still wasn't wearing a coat. She had to bring Leo, her little boy, with her because her Mum wasn't well and couldn't look after him. Leo obviously had an awful cold and was thoroughly miserable, sniffling and crying – really a poor little thing. They both looked utterly exhausted. I just wanted to give them a warm bath and tuck them up in bed.

'Then Ruth told me, "I'm pregnant again." I felt absolutely dismayed. "Oh," I said. I was trying to sound neutral but I'm sure my face told a different story. "It's all right," she said. "The new baby's Dad is a real smasher." The choice of that word "smasher" sent a jolt through me. One of the things Ruth has told me is that Leo's father was violent towards her and that's why she split up with him. So now I'm sitting here wondering about this, her getting pregnant and planning to go ahead and have this second baby, when she's not coping with the first one. Would you see that as an example of self-harm?'

Rather than responding directly, I invite the other members of the group to respond to what Sheila has said. Like Sheila, they are upset by the story they have heard. They empathise with her sense of dismay and helplessness. Most of them say that this is self-harm, just as surely as deliberately cutting your arm is self-harm, but two group members are unsure about this. It seems to them 'too different'.

The next contributor, Lynn, tells us about a client, Bernie: 'Bernie is very attached to his running schedule. I don't see anything wrong with this. I don't run myself but I like to do a lot of walking and, on the whole, I think that exercise is beneficial, emotionally as well as physically. But I was very concerned about what Bernie told me last week. He had been in bed for two days with a bout of flu and had a high fever. In fact, I knew this because he had rung me to cancel a session. The next day, he went out running in the park, aiming to do an extra long run to make up for lost time. Along the way, he virtually collapsed. After sitting on a park bench for a while, he was able to use his mobile phone to call a taxi to take him home.'

Lynn says that she is wondering now whether Bernie's behaviour should be seen as a kind of self-harm. She notes that, in punishing himself for what he perceives as his weakness, he has set back his recovery and made himself feel very unwell again. She asks the group what they think. This time, opinion is more evenly divided. A number of people say that the story makes them feel anxious about Bernie. He could have brought a heart attack upon himself. He could have caught pneumonia. He could have died. Others say that it's normal, after all, to push yourself to achieve your best and that people do make mistakes and then find that they have gone beyond their personal limits.

Jane tells the group about a man in his fifties whom she has been seeing in the context of her work as a bereavement counsellor. (Later, as part of her MA submission, she writes an essay about this client and his 'accident proneness', which she also makes available to me.) 'Harry' has a history of falls, injuries, illnesses and frequent childhood hospital admissions 'too numerous to mention'. During the eight months of counselling, he has cut himself twice, burned himself while cooking, sustained a scald, painfully stubbed his toes six times, trapped his fingers and cut himself by accidentally breaking an ornament that belonged to his mother.

The past is marked by four life-threatening 'accidents' which have left him a chronic invalid, having to walk on sticks and practically housebound. The first of these was a very serious car accident at age nineteen, in which a girl was killed. It happened shortly after the end of Harry's first sexual relationship, which Harry accused his mother of 'deliberately trying to sabotage'. Twelve years later, working as an engineer in a job his father had found for him, Harry electrocuted himself. Just before this, he saw his father's contemptuous face, thought 'I shouldn't do it' and then connected the wrong wires. At forty-three, Harry fell from his bike into the path of a lorry and sustained several fractures. Finally, eight years ago, he fell from a ladder that he knew had 'rotten rungs' and sustained a back injury 'that still gives him gyp'. At the time he had been depressed, not caring what happened to him.

Following each of these 'accidents', Harry was hospitalised. He describes not wanting to leave the security of the 'womb-like' hospital, which felt calm and safe. He says he felt 'cosseted and cared for', that his mother had become a 'ministering angel' and that he was able to relinquish all responsibilities and become a total child.

The final person to speak is Rachel and she chooses to speak about herself. She describes her difficulties in controlling her workload. At her busiest times, she sees thirty clients a week. She has set up a small voluntary organisation and, connected with this, attends training sessions on budgeting, quality assurance and other organisational matters. She runs a training course on bereavement counselling and is a member of her local Community Health Council. At home, she has primary responsibility for two teenage children, one of whom has a medical condition that requires ongoing management.

Rachel tells us that she sets no limits on the number of concessionary counselling places she offers. She finds herself unable to say no to 'needy' clients and is aware that this is linked to a feeling of neediness in her. At present, she is sleeping fitfully – work matters go round and round in her head and keep her awake. A few months ago, her blood pressure became dangerously high and is now controlled by medication. She concludes by saying that she recently had a dream in which her family doctor told her that she had, at the most, five years to live. She awoke in great distress, thinking of her children and the loss and pain they would suffer when she died, then thought fleetingly that dying would be something of a relief.

On the basis of these communications, four vignettes were written summarising the situation with 'Ruth' and 'Bernie' and 'Harry' and 'Rachel'. Each of these was used alongside the vignettes of 'Sarah', 'Ellen May', 'Peter' and 'Kate' in the second phase of the research.

'Qualitative leap' and 'continuum' models of self-harm

The second phase of the research involved presentation of the vignettes at a number of different conference venues and gatherings of clinicians and researchers. Many of those present were counsellors or psychotherapists. Practitioners from other professions and, in some cases, service users were also represented. Each session began with a presentation describing two conceptual frameworks for thinking about self-harm and introducing the idea of a 'casha'. Following the presentation, participants were asked to consider and comment on vignettes involving actions, or failures to act, which might or might not be seen as examples of self-harm. A count was made of those who would see a vignette as describing self-harm and those who would not and percentages were calculated.

At each presentation, I begin by suggesting that the current definition of self-harm is relatively narrow, in the sense that it is used almost exclusively in relation to severe and highly visible examples of self-harming behaviour. According to this understanding, only a small minority of individuals harm themselves and their behaviour is in a category of its own, in no way akin to 'normal' behaviour. I describe this as the 'qualitative leap' model of self-harm, since the behaviour of individuals who self-harm is seen as qualitatively different from that of 'normal' individuals.

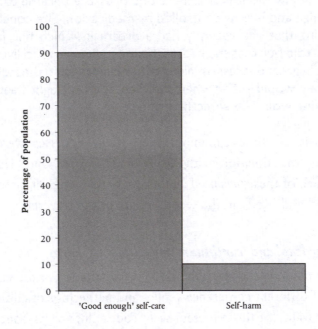

Figure 2.1 Qualitive leap model of self-harm

Figure 2.1 depicts this commonly held view of self-harm in the form of a bar chart. Self-harm is identified as belonging in a category of its own, a world away from ordinary self-care. The fact that individuals who harm themselves are often seen as suffering from a particular kind of illness or disorder is consistent with this version of events. It becomes clear during the discussion phase of each event that there are practitioners present who have come across examples of a psychiatric diagnosis such as 'borderline personality disorder' being made on the basis of self-harming behaviour alone. Such anecdotal accounts are in line with the findings of the National Self-Harm Network (Pembroke 2000) and the Bristol Survey (Arnold 1995). They suggest that reluctance to disclose self-harming behaviour, something that commonly comes to light in counselling and psychotherapy encounters, is grounded to some extent in a realistic fear of being seen as 'crazy' and being stigmatised.

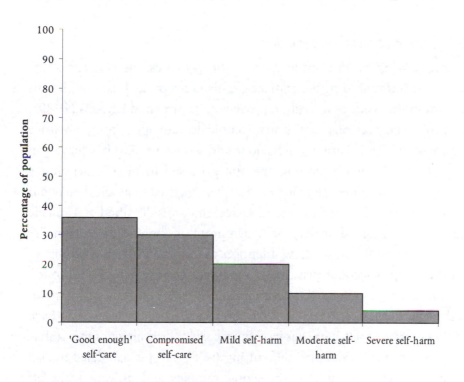

Figure 2.2 Continuum model of self-harm

The presentation continues with the introduction of the 'continuum' model of self-harm (see Figure 2.2). In contrast to the 'qualitative leap' model, this version of events suggests a gradation from 'good enough self-care' to 'compromised self-care' to 'mild self-harm' to 'moderate self-harm' and, finally, to 'severe self-harm'. (The percentages given in the charts are indicative only. As no relevant statistics are available, estimated figures based on clinical experience have been used.) This model suggests that self-harm is not a discrete phenomenon. An 'in-between' area comes into view, which both separates and connects self-care, with all of its vicissitudes, and self-harm.

At each of the research events, the idea of a self-harm–self-care continuum is received with enthusiasm. Many practitioners express strong support for this perspective, echoing and expanding upon my desire to create a conceptual space in which to discuss behaviour which expresses self-harming tendencies but falls outside current stereotypes of self-harm.

Self-harm and social transgression

Before moving on to consideration of the vignettes, the concept of the 'casha' is introduced to the audience. This concept, as I explain, has its origins in the work of the cultural psychiatrist Armando Favazza (1989a, 1989b), who was one of the first people to attempt a comprehensive exploration of self-harming behaviour and whose writing has played an important role in legitimising the study of self-harm. Challenging a number of prevailing stereotypes, Favazza insisted that the behaviour should not be trivialised as 'attention-seeking', misidentified as a suicide attempt or regarded merely as a symptom of borderline personality disorder. In addition, he drew attention to culturally accepted forms of self-harming behaviour that can be observed in every part of the world.

Self-harm can take the form of self-injury, internal self-harm or self-neglect, referred to later in the book as 'self-harm by omission'. Each of these forms of self-harm has its counterpart in the domain of the 'casha'. To give just a few examples, self-cutting (self-injury) is paralleled by nail biting, gnawing of cuticles, squeezing pimples and picking scabs off wounds. Overdosing on prescribed medicines (internal self-harm) is paralleled by over-consumption of alcohol, over-eating, smoking and, as noted above, over-working. Self-neglect (self-harm by omission) is paralleled by 'accident-proneness', self-imposed sleep deprivation and a failure to seek treatment for medical and dental problems.

'Cashas' are omnipresent features of ordinary 'good enough' self-care. In every society, certain behaviours that regularly lead to injury or damage to health are deemed permissible, a situation that perhaps reflects an implicit understanding of the need to offer channels for the expression of aggressive and destructive tendencies. For example, players and spectators accept that certain ball games, for example rugby and football, involve rough physical contact and regular minor injury. Provided the rules are not broken, this is seen as part of the game and part of the enjoyment. Richards suggests that the game of football, in particular, offers a channel for aggressive energies and acts as a civilising influence in the psychological sense:

> This modification of aggressive energies is perhaps aided by our memories of how as babies we express vigour and obtain pleasure through kicking movements, as well as using our feet to struggle against a restraining parent. (Richards 1994, p.34)

'Cashas' also offer possibilities for physical self-soothing. When we see that a person's cuticles are raw and bleeding, we are prepared to look the other way. When a person is chain-smoking on the morning of an examination, we are more likely to sympathise than to condemn. Most of us know from our own experience the soothing distraction that such activities can provide. At a certain point, a particular kind of behaviour may cease to be acceptable and come to be regarded as self-harm, either because the behaviour has moved beyond some unmarked limit or because the situation has changed. I have in mind, for example, behaviour such as continuing to smoke after cancer or heart disease has been diagnosed or continuing to engage in extreme sports during pregnancy. When there is a transgression of limits, acceptance is replaced by disapproval and intolerance.

The point at which a particular kind of behaviour is deemed to have gone beyond what is acceptable varies between cultures, sub-cultures, generations and individuals. Consequently, behaviours that attract the self-harm label *always* combine an element of self-inflicted illness or injury and an element of transgression, with the breaking of unspoken cultural rules. This element of transgression is important, being inherently meaningful. It tells us that the person concerned is unable, at the current time, to manage his or her psychological needs without recourse to socially proscribed action or inaction. Such breaching of the limits in itself speaks of a heightened state of distress, of a certain level of desperation.

Selection of the clinical material

At the end of the presentation, the audience is invited to ask questions and make comments. Then typescripts of two vignettes, similar in length and style to the vignette of 'Sarah' included in the Introduction, are distributed to those present. Participants are asked to read either one or two vignettes (depending on the time available), discuss them in small groups and consider their response to the questions: 'Is this an example of self-harm?' and 'If so, is the self-harm mild, moderate or severe?'

Table 2.1 Summary of results		
Name	*Behaviour*	*% regarding behaviour as self-harm*
Ellen May	Anorexia and bulimia, including damage to the throat	100%
Sarah	Neglected eczema and skin infection	95%
Harry	'Invited' accidents, both major and minor, leading to chronic illness and disability	90%
Peter	Frequent minor accidents, sexual risk-taking, hidden drug and alcohol abuse	80%
Kate	Over-riding of physical symptoms, leading to aggravation of RSI and permanent disability	70%
Ruth	Failures of self-care, leading to second unwanted pregnancy	60%
Bernie	Inappropriate and excessive use of exercise	50%
Rachel	Overworking, sleep disturbance, exhaustion, high blood-pressure	50%

For a clinical example to become eligible for inclusion in the book, 70 per cent or more of those present need to decide that the behaviour in question qualifies as self-harm. Thus, some potential case examples are excluded at this stage, on the basis that the votes in favour of their counting as an example of self-harm fall below the cut-off point. (See Table 2.1 for a summary of the results.) Among the examples 'voted' to be examples of self-harm, those of 'Harry' and 'Sarah' have not been included as longer case studies, as it was not appropriate to ask the client for permission to publish a detailed account.

Further discussion is invited and a number of interesting themes emerge. Many people say that they have found it difficult to arrive at a decision. The line dividing a 'casha' from an act of self-harm is described as 'fuzzy' and 'elusive'. Practitioners who have decided that a particular clinical example does not qualify as self-harm are given the opportunity to comment on their decision. The reasons they name fall into two main categories. The first is that the behaviour in question is 'passive' rather than 'active'. This comment is made by the three out of the seventy practitioners who do not see Sarah's behaviour as an example of self-harm. The second is that the behaviour is so common and generally accepted that it counts as an example of a 'casha' rather than as an example of self-harm. This is said most often in relation to the vignettes describing 'Bernie', 'Ruth' and 'Rachel'.

The question of 'severity' raises a number of complications. For some practitioners, the intention behind the action is the most important consideration, while others are more swayed by the level of the physical damage itself or by the 'shock value' of the behaviour. In every case, some practitioners rate the self-harm described in a particular vignette as 'mild', while others assert equally strongly that it is 'severe'. As a consequence of these exchanges, I find myself moving away from the terms 'mild', 'moderate' and 'severe' and towards the terms 'hidden', 'low visibility' and 'high visibility' self-harm, a change that is reflected in the title chosen for the book.

Self-care and its vicissitudes

Writing of 'cashas', I find that it is 2.00 am and I am still at my keyboard. I am tired and tomorrow is a busy working day. Shall I spend another hour on this book chapter or go to bed? This decision, like so many others, will be guided by a number of factors, of which physical self-care is just one. My need for sleep, fast becoming desperate, is in conflict with my need to keep anxieties concerning deadlines within tolerable bounds and with the sense of well-being that comes from completing a task and feeling I have done it well.

Similar situations are by no means uncommon. A concern for physical self-care will often come into conflict with other concerns or desires – sexual desire, a desire to enjoy being sociable or a desire to seek out new experiences. We speak of a 'lovesick' teenager and know that food and sleep are of very minor importance to this particular individual at this particular time. Recent research suggests that long flights pose a small, but nevertheless measurable, risk of DVT (deep vein thrombosis). But this will not, on the whole, deter us from visiting a far-off country we have long dreamt of seeing, or one where we have dear friends or relatives.

On many occasions, then, best physical self-care and best emotional self-care stand in opposition to each other and we are faced with a choice. Interestingly, automatic prioritisation of physical self-care emerges as a poor solution. Individuals who follow this path, rather than serving as models of healthy functioning, tend to be self-absorbed, rigid in their behaviour or even obsessive. They *must* have their eight hours' sleep and no exception can be made, even for a particularly important or enjoyable event. They become anxious if they cannot eat particular foods that they regard as healthy. One client came to see me through an employee assistance programme when he heard that his contract was not going to be renewed. It emerged that his work involved travelling abroad and that he didn't feel able to do this unless he could take along a supply of particular 'healthy' foods sufficient to last him for the whole trip. His avoidance of longer trips abroad had indirectly led to his losing his position and he was distraught about this turn of events.

The idea of a connection between the everyday vicissitudes of self-care and behaviour typically described as self-harm offers the possibility of a shared understanding between practitioners working with self-harm and the clients themselves. When asked about the reasons for their behaviour, many clients say in one way or another that they harm themselves physically in order to cope emotionally. One client told me: 'Cutting isn't the problem for me – it's the solution. If I don't cut myself, I can't cope. I feel I'm going to go crazy.' In the largest survey of its kind undertaken in the UK (subsequently referred to as the Bristol Survey) 'relief of feelings' was the most common reason given for self-harming behaviour (Arnold 1995). It seems reasonable to suggest that we are all striving to 'cope' and to 'relieve our feelings' when we unconsciously weigh the balance between physical care and emotional self-care. Under normal circumstances, we are able to find a balance without recourse to self-harming behaviour, although we may at times find ourselves relying heavily on 'cashas'. In extreme circumstances, physical self-harm may be resorted to as a desperate and paradoxical form of emotional self-care.

The Bristol Survey raises further questions with regard to what does and does not constitute self-harm. Should we, for example, have a category of 'self-harm by proxy', where a person puts himself or herself in the way of harm but the damage is actually inflicted by a third party? Should we include emotional (and/or financial) self-sabotage?

> There were many other ways in which women saw themselves as self-harming. These included overwork, over-exercising, excessive shopping, abusing glue/solvents, suicide attempts (other than overdoses), staying in abusive relationships, unnecessary and repeated risk-taking, self-sabotage (for example in career, academic work, relationships), and smoking. (Arnold 1995, p.8)

It is possible, and I think important, to make a distinction between psychological self-sabotage and physical self-harm. Nevertheless, this still leaves a grey area, an 'in-between' area, where we are confronted by the question of what counts as self-harm, what does not count as self-harm and on what basis a distinction is being made.

Returning to the scenario suggested by 'Woman A', are we now any better equipped to decide whether it is useful to refer to everyday behaviour such as 'worrying' and 'doing too much' as self-harm? That such behaviour can contribute to physical illness or injury is not in doubt, and this is also true of smoking, excessive consumption of alcohol, over-eating to the point of obesity and much else besides. It seems important, however, if the term 'self-harm' is to retain any specific meaning, to make a distinction between behaviours that are physically harmful but commonplace and those that are physically harmful but fall outside the accepted limits. According to these criteria, worrying and 'doing too much' do not qualify as self-harm.

The dividing line between a 'casha' and an act of self-harm may in some cases involve a difference of frequency or intensity rather than a difference of kind. I have already referred to picking scabs as 'culturally acceptable' but, taken to extremes, this same behaviour can shade over into self-harm:

> A client, Linda, picked her skin excessively, particularly in the bath, causing sores that formed scabs, which she then picked off. She told me that, underneath her clothes, she was a mass of sores and small bleeding wounds. She also had a never-ending succession of colds and sore throats and, although she invariably attended for her session, she was never really well. (Turp 1999a, p.318)

Defining self-harm

As will by now be clear, defining self-harm is not an exact science. There are choices to be made about where and on what basis various lines might best be drawn. A tentative definition is set out below. I have made an effort to take into account the significance of emotional responses evoked by self-harm and the understanding that such responses are shaped both by individual subjective factors and by the cultural context in which the behaviour in question is embedded. The definition is offered as a guide to the way in which the term 'self-harm' is used and understood in this book. It is not intended as any kind of final word.

Self-harm is an umbrella term for behaviour:

1. that results, whether by commission or omission, in avoidable physical harm to self

2. that breaches the limits of acceptable behaviour, as they apply at the place and time of enactment, and hence elicits a strong emotional response.

Criterion 1 encompasses both external and internal self-harm. It refers to self-harm resulting from both active and passive behaviour (self-harm by omission). Eating disorders and alcohol and substance abuse are encompassed by the definition, although it needs to be added that these forms of self-harm have distinctive characteristics of their own.

Criterion 2 makes reference to the response, or imagined response, of individuals exposed to the behaviour concerned or to a description of that behaviour. While a 'casha' may provoke mild disapproval or concern, self-harm tends to stir up more disquieting emotions – for example, extreme sadness, dismay, alarm, horror, guilt, anger or disgust. This part of the definition involves consideration of subjective responses to the behaviour in question. As such responses are culturally embedded and vary between time and place as well as between individuals, 'The Many Faces of Self-Harm' (Turp 2002) are to some extent the changing faces of self-harm. In these shifting sands, a stance of interest and ongoing curiosity is likely to be of greater value than an attempt to achieve final closure.

3

The Capacity for Self-Care:
Observations of Esther

> Health here includes the idea of tingling life and the magic of intimacy.
> All these things go together and add up to a sense of feeling real and
> being, and of the experiences feeding back into the personal psychical
> reality, enriching it and giving it scope. (Winnicott 1986, p.31)

This chapter and the next are concerned with 'health' and 'normal
development'. We tend to take it for granted that we know what we mean
by these terms but detailed investigation reveals a mixed, subtly shaded
picture. The question of self-care is, I believe, inseparable from the
question of self-harm. It can be difficult, however, to shift our gaze away
from self-harm, with its 'noisy' and disturbing quality, and on to self-care,
which tends to be quiet and unobtrusive. In other words, it is easy to
become preoccupied with what goes wrong, without a clear understanding of what goes right, when it does go right.

The observation extracts presented in this chapter and the next offer
food for thought with regard to the possible origins of a capacity for
self-care. I hope they capture, too, something of the 'tingling life and the
magic of intimacy' referred to by Winnicott above and, in doing so,
demonstrate that self-care and overall healthy functioning are closely tied
together. The extracts are grouped under a number of headings. Those
discussed in this chapter concern especially the internalisation of a caring
figure or 'good object', experienced as capable of generating and
sustaining a capacity for self-care.

Physical dependency in infancy

Object relations theory is based upon certain understandings relating to the nature of pre-verbal experience, at a time when dependency is uppermost and primitive emotions hold sway. The mother's intuitive understanding of her infant's changing bodymind state and her ability to respond appropriately are seen as laying a foundation for adult mental health. This perspective offers a starting point for thinking about the processes likely to be involved in the establishment of a capacity for self-care.

The first and most obvious statement to be made is that we are endowed at the beginning of life with a very limited capacity for self-care. We have a will to survive and a potential for self-care, but are dependent on others for both physical and emotional care. At the beginning, this dependency is absolute. If we are not fed, we will starve. If we are not cleaned and changed, we will lie in our urine and faeces. If we are not wrapped and dressed, unwrapped and undressed, then we will be too cold or too hot. If we are not watched over, then any accident may befall us. We are equipped neither to appreciate the difference between what is safe and what is dangerous nor to take evasive action. Our well-being is heavily dependent on experiences of appropriate responsive handling, in the absence of which we are vulnerable to the well-documented effects of touch deprivation (Hopkins 1990; Spitz 1945; Turp 1999b), including failure to thrive and, in extreme cases, failure to physically survive.

In the early weeks of life, our capacity to regulate levels of arousal, to soothe ourselves when we need soothing and to enliven ourselves when we need to be enlivened is very limited. Research has shown that premature infants are unable to regulate even basic physiological functions, such as body temperature and heart rate. A number of studies, including Field (1995) and Ludington-Hoe *et al.* (2000), have described the progress of premature infants who receive 'kangaroo care', spending their early weeks in almost continuous skin-to-skin contact with the mother, living chest-to-chest inside her T-shirt instead of inside an incubator. It has been found that the mother's body temperature and heart-rate continually adjust in order to keep the infant's temperature and heart-rate within the ideal range. Recent research in the field of neuroscience has shown that full-term infants also depend on maternal regulation of physiological functioning, although their situation is somewhat less fragile (Schore 1994).

From this position of absolute dependence on maternal care, most of us eventually achieve an adequate level of self-care.

Psychoanalytic infant observation

The process of psychoanalytic infant observation involves weekly visits to a family, each lasting one hour. The observations begin as soon as possible after the baby is born and usually continue until the child is two years old. Psychoanalytic infant and young child observation offers a privileged perspective on normal development as it unfolds in a family setting, giving the observer an opportunity to tune in to the dynamics in play in the family and in the internal world of the infant. According to a object relations viewpoint, these dynamics remain operational, although less readily visible, in the internal world of the adult.

The position taken up by the observer in the family being observed is that of a visitor rather than of an expert: 'Although required to refrain from initiating activity and interaction, he is expected to maintain a friendly and receptive attitude to the family, of whom he is a privileged guest' (Briggs 1997, p.27).

Psychoanalytic infant observation began its life as a tool for teaching. Over time the student's immersion in and reflection on the family dynamics that make up the world of the infant has emerged as a sensitising experience second to none. More recently, its status as a research methodology has been rising. Reid (1997) argues that psychoanalytic infant observation has the same structured form as a psychoanalytic clinical encounter, the same clear rules of engagement and the same potential for the generation of new ideas. She suggests that it constitutes a second core methodology to stand alongside the clinical case study (described by Michael Rustin (1997) as the equivalent of 'Pasteur's laboratory') in the field of psychotherapy research.

Each of these two research methods meets the stringent ethical requirements of psychoanalytic research:

> The control of the outside world routinely sought by normal sciences is made impossible and undesirable for psychoanalysis by its distinctive commitment to the autonomy of its human subjects. (Miller *et al.* 1989, p.62)

Infant observation and case study methodologies involve 'participant observation', and are similar in this respect to methodologies used in anthropology and some branches of sociology. Rather than claiming objectivity or detachment, the observer notes his or her subjective responses to the drama being played out and these responses form part of the observation itself. The presence of an observer inevitably affects members of the family and the dynamics being observed. Happily, there is evidence to suggest that the effect of the observer's regular and non-judgmental presence is a beneficial one, a situation that enhances the ethical acceptability of observations of this kind.

Having come across various accounts of subtly beneficial effects, I was interested by events that took place at the end of one of my own periods of observation, described in Turp (2001). The baby's mother ('Jenny') told me with much feeling how important the observation had been to her. She said that her own mother had been disapproving of her and disparaging of her style of mothering and this had to some extent spoiled her experience of her first child as a baby. To her, my friendly interest felt wonderfully supportive and enabled her to fully enjoy mothering her second baby.

The growth of psychoanalytic infant observation has also been part and parcel of an ongoing psychoanalytic interest in health and everyday living. It is an area of study where theory is used with a light touch. Observation and description are given priority and theory remains closely linked to the material itself. I have been much influenced by this approach in relation both to the observations presented here and the clinical material presented later. I am aware, of course, that the construction of any kind of a narrative involves some 'shaping' of the material. Nevertheless, I have been scrupulous in my efforts to select and adjust the theory to match the events, rather than re-shaping the events so that they fit comfortably into a pre-existing theoretical framework.

The extracts presented in this chapter and the next come from my observation of 'Esther'. I first met Esther a week after she entered the world. She arrived via a planned Caesarean section, which took place five days before her due date. When her mother, 'Helen', returned from hospital, I visited to make my first observation and enquired about Helen's health. 'Oh, it's a bit uncomfortable,' she said, 'but nothing compared to what you get.' She and her husband Rob gazed lovingly down at Esther, asleep on her mother's lap. To this couple, as to many parents, their baby is a source of wonder, inherently loveable and deserving of the best possible care.

Parental sensitivity

From the start of life, Esther's parents do their best to 'read' how she is and to respond to her (imagined) internal state and to her preferences. In this way, they indicate to Esther that she is deserving of their attention, interest, concern and respect.

Observation at 3 months

Helen puts Esther in her rocker chair and gives her a toy doll ('Katy'). Esther cries. 'Don't you want to go in there?' says Helen and immediately lifts her out. They sit at the kitchen table together and Helen makes Katy sing and dance.

Observation at 4 months

Rob is looking after Esther. She has just started eating solid food and he is about to prepare her lunch. He tells me seriously, 'She likes a little pureed carrot and apple, but she doesn't like courgette.'

Observation at 7 months

Rob is telling me about last Friday, when Esther 'cried and cried'. He says, 'I wonder what it's like for her, not to be able to tell us what's wrong.' He turns to Esther and continues: 'You definitely had a pain, though, didn't you? Maybe it was a sore throat? You felt better when you'd had some Calpol, though, didn't you?'

Observation at 7 months

Esther is in the kitchen in her high chair. She is banging plastic cups together noisily, then banging down on the tray of the chair so that the cups dance around and eventually fall on the floor. When they have gone, she sits quietly for a minute then rubs her right eye and begins to play with her left ear. Helen says to me, 'She's tired. She hasn't had a sleep this morning.' She adds, 'It's funny. My Dad pulls his ears as well when he's tired.'

Because her needs are well intuited and responded to, Esther soon becomes adept at indicating them more clearly.

Observation at 8 months

We are upstairs. Esther has been crawling around and playing happily but now each book and toy is discarded after only a few seconds and her face wears an expression of discontent. She points at her cot and says, 'Uh! Uh!' Helen says, 'She does that now when she's tired', then to Esther, 'You want to go for a little sleep, don't you?'

Observation at 8 months

Rob is looking after Esther. We are in the kitchen catching up on Esther's progress and drinking a cup of coffee. Esther is crawling around taking toys out of her big basket near the window and playing with them. Suddenly she begins to cry. We look towards her and Rob says, 'What happened? Did you bang your head?' In response, Esther crawls to the window and mimes bumping her head on the window ledge. Then she puts her hand to her head. Rob says to me, 'Hey, look at that. She showed me what happened', and then to Esther, 'That was very clever, you know.' He picks her up and gives her head a rub and a kiss.

Recognition of achievements

Like many parents, Helen and Rob take great delight in their daughter's achievements. Many of these 'achievements' involve her simply being who she is and doing the things she likes to do. We can imagine that, through the process of internalisation, parental pleasure in Esther's accomplishments serves as a building block for her sense of self-worth and thus for her future self-care.

Observation at 5 months

Esther is held by Helen with her legs astride, one each side of her thigh. She is kicking her legs and waving her arms up and down. Helen rocks her from side to side. 'Are we going bicycling? Is it the Tour de France?' Esther says, 'Aah! Aah!', with great animation. Helen takes her over to the mirror. 'Who's that big girl? It's a kicking girl. Look at those strong kicking legs!' Esther kicks and cycles some more, watching herself in the mirror and panting a little.

Observation at 6 months

Rob is giving Esther her lunch. 'Show Maggie how you can drink from your cup, even though you're very little.' Esther clasps the cup with both hands and chews the spout noisily, not in fact drinking. With the spout still in her mouth, Esther looks up at Rob in a questioning way. He laughs with me and Esther joins in with the joke, laughing delightedly herself. Rob tells her she has done very well.

Observation at 13 months

Esther is sitting on the floor playing with a soft toy lion. Rob says, 'It's really exciting, you know. She can walk!' He turns to Esther. 'Let's show Maggie your walking skills.' He picks her up and sets her on her feet about a metre away from him. 'Walk to Daddy.' Esther looks across at me and gives a shy smile, then takes two steps to Rob, who scoops her up. She points to her dog-on-wheels and shouts. Rob gets it for her and she walks up and down the kitchen with great élan, pushing the dog by the handle. Each time she passes me, she turns and gives me a huge self-satisfied smile.

Stern (1999) refers to 'vitality contours' – sequences of action and interaction characterised by rising and falling tides of excitement. He notes that such sequences both reflect and contribute to emotional attunement between parent and infant. Many examples can be seen in the observations of Esther, including those included above. In this family, as in many others, the use of humour plays an important part in the creation of shared feeling states. Esther is regularly invited to share a joke and, although the verbal content is certainly lost on her, she responds with alacrity.

Evolving concern for others

Where self-worth develops in a satisfactory manner, we may expect to begin to see the concerned and respectful behaviour towards others that is also evidence of the establishment of a good internal object and an associated capacity for gratitude and generosity (Klein 1957). The following observation speaks of the role of good care, including the infant's gratitude in relation to that care, in the establishment of a good internal object and hence in the shaping of relationships with others. As Esther learns to talk, her self-confidence grows. She is a sociable and chatty toddler who knows that she will be listened to and that what she has to say will be received, considered and responded to with due care and attention. By the age of 18 months, she is showing evidence of an internal resource that finds expression in a generosity towards others and a genuine concern for their pleasure, comfort and well-being.

Observation at 22 months

The family has visitors. Esther is keen to see everybody seated and says to me in a solicitous tone, patting a particular chair, 'Maggie, You sit *here.*' Rob says, 'Where shall I sit, Esther?' '*Here,*' she says, pointing to another chair. Esther brings me a crisp, then a biscuit, then takes these items around to other people, saying in a questioning voice, 'You like a crisp?' 'You like a biscuit?'

Maternal care, self-worth and self-care

Object relations theory revolves around the interaction between infant desire and phantasy, maternal response and the consequent shaping of the internal world of the infant. An underlying and widely accepted premise is that internal objects colour our every encounter with the external world. Good internal objects are the source of resourcefulness, authenticity and self-worth. They underpin resilience in the face of life's challenges and the capacity to recover from life's disappointments.

Klein described the good internal object as deriving on the one hand from the nourishing and comforting qualities of the breast and on the other from the contribution made by the infant's own capacity for love and gratitude.

> The close bond between a young infant and his mother centres on the relation to her breast. Although, from the earliest days onwards, the infant also responds to other features of the mother – her voice, her face, her hands – the fundamental experiences of happiness and love, of frustration and hatred, are inextricably linked with the mother's breast. This early bond with the mother, which is strengthened as the breast is being securely established in the inner world, basically influences all other relationships, in the first place with the father; it underlies the capacity to form any deep and strong attachment to one person.

With bottle-fed babies the bottle can take the place of the breast if it is given in a situation approximating to breast-feeding, i.e. if there is a close physical nearness to the mother and the infant is handled and fed in a loving way. Under such conditions the infant may be able to establish within himself *an object felt to be the primary source of goodness*. In this sense he takes into himself the good breast, a process which underlies a secure relation to the mother. (Klein 1952, p.99, my italics)

Klein's thinking on good and bad internal objects continued to develop throughout her long career. Contemporary Kleinian Meira Likierman has this to say in reference to one of Klein's last papers, 'Envy and Gratitude', published in 1957:

This is a final confirmation that the first good object has a unique place in mental life, as it does throughout the life cycle, since the human individual continues to depend on the self-nourishing creative core that was introjected in infancy. (Likierman 2001, p.173)

Advances in developmental psychology have refined our understanding of the capacities – social, emotional and cognitive – of new-born and young infants. It has been suggested in some quarters that Klein overemphasised the importance of the feeding relationship. Stern (1977, 1985, 1999) has highlighted the 'dances of reciprocity' and echoing and re-echoing 'vitality contours' characteristic of periods when the baby is alert and not feeding. In similar vein, Trevarthen (1979, 1998) has called our attention to early patterns of vocal interaction that prefigure actual verbal conversations, where mother and baby take it in turns to 'speak', each waiting for the other to respond before continuing. In the passage cited above, Klein also refers to the mother's voice, face and hands, and to bottle-feeding, suggesting that these new contributions constitute an adjustment of emphasis rather than a total change of view.

The establishment of the good internal object is immediately relevant to self-care, for self-care must surely be grounded in a sense of self-worth, in the understanding, conscious or unconscious, that one is deserving of care, that it is right that one should be treated with proper care and respect. While many factors, including academic and work achievements, contribute to self-worth, the feeling that one is deserving of care and should be treated well *simply on the basis of being oneself* remains the most significant. Many of us have encountered people who have achieved a great deal in the external world but who are nevertheless plagued by feelings of worthlessness and inadequacy. High on the list of such individuals are those who physically harm themselves, who often speak of being bad, of feeling bad and of having to purge a feeling of badness: 'Sometimes at night I would walk for hours in the rain wondering why I'd been born so bad, useless and ugly. The only way I found of coping was to self-harm' (Arnold 1995, p.13).

Self-care and 'entitlement'

Krystal (1988) suggests that the core of post-traumatic disturbance is a loss of integration and, particularly, *a loss of the ability to carry out self-caring and self-integrating functions.* He argues that a capacity for self-care involves not only a concern for one's own physical safety and enjoyment but also a sense of entitlement with regard to the exercise of self-caring functions. One aspect of 'good enough' mothering (Winnicott 1960b) is the physical comforting and soothing of the infant. Another is the communication of the idea that the infant has a right to exercise this function for himself or herself, that it is not reserved for the maternal figure alone:

> The availability of a good self object not only allows the grandiosity of the child to unfold appropriately but also permits the feeling that it is proper for him to 'take care of himself'. In other words, infantile omnipotence permits the fantasy of self-care when the actual capacity for it is nil... If the child's grandiosity includes a long enough period of his fantasies of 'providing for himself' the loving and soothing functions, these may become relatively guilt free. (Krystal 1988, p.194)

Krystal implies that a capacity for self-care is a 'given'. He states that where there are failures of self-care, this is not because there is a 'deficit' but because the individual in question feels that to care for himself would be to usurp the maternal function:

> It is that he is unable to acknowledge, claim, and exercise various parts and functions of himself; he experiences these as being part of the object-representation, not of the self-representation. Without being consciously aware of it, he experiences himself as unable to carry out these

functions because he feels that they are prohibited to him, being reserved for the parental objects. (1988, p.174)

With recent neuroscience findings in mind, I would like to suggest that problems can arise in two distinct areas. It seems unlikely that self-care is an emergent 'given', as Krystal suggests. The infant is ill equipped to organise and manage biological functions on his or her own. This has been found to be the case with regard to homeostatic regulation of digestion, sleep, and of many other basic physiological functions. There is little reason to suppose that the situation with regard to self-soothing and self-comfort is different. Almost certainly, the neural networks involved in these functions, in common with other neural networks involved in physiological self-regulation, are dependent upon stimulation in the form of positive interactions with primary caretakers (Schore 1994).

The value of Krystal's work lies in the attention he draws to the fact that maternal comfort and care is not in itself *sufficient* to ensure an effective adult capacity for self-care. The infant needs both to be responsively and affectionately cared for and to acquire a sense of agency, of entitlement to the independent exercise of self-caring functions. Without this, the caring function remains 'walled off' within the maternal object. When this is the case, the individual finds himself or herself in the grip of an unconscious prohibition:

> The conflict is generated by the infantile view that it is the prerogative of the mothering parent to lend all the organizing, nurturing and, in fact *life-maintaining* powers to the child. The mother seems to have the exclusive right to provide loving, comforting and soothing, as if she had cornered the love market. (Krystal 1988, p.182)

Krystal's work enables us to understand how a client who describes being well cared for or even 'wrapped up in cotton wool' as a child may nevertheless have difficulties with self-care in adult life.

In the observations presented above, we see how a sense of entitlement might begin to be established in infancy. Helen and Rob care lovingly for Esther and in addition actively support her gestures towards autonomy in the arena of self-care. Helen does not say: 'You're tired. You are going to sleep.' She takes her cue from Esther's action of pointing to her cot and says: 'You want to go for a little sleep, don't you?' Rob does not tell me: 'I give her courgette because I know it is good for her.' He says 'She *doesn't like* courgette', the implication being that this is a matter of some importance and that her wishes are to be respected. In these and in many other small ways, Esther's parents communicate to her that she has a right to begin to determine what she needs, what is right for her, and that her 'views' will be taken into account. Thus her capacity for self-care is both being established and becoming available to her as something that she is entitled to exercise for herself.

4

Bodily Integrity and Psychic Skin: Observations of Esther

> The mother's capacity to respond to her baby's experience seems to be felt by the baby at first as a gathering together of his bodily sensations, engendering the beginnings of a sense of bodily integrity (Shuttleworth in Miller *et al.* 1989, p.32)

Other themes that emerge from observations of Esther call to mind Winnicott's work on bodily integrity and post-Kleinian work on the significance of skin, in both the physical and the metaphorical sense. These themes are explored here through observation extracts grouped under the headings of 'Touching and being touched' and 'Physical enjoyment and physical hazards'. Observations presented later in the chapter relate to the management of 'impingements' and potential disturbances of 'continuity of being' (Winnicott 1960b).

The first set of observation extracts testify to Esther's fascination with her own skin and the skin of others, and perhaps also to an emerging sense of what it means to be embodied within a skin.

Touching and being touched

From the start, Esther is carried a great deal, especially by her mother. Usually, when I arrive, Helen comes to the door with Esther on her hip or shoulder. When Esther is picked up, put down and has her nappy changed, I am aware of a respect for her as a whole person who deserves to be treated with care and consideration. This respect is characteristic of both parents in their interactions with Esther. The following sequence of observations shows Esther beginning to learn about touching other people (and cats) without hurting them.

Observation at 4 months

Helen comes to the door carrying Esther. She says, 'Look. It's Maggie.' Esther gazes at me long and hard. Then she turns back to Helen and very gently fingers her face and neck. She catches a strand of Helen's hair and holds on to it. 'I hope you're not going to pull that hair hard,' says Helen, half-joking.

The builder arrives and Helen stays at the front door, talking to him and to Esther. Helen needs to choose a new front door and we go out into the street to look at other people's front doors. 'Yes, I think that's the door we want, isn't it, Mouse?' says Helen. Esther holds on to the strand of hair, not pulling it, her face calm and alert.

Observation at 5 months

The builder is again in residence and Helen is carrying Esther so that Esther looks out over her shoulder. She takes a strand of Helen's hair, fingers it and pulls it gently. She lets go and takes hold of Helen's hand and tries to put it in her mouth, sucking noisily on her knuckles. Then she does the same with Helen's cheek, opening her mouth wide but not hurting or biting. Helen says, 'That *is* a big kiss!'

Observation at 7 months

Rob is carrying Esther. He speaks to me and, as he does so, Esther fingers his chin gently. The cat comes into the kitchen. Esther spots it immediately, makes small, excited sounds and reaches her hands out towards it. Rob holds her where she can touch the cat and she takes hold of its tail. 'Gently,' says Rob and Esther is quite gentle but nevertheless attempts to put the cat's tail in her mouth. 'No, not in the mouth,' says Rob. The cat escapes and runs out of the room.

Physical enjoyment and physical hazards

As with all infants, the possibility of accidental injury increases once Esther becomes mobile. When she starts to crawl, I notice that her parents are very protective towards her. I sometimes see Helen insert a hand between Esther's vulnerable head and the wooden leg of the kitchen table that she might otherwise bump into. Once she can walk and run, it becomes more difficult to protect her. Increasingly, Esther expresses her determination to be allowed to experiment. Her enthusiasm for using her new skills outpaces her competence but she remains undaunted. Soon she is running with gay abandon up and down the hall. Helen and Rob are obliged to live with the fact that their daughter will at times hurt herself in minor ways.

Observation at 16 months

We are in the kitchen. Rob pulls out Esther's big 'dog on wheels' that she can pull around by the handle. She pulls it up and down the kitchen with great enthusiasm, emitting high, squeaking sounds and occasionally looking over at me to see if I am watching. Rob says, 'She's running now and it gets scary. She's had some real spills. Last week she surfed down the stairs on a suitcase. And last Sunday when we were walking in the cemetery, she ran and ran and then of course she fell and grazed her knee.'

His voice suggests that he is partly anxious and partly admiring of his plucky and adventurous daughter. The need to manage a tendency towards recklessness and/or a tendency towards timidity and excessive caution is an aspect of self-care that will be a lifelong concern. It is one of the things that Esther, as yet, has little capacity to manage for herself. Instead, Rob and Helen do their best to ensure their daughter's safety and at the same time to respect and support her healthy sense of adventure.

Each of these observation extracts relates in some way to the question of bodily integrity or, to use Winnicott's phrase, 'the psyche indwelling in the soma' (1960b, p.45). The question of 'bodily integrity' is an interesting one. It is something that we intuitively recognise and yet it is not easy to describe the basis for our perceptions. I notice that Esther's movements become increasingly smooth and well co-ordinated and that they span a full range, from energetic and exuberant to finely tuned and painstaking. Most of all, she looks 'all of a piece' or in the French phrase *'bien dans sa peau'* – 'at home in her skin'. Winnicott writes of 'what might be called "in-dwelling": the achievement of a close and easy relationship between the psyche and the body and body functioning' (Winnicott 1962b, p.69).

One reflection of a good quality of psychosomatic indwelling is the active enjoyment of physical self-expression: 'In health, the use of the body and all its functions is one of the enjoyable things, and this applies especially to children and to adolescence' (Winnicott 1986, p.29). Such enjoyment is readily observable in Esther's vigorous kicking as a small infant. It develops further as she extends her range of motor skills to include sitting, crawling, walking and running. In Turp (2001) I examined the possibility that in adult life as well, skilled and/or vigorous physical activity helps to sustain a good quality of 'indwelling'.

'Impingements' and 'continuity of being'

A major area of concern in Winnicott's work is the preservation of 'being', dependent from the outset on maternal protection from 'impingements':

> With 'the care it receives from the mother' each infant is able to have a personal existence, and so begins to build up what might be called a *continuity of being*. On the basis of this continuity of being the inherited potential gradually develops into an individual infant. If maternal care is not good enough then the infant does not really come into existence, since there is no continuity of being; instead the personality becomes built on the basis of reactions to environmental impingement. (1960b p.54)

The following observation shows a potential impingement being managed in a way that protects Esther's experience of continuity of being.

Observation at 7 months

When I arrive, Helen tells me, 'I'm going to wake her up. She's been asleep too long. She's been sleeping so badly at night ever since she had that cold.' (Looks at me and laughs.) 'She's had to come back into the big bed!'

We go upstairs and I see that Esther is fast asleep on her back in her cot with a cover over her. Helen gently removes the cover and begins to stroke Esther's forehead. 'Are you going to wake up?' After a minute or two, Esther stretches, extending her left leg and pointing the toe. She opens her eyes, sees Helen and smiles. She turns her head and spots me and gives me a long, serious gaze. Then she looks back at Helen and smiles again and begins to coo gently.

Helen speaks in a slightly more animated way. 'You had a croissant for breakfast and then a long, long sleep. It's not a bad life, is it? Are you ready to wake up now?' Esther smiles more widely and kicks her legs. Helen laughs and gives Esther a little tickle in the chest. Esther becomes more enlivened and drums her legs up and down on the cot. 'Do those legs still work?' says Helen. 'Yes! They work very well.'

Esther becomes still again and Helen passes her a knitted rabbit. Esther puts its leg in her mouth and chews with an expression of great thoughtfulness. Rob comes in and says, 'Are you chewing Minty's foot?' Looking at Rob, Esther becomes very animated and kicks and drums her legs vigorously on the mattress. Helen and Rob both laugh. Helen says, 'Do you get very far on that bicycle? How fast can that baby go?'

Now Esther is fully awake. She reaches her arms out to Helen, who picks her up out of the cot.

Esther is disturbed from her sleep in a very gentle way and allowed to wake up gradually, at her own pace. Her parents respond to the ebb and flow of her energy and activity, closely matching their own level of liveliness to that of their daughter. Their sensitivity and respect for Esther's timing ensure that a potential impingement – being forcibly woken from a sleep – does not become an actual impingement.

Winnicott's work on 'being' and 'continuity of being' is complementary to his reflections on 'the psyche indwelling in the soma' (1970). In his account, overall well-being is absolutely tied in with the provision of an environment that allows the infant to inhabit the psyche–soma with a minimum of disturbance.

> In the ordinary course of events the mother tries not to introduce complications beyond those which the infant can understand and allow for; in particular she tries to insulate her baby from coincidences and from other phenomena that must be beyond the infant's ability to comprehend. (Winnicott 1949, p.245)

Winnicott highlights the particular role played by touch and physical care, in the form of responsive maternal 'handling', in supporting psychosomatic indwelling. Abram offers this summary of Winnicott's work on the nature and consequences of impingements:

> If the infant is properly protected at the beginning – if he has good enough ego support from the environment – then he will gradually learn to meet the impingement, which will result in a strengthening of his self-awareness. However, if the impingement is too early or too intense, the result will be traumatic, and the infant can do nothing but *react*. It is the *reactions* to impingement happening over a period of time that cause damage to the personality and result in fragmentation. (Abram 1996, p.163)

Later in the book, when I am describing psychotherapy encounters, I will refer to thoughts, images and physical sensations that float into awareness in the presence of particular clients. A number of these 'unexpected guests' seem to gesture towards situations where an infant has been subject to impingements that have been 'too early or too intense' and have therefore been traumatic.

Physical skin and psychic skin

There are many points of contact between the scenario described by Winnicott and post-Kleinian thinking on the subject of skin. Literature in this subject area, including seminal contributions from Bick (1968), Pines (1977) and Anzieu (1989), is extensive and relatively well known. A theme that runs through much of the work is the role of 'psychic skin' in mediating the relationship between inner and outer worlds. In health, the skin allows messages from the external world to be received while at the same time maintaining a boundary between what is inside and what is outside the individual. Physically speaking, these 'messages' come in the form of different touch sensations and of cold and warmth. In the case of 'psychic skin', the reference is to a degree of psychological sensitivity and permeability. Where there is a suitable degree of permeability and resilience, the individual is able to sense and take on board the emotions of others without becoming swamped, and at the same time to effectively communicate his or her emotions. It is the skin, both literal and metaphorical, that holds the individual together, safeguards coherence and yet permits the interpenetration of internal and external worlds of experience.

Freud denotes the 'id' (literally the 'it') as the well-spring of instinctual drives, as body-based. Interestingly, he also describes the ego as 'first and foremost a bodily ego' (1923). He suggests that the early development of the ego depends on a sense of the skin, which forms a boundary between the inner and outer worlds of the individual. In similar vein, Winnicott refers to 'the perpetual *human* task of keeping inner and outer reality separate yet interrelated' (Winnicott 1953, p.230). These ideas are extended further in post-Kleinian thinking. Bick (1968) describes how the skin is not at first experienced as having a sufficient binding force to hold the infant together. The infant relies on maternal care, including being wrapped in clothes and being held and fed at the breast, for a sense of proper enclosure and embodiment.

Drawing on her own infant observations, Bick suggests that repeated failures of maternal care force an infant into excessive reliance on inanimate objects for a sense of being held together. The infant defends against the threat of psychological disintegration – 'falling apart' – by concentrating intensely on, for example, a moving curtain or a patch of light on a wall. Or he distracts himself through constant activity and use of 'muscularity'. Where such devices are relied upon to excess, a distortion of psychic skin functioning develops. Bick's concept of 'second skin' formation involving toughening and impermeability describes such distortion. A 'hippopotamus hide' develops that protects the infant against the threat of disintegration but at the same time impairs his capacity for relationship. This state of affairs may be expressed either in avoidance of relationships or in 'adhesive' relating, expressed in clinging and over-dependent behaviour.

Briggs (1997) extends Bick's work, exploring the complementary possibility of 'porous' skin, skin that is slack and, metaphorically speaking, falling in holes. This situation can find expression in a number of ways, including psychosomatic illness and an air of drifting and incomplete presence. My first observation was of an infant, 'Emma', whose mother was (in my estimation) suffering from undiagnosed post-natal depression. Emma was left for long periods in her rocker chair and later her high chair. She was carried and held very little and often appeared glazed-over and inert, having apparently been dropped from her mother's mind. At one point, the situation led me to note: 'Emma seems to express a weakened sense of skin, barely any skin at all… Instead of manic activity and overde-veloped physicality, I witness a sagging posture, half-hearted crying, and a lack of physical vigour' (Turp 2001, p.96).

There is, I believe, a particular connection to be made between porous skin phenomena and what I refer to as self-harm by omission. By this I mean behaviour that leads to significant injury or damage to health through inaction rather than through action. Examples include failures to ensure adequate sleep or nutrition, failures to seek urgently needed medical attention and accidental injuries associated with states of distraction and dissociation. The vignette of 'Harry' (Chapter 2) and the case examples of 'Peter' and 'Kate' (to follow) are concerned primarily with difficulties of this nature.

Prior to training as a psychotherapist, I was a social worker for many years. When I first read Bick's work, I was painfully reminded of the children I had worked with, many of whom had chaotic home backgrounds and had experienced periods of being 'looked after' by the local authority. The self-harm I witnessed, involving attacks on an already scarred skin and a tough and confrontational self-presentation alternating with expressions of extreme dependency seem also to speak of the development of a toughened and/or porous 'second skin' that is both a necessary protection and a distressing liability.

Returning to the subject of the good care enjoyed by Esther, we can see from the observations that she has a very tactile relationship with both of her parents. The responsive touch experiences described in the observations are a source of pleasure for all parties. As well as benefiting from the responsive handling, Esther enjoys her parents' enjoyment and the sense of a shared feeling state. Each of these aspects of experience contributes to a robust sense of oneness and bodily integrity.

Holding, handling and containment

Winnicott emphasises that either a major impingement or an accumulation of minor impingements can constitute a trauma, as described in Chapter 1. An impingement is an event that 'pierces' the individual rather than being processed in the usual way. Because it is unprocessed, it lives on in an unintegrated state, making its presence felt in physical symptoms and/or disturbances of self-care.

The maternal functions that protect the infant from impingement are described by Winnicott as 'holding' and 'handling' and by Bion as 'containment'. Both theoretical formulations speak of the need for 'primary maternal preoccupation' (Winnicott 1956) or 'maternal receptivity' (Bion 1962), phrases that refer to the mother's capacity and willingness to take on board the infant's experience with all its attendant and often intense emotion. Winnicott suggests that it is the mother's identification with the infant – her unconscious memory of her own infant experience – that underpins her capacity to intuit and respond to the infant's unspeakable states of mind.

Bion emphasises the communicative aspects of projective identification, the unconscious process via which the infant stirs up in the mother emotions that mirror those that threaten to overwhelm the infant himself. In both accounts, it is taken for granted that, in the early weeks and months of life, an infant will encounter situations that he is not psychologically equipped to manage. Perhaps he has to have an injection or perhaps he wakes up and his mother isn't there and, in a state of terror and imagined abandonment, he 'falls apart'. Unlike other experiences, where there is a sense of an 'I' having an experience, these experiences 'have' the infant. They overwhelm him completely. It is quite beyond him to process the feelings involved, to make any kind of sense of them. All he can do is 'project' his experience, throw it away from him. This projection often takes the form of wailing or screaming. The infant may hiccup and sob. Arms and legs fly out and flail, giving a physical impression of fragmentation and panic.

In normal circumstances, these projections exert a powerful effect on the infant's mother or other close carer. Her receptive state equips her for the task of intuiting the infant's state of mind and bringing her adult capacity for thinking into play. This is done quite automatically as a normal part of loving and attending to the infant. Hence the mother receives, acknowledges and thinks about the experiences being communicated and returns them to the infant in a detoxified and manageable form.

Narratives of continuity

These are matters to which I shall return when considering the case study material. At this point, I want to look more closely at the aspects of 'holding' or 'containment' that relate particularly to what I describe as the creation and preservation of a 'narrative skin', a phrase also used by Scott (1998). This final observation extract shows Rob 'pacing' actions and narrating them, organising them in a time sequence, as he changes Esther's nappy.

Observation at 3 months

Rob takes Esther upstairs to change her nappy and I follow behind. He lays her down on the changing mat very carefully, talking to her as he does so. 'That's a bit cold, isn't it? Is it OK for you?' He takes off her fabric shoes. Esther lies with her hand half in her mouth and gurgles at Rob. She reaches with her other hand to take hold of one of the shoes lying next to her, brings it to her mouth and chews it. Rob talks her through the nappy change, 'Trousers off. One leg. Two legs. Now comes the nappy...' Esther is very relaxed and co-operative.

Rob picks Esther up when he has finished and walks around with her. She sits in the crook of his arm, looks over at me and smiles perkily.

The overall feeling of this observation is that great care is being taken to ensure that Esther's continuity of being is not unduly disturbed. In respecting Esther's right not to be unduly disrupted, her parents are perhaps laying the foundations for adult self-care that includes the capacity for 'Saying No' (Asha Phillips 1999) to demands that are excessive or that require the sudden and unreasonable interruption of an activity that is already under way.

The preservation of 'continuity of being' can be thought of as an additional psychic skin phenomenon, one with a significant temporal element. It is easy to see how the creation of a 'narrative skin' might protect against the threat of internal chaos and fragmentation. A web of words is woven around Esther and this in itself soothes and contains. Events are organised into an orderly sequence and the feeling of this rhythm and orderliness helps to sustain her sense of continuity.

The provision of a narrative skin involves maternal holding-in-mind that is sustained over time. At the beginning, when symbolic functions are in the early stages of development, physical 'handling' as well as 'holding in mind' is essential. Observations presented by Amez and Botero (2000) describe the plight of a premature infant whose 'kangaroo care' is interrupted. When the infant has to be admitted to hospital, her mother's holding-in-mind continues, in the sense that her thoughts are constantly with her daughter and she visits her as much as possible. However, the hospital policy militates against the continuation of 'kangaroo care' and, without physical continuity, the infant is unable to benefit from this hold-ing-in-mind. The web of thoughts and words is not effective in the absence of the accustomed skin-to-skin contact. This child comes very close to dying but, thankfully, just manages to pull through.

Problems also arise if the mother's narrative involves a fantasised rather than a realistic version of events. During my observation of 'Emma', referred to briefly above, Emma's mother, 'Louise', became keen to return to work and, perhaps because of doubts about her own maternal capacities, was extremely enthusiastic about the child-minder she found and about Emma's relationship with the other children in the household. Relieved of continuous responsibility and thus of some of her own difficult feelings, Louise seemed to become more able to hold Emma in mind. It was clear from the observations undertaken at home that she felt much more able to engage with Emma and the mother–daughter relationship finally seemed to be going well. Louise encouraged me to undertake two observations at the child-minder's home, which I did. To my dismay, on both occasions Emma, now 11 months old, was almost entirely 'forgotten', unable to join in with two older, more confident and more boisterous children. She spent the major part of both observation periods in a regressed state, curled up on the floor with a very large Teddy Bear, sucking a bottle.

Within a few weeks, Emma's development seemed to have ground to a halt. After three months, she developed a large neck abscess that had to be drained and this necessitated her and her mother spending several days together in hospital. It seems not unreasonable to view this incident as a psychosomatic crisis, precipitated by the interruption in the experience of good holding and of the provision of a narrative skin that Emma was just beginning to enjoy. Perhaps because her early experiences had been less than ideal, Emma did not have the resources at 11 months to conserve her sense of continuity during the long hours in the child-minder's home. Following the period of hospitalisation, the mother–daughter relationship took another step forward, becoming close and affectionate, the hours of child-minding were reduced and Emma's development accelerated in every way.

I have given some examples of the way in which Helen and Rob verbally organise Esther's experiences into an orderly sequence of events. On many occasions, I observe a narrative skin being sustained and, when it has been disrupted, being restored. Although subject to the inevitable disruptions that are a part of the life of every family, Rob and Helen manage on the whole to conserve the orderly and familiar rituals of the day. Like most parents, they have an intuitive sense of the importance of such rituals, which bestow a sense of rhythm and predictability and so bring the complexities of the day within the grasp of the infant. Although there is a great deal that is novel for the infant in every new day, something is also conveyed that speaks of an underlying pattern and order. In simplifying and highlighting regular patterns of events, rituals serve as an aspect of parental protection from 'impingements', from 'complications beyond those which the infant can understand and allow for', referred to above (Winnicott 1949).

In the observations we can see how, from very early on, sequences of events are accompanied and supported by verbal narratives. Helen seems to recognise the importance of offering Esther a narrative of the day so far: 'You had a croissant for breakfast and then a long, long sleep. It's not a bad life, is it? Are you ready to wake up now?' Sorensen refers to this type of narrative as 'a linguistic mode relative to the sequence of events' (2000, p.49). The phrase 'narrative skin' seems to me to convey in a less technical way the sense of what is meant. As Esther's capacity for symbolisation develops, we can imagine that she will be well equipped to create her own 'narratives of continuity' in the future.

The space allocated to exploring this train of thought reflects the potential value of a concept such as a 'narrative of continuity' in relation to the question of self-harm. Individuals who harm themselves often convey a sense that they are threatened by chaos or have already been invaded by feelings of chaos. The involvement of skin – physical skin – in many acts of self-harm is also striking and presumably meaningful. Thus the concepts of 'psychic skin' and 'narrative skin', which have their origins in infant observation studies, offer a particularly useful framework for thinking about potential meanings of self-harming behaviour in adult life.

5

Themes and Theoretical Frameworks

A conscientious, detailed, and interesting report of even a single case is like a fine portrait; we can return to it again and again when we wish to understand. Its helpfulness is in depth rather than in breadth of view. (Cobb in Sifneos 1965, p.xi)

When Sifneos, a psychiatrist, asked his patient for permission to write about their work together, the patient apparently replied, 'Tell it like it is, doc!' The clients whose stories appear in the following chapters have also given permission for publication. In a spirit of gratitude and respect, I shall also do my best to 'tell it like it is'. This chapter serves as an introduction to the case studies, setting out some of the ideas that inform the style of presentation and the theoretical discussion of the material.

The value of description

The rallying cry of that philosophical movement known as phenomenology, founded by Edmund Husserl (1859–1939), was 'to the things themselves' ('*zu den Sachen selbst*'). I am not concerned here with the elaborate theories of logic, epistemology and ethics developed over time by Husserl, Brentano and Heidegger (readers who are interested will find an excellent account of these in Moran 2001) but with what David Bell refers to as 'concrete phenomenology'. This concerns the endeavour to set down experiences in the form: 'This is what it is like for me.'

Phenomenology – at least in one sense of that term – is the attempt to capture in all its concrete immediacy the intrinsic nature of one's experience, exactly as it strikes one, and without any embellishment, explanation, extrapolation, interpretation, inference or resort to theory. In this spirit, one might, for instance, try to put into words just what it feels like to experience vertigo, or grief, or hunger. Or again, one might try to capture the complex web of sensations, feelings, thoughts, images, memories, desires and emotions which occur, say, on taking a sip of tea in which a few crumbs of petite madeleine have been soaked. (Bell 2001, p.34)

Bell identifies a particular problem with concrete phenomenology, namely a tendency towards dogmatism – with 'this is what it is like for me' being replaced by 'this is what it is like'. He identifies examples of such slippage in Sartre's *La Nausée* and in contemporary work by Sokolowski (2001):

Take, for example, the description Sokolowski offers of 'the phenomenon of memory', or 'the experience' one undergoes when one remembers something. He simply asserts that 'what happens in remembering is that we relive earlier perceptions'. Should anyone object to this characterization, the author's response is simply to insist, and to keep on insisting, that: 'such reliving of experience is just what remembering is. It is quite marvellous, but that is how we are wired.' (Bell 2001, p. 34)

The tendency towards dogmatism within phenomenology is linked to a belief in the possibility of '*époché*'. The law of *époché* calls for the 'bracketing off' of assumptions, a procedure that supposedly releases the individual from the distorting effects of theories and presuppositions. The claim that this is in any way possible, that one can speak, as it were, from a 'neutral' position, is strongly challenged in postmodern writing.

Psychoanalysis is 'phenomenological' in the sense that it too is concerned with rich descriptions of subjective experience. These come into the service of the primary aim of assisting the client in his or her search for personal meaning, by uncovering and deciphering invisible currents that lie beneath the visible surface: 'One comes to see that it is not so much the nature of the act that counts but its meaning' (Chasseguet-Smirgel 1990, p.77).

If the elucidation of meaning is to proceed fruitfully, the theories we bring into play need to be grounded in robust descriptive accounts, accounts that do justice to the complexity of the situation. Good description provides a secure base from which to work and offers a measure of protection against stereotyping and other flights from thoughtfulness.

Intersubjectivity and postmodernism

Merleau-Ponty develops the idea of intersubjectivity, rooted in Heidegger's notion (1927) of 'being-in-the-world' ('*Dasein*'), emphasising the fundamentally interpersonal nature of being: 'My existence as subjectivity is merely one with my existence as a body and with the existence of the world' (Merleau-Ponty 1962, p.408). Intersubjectivity informs the work of a number of contemporary developmental psychologists (Stern 1977, 1985, 1999; Trevarthen 1979, 1998) and psychoanalysts (Bollas 1987, 1993; Casement 1985; Crossley 1996; Elliott and Frosh 1995; Lacan 1979; Ogden 1997, and many others).

Merleau-Ponty's work is also the starting point for the development by Diamond (2001) of an interpersonal understanding of bodily experience:

> Merleau-Ponty made the following points. The infant does not start life in an interior mental space but is, from the first, situated outside in its bodily behaviour and intentions that are orientated towards others. The infant and others do not coexist as disembodied psyches but share an embodied space, where communication is formed in bodily actions. (p.49)

The client who self-harms likewise shares an 'embodied space' with the psychotherapist. The action described can only be understood in the context of its enactment and its telling. This sharing of an embodied space is the context for the operation of projective identification, particularly in the form of unconscious somatic communications, a phenomenon that pervades the clinical encounters I describe.

In postmodernism, the constant 'embeddedness' of the individual within a culture is emphasised. Much of what we are, what we perceive and what we believe is socially constructed. We cannot step outside our embeddedness, hence we cannot 'bracket off' our assumptions. We are called upon, however, to take up a critical stance towards taken-for-granted knowledge:

> Postmodernism questions the basis for all knowledge and expertise and asks us to challenge our assumptions and beliefs, the things we hold most dear. How do we know what we know? How is knowledge constructed? How do we use knowledge, whoever or whatever or wherever we are? (Taylor and Loewenthal 2001, pp.64–65)

A highly relevant postmodern theme is the ephemeral quality of what we take to be 'true' and 'real'. If perception involves an unconscious and culturally shaped act of interpretation, as has been shown to be the case (see, for example, Lesser 1996), then the stories we tell ourselves, based on our perceptions, are not undistorted reflections of 'objective reality'. Inevitably, they are our individually and culturally shaped versions of events.

> It is especially important to emphasize that narrative is not an alternative to truth or reality; rather it is the mode in which, inevitably, truth and reality are presented. We have only versions of the true and the real. (Schafer 1992, p.xiv)

In psychoanalysis, as in sociology and anthropology, a number of contemporary research methodologies involve participant observation. The involvement of the observer and his or her effect on the 'material' being observed is explicitly acknowledged. This is true of psychoanalytic infant observation, case study research methods (Yin 1993) and discourse analysis (Parker 1992; Potter 1997; Taylor and Loewenthal 2001). In the following chapters, I set out through the presentation of 'live' examples a descriptive version of some aspects of the 'true' and the 'real' in relation to the subject of self-harm. My account is just one of an infinite number of possible versions of events, necessarily informed by my own stance and position as well as by the client's words and behaviour.

Self-harm stereotypes

In Chapter 2 I suggested that self-care and self-harm are issues that concern each of us personally. If this is accepted, then a mental step is taken towards the client, and the possibility of a good therapeutic alliance is enhanced. Favazza (1989a, 1989b) has described self-harm as 'a purposeful, if morbid, act of self-help'. He is suggesting – and my own experience points in the same direction – that people harm themselves physically in order to feel better emotionally. When a capacity for self-care is in good order, this kind of 'self-help' is not much called for and our lapses will be limited to the domain of the 'casha'. A person may perhaps miss a meal or a night's sleep in order to finish a piece of work or deliberately eat junk food or drink heavily when he feels angry with himself or with the world. When the same dynamics are enacted at higher levels of intensity, self-directed violence or potentially catastrophic lapses in physical self-care come into play and we speak of self-harm.

I have noted that most of the available literature is focused on highly visible acts of self-harm, in particular dramatic episodes of self-cutting, self-burning and overdosing. I have acknowledged also that this literature is a valuable resource for practitioners who encounter repetitive and severe self-harming behaviour. For all its usefulness, it is also, unfortunately, a literature that reinforces a tendency to locate individuals who self-harm in a separate enclave, to identify them as 'not like us'.

Viewed psychoanalytically, this depiction of self-harm as a separate and circumscribed phenomenon suggests the operation of unconscious processes of splitting and polarisation (Klein 1946). These processes are fuelled, according to Kleinian thought, by an underlying dread that bad will win out over good, in this case that self-destructive tendencies will contaminate and overwhelm self-caring tendencies. It may be that when others give active expression to dangerous impulses, we experience an internal pressure to distance ourselves, to emphasise the difference between 'us' and 'them'. Psychoanalysts are not immune to the unconscious imperatives that drive such defensive strategies. They do, however, have the potential advantage of a language in which to speak of the processes involved.

Wise (1989), Arnold (1995), Pembroke (2000) and Gardner (2001) have also commented on the prevalence of stereotyping in relation to the phenomenon of self-harm. The self-harming individual is widely depicted as (a) always female, (b) always angry, (c) suffering from borderline personality disorder and (d) a victim of childhood sexual abuse. With regard to the latter, Favazza sounds a welcome note of caution:

One caveat I would encourage readers to keep in mind is that childhood physical and sexual abuse so dramatically and accurately described in the book applies to 50 to 60 percent of self-mutilators, which means that a fair number have *not* been abused. On several occasions I have had to rescue patients from therapists who were frustrated at not being able to find the cause of an individual's self-mutilation and therefore assumed that he or she must have been abused. (Favazza in Strong 2000, p.xiv)

I have reason to echo Favazza's concern. Some months ago, I received a telephone call from a counsellor whom I did not know but who had read my work. She told me she had recently been referred a client who harmed herself and added, 'I suppose that means that she has been sexually abused.' I felt it important to emphasise, in as helpful a way as possible, that the exploration of self-harming behaviour cannot be pre-empted in this way. The meaning of self-harm remains to be discovered anew in each individual case and fixed assumptions can only stand in the way of a genuine face-to-face encounter. Taken together, the case studies that follow present a complex and multi-faceted picture, challenging stereotypic conceptions of self-harm. I hope that they will serve as a resource for other practitioners, supporting their efforts to maintain a willingness not to know, to wait, in Bion's words, 'without memory or desire' (1967b) and to help the client tell and retell in all its various versions his or her particular story.

Psychoanalysis in the postmodern era

Psychoanalysis is a broad church. My own particular point of view, which is one among many, could be described as a contemporary object relations approach that bears the mark of phenomenological and postmodern concerns. Adam Phillips has described psychoanalysis as 'a story – and a way of telling stories – that makes some people feel better' (Phillips 1993, p.xvii). This description succinctly captures the 'meaning-making' quality of the psychoanalytic encounter that I consider to be its most important characteristic. In previous work (2001), I have suggested that postmodern tendencies are prefigured in Winnicott's work, in his refusal to 'sum up' his ideas and in his openly expressed opposition to any total system of ideas (see Rodman 1987). For Winnicott, there could never be a closure, a final explanation, of human experience and behaviour. Winnicott's spirit is alive and well, I hope, in this book.

As a psychoanalytic practitioner, I rely on a theory base to help me to think about the situations I encounter, to begin to make sense of what currently seems to the client to be without sense or meaning. Psychoanalytic theory provides a range of eloquent narratives that speak to the experience of many people who find themselves in trouble and close to despair, and in this resides its positive potential. I am aware that psychoanalytic theory also has a negative potential. In the course of my work I have come across incidents, fortunately few and far between, where self-harming individuals have had psychoanalytic theory applied to them in a high-handed and doctrinaire way and have felt demeaned by this experience.

Postmodern discussion of ethical issues has highlighted the dangers of overarching 'meta-narratives', particularly the danger of drowning out or distorting the voice of the individual (see, for example, Levinas 1961). In an effort to minimise this danger, I have included in the case study chapters copious examples of the verbatim exchanges between the client and myself. The client's voice, his or her version of events, his or her choice of words, is present in the case studies. The only exception is the case of 'Lorraine', where I supervised the work rather than undertaking it myself. The inevitable operation of selective memory and narrative smoothing prevents me from claiming that I am presenting the client's 'true voice'. Nevertheless, this is an attempt, albeit imperfect, to include the client's point of view and to ensure that it has a place alongside my own musings and interventions.

The theories we have at our disposal do not consist of indisputable sets of facts and explanations. Theory is no more, and no less, than a valuable tool for thinking. It is in this spirit that it is invoked in relation to client narratives that follow. It is the process of meaning-making, not the presentation of a formulaic explanation, that is at the heart of the matter and has the potential to be therapeutic.

Examples from counselling and psychotherapy

At the beginning of my career, I shared the widespread assumption that self-harming behaviour was in its essence highly visible, possibly even dramatic, and it is only over time that I have come to question that point of view. Over the years, I have only occasionally worked with clients who persistently and violently harm themselves. I have, however, repeatedly encountered other kinds of self-harm, self-harm that is perpetrated occasionally, self-harm that is gradual and arises from lapses in self-care, self-harm that is invisible or close to invisible and has not previously been disclosed. The research presented in Chapter 2 suggests that the same is true for many colleagues.

I have come to realise also that overlaps between different kinds of self-harm are very common. Overlaps are reflected in the case studies that follow, with most of the clients manifesting several kinds of self-harming behaviour. 'Peter', whose presenting problem is a habit of lashing out at inanimate objects and injuring himself, also describes sexual risk-taking, chronic overwork and abuse of alcohol and drugs. 'Ellen May', whose bulimic vomiting is so severe that her throat bleeds, also 'forgets' to take the anti-anxiety medication prescribed to mitigate her severe attacks of agitation and panic. My experience is in line with the findings of the Bristol Survey. Of the women who took part in that research and spoke about self-cutting, 53 per cent also referred to eating problems, 39 per cent referred to overdosing, 37 per cent referred to alcohol misuse and 35 per cent referred to drug misuse.

In presenting individual clinical examples, I am continuing a long-standing psychoanalytic tradition, one that began with Freud and Breuer's publication of their first famous case study (1893). Psychoanalytic theory has evolved out of the discussion of individual clients, out of their self-descriptions, the ways in which they relate to us and the quality of their presence, the whole experience of being in the consulting room with the particular individual in question. Each of the short vignettes and the longer case studies in the book logs an aspect of a client's voyage of discovery in the vessel that sails under the name of 'psychoanalysis', 'psychoanalytic psychotherapy' or 'psychodynamic counselling'. For simplicity, I refer to each helmsperson as a 'psychotherapist' and to each voyager as a 'client'.

In leaning heavily on individual narratives, I have come up against the usual dilemmas concerning client confidentiality and considered various courses of action. Case studies compiled from material taken from several client encounters sometimes lack conviction or give an impression, once selected and spliced together, of something unrealistically neat and tidy. Orbach arrives at an unusual solution, well suited to her stated aim of showing what psychotherapy is like for the therapist and how the therapist's reflection on her own 'bodymind' state assists in the work: 'I decided to do this by creating a set of stories between imagined patients and a fictionalized therapist, told from the perspective of the therapist' (Orbach 1999, p.3). One of my own aims is to argue for verbal therapies to be more widely offered to people who harm themselves – and a 'created set of stories' could not, of course, be offered as evidence in support of such an argument.

With these thoughts in mind, I decided some years ago to ask certain clients during the closing stages of their therapy whether they would be happy for me to refer to our work together in possible future publications. On each occasion, I suggested that they should think the matter over for a week or two prior to a further discussion. Some clients did not want their stories disclosed and their decision has, of course, been strictly respected. Some clients asked a number of questions, then gave permission in a thoughtful way, sometimes giving as their reason a wish for the work to be helpful to others who found themselves in similar difficulties.

There were a few rather difficult cases, always where the work had not gone well or the ending was unsatisfactory, where permission was quickly and carelessly given. Whether or not to take advantage of such hastily granted permission has been the subject of much soul-searching and discussion with colleagues. In the event, I decided to take the granting of permission more or less at face value. The fact is that permission is more likely to be given in a thoughtful way when the client has progressed well in the work and is happy with the outcome. To present only examples where this has been the case would be to present an idealised and unrepresentative picture. I have described in detail work with four of my ex-clients and with one client (who also gave written permission) seen by a counsellor who comes to me regularly for supervision. I consider myself most fortunate not to have had to 'compile' cases or alter significant details and I am extremely grateful to those clients who so generously gave permission for publication. In the case studies that follow, only identifying data such as names, locations and occupations have been changed.

Each of the following five chapters is organised around an individual theme. The themes are explored through the presentation of case material from work with 'Lorraine', 'Ellen May', 'Tracey', 'Peter' and 'Kate'. The clients in question come from different income brackets and age groups. Some of them have paid employment and some do not. Some have a history of obvious and easily identifiable abuse and others do not, although each of them has suffered difficult childhood experiences of one kind or another. In some cases, self-harming behaviour appears as a 'presenting problem'; in others it takes a more subtle and elusive form and comes into view only as the therapeutic alliance deepens.

Because I describe the people who find their way to my door, or to the door of counsellors whom I supervise, what is on offer here is by no means a comprehensive overview. There are groups of people I do not have occasion to work with, either directly or indirectly, and who are therefore not represented. For example, I do not work with people whose state of mind calls for the level of containment and support that can only be offered by an institution. Most of my clients are white and I am unable to offer examples of the role played by racial abuse in self-harm, although there is evidence to suggest that racism is a significant factor in some cases:

> A young woman called Humerah tells Syal how, when she was 14, she would be alone in the house during school holidays. 'The National Front people used to ring up and give me delightful messages. I just thought I'd try out what the razor was really like because I just felt so numb, so alone and pretty desperate. It just made me feel something, and that was important.' (*The Guardian*, 12/7/2000)

There are other omissions as well. I tend not to see people in the immediate aftermath of an overdose that has led to hospitalisation (although I regularly see people who have taken overdoses in the past), and I do not have contact with prisoners or with youth offenders, although I am aware of the high levels of self-injury prevalent in those populations. Such omissions are regrettable but inevitable in a book that leans heavily on the author's clinical experience.

6

Trauma and Dramatic Repetition: Working with Lorraine

> I became trapped in a world of my own, suffering the hurts and pains in silence. Cutting was my only release from the unbearable chaos inside me. ('Woman B', Arnold 1995, p.13)

The first two case studies presented describe self-harming behaviour that lies somewhere between the 'high visibility' examples of self-harm with which we are most familiar and the 'hidden' examples that follow.

The first client, 'Lorraine', has made two suicide attempts in the past, both involving over-dosing on prescribed medication. When she first comes along, she is cutting herself on the arms about once a month, at times when she feels overwhelmed by emotion and finds herself in a strange and distressing state of mind. Her self-cutting does not have the entrenched and ritualistic quality that can be a part of the picture when it has been heavily relied upon over a long period of time. In contrast to some of the young women described in Gardner (2001), Lorraine wants very much to stop cutting herself and sees this as one of the major goals of counselling.

The findings of the Bristol Survey suggest that self-cutting is the most common type of self-injury, as indicated in the table reproduced below:

Table 6.1

Type of injury	% of sample
Cutting	90
Inflicting blows	32
Burning/scalding	30
Picking/scratching	12
Pulling out hair	7
Biting	5
Swallowing objects	4
Other	5

The researchers note that:

- cutting was by far the most common type of injury reported, with 90 per cent of respondents saying that they had cut themselves. Women used such implements as knives, razor blades and broken glass. The area most commonly cut was the arms and/or hands, while a fairly large proportion cut their legs and some their stomach, face, breasts or genitals. Some women reported cutting several areas of their bodies or 'all over' (Arnold 1995, p.6).

According to the survey:

- the 'treatment' women most commonly reported to be helpful was talking; to be able to talk to someone supportive about their feelings

- some women said counselling had finally enabled them to turn their lives around after many years of distress and self-injury, and, in some cases, repeated hospital admissions (Arnold 1995, p.20).

In spite of this, it emerged that:

- counselling and psychotherapy were very seldom offered. Some women were told that it would be 'dangerous' for them to uncover the feelings and experiences which underlay their self-injury (Arnold 1995, p.19).

These findings are relevant to the situation described in this chapter. By the time she arrives, Lorraine has struggled for a long time to gain access to counselling. In years of involvement with social services and mental health services, it has never been offered. She has several times asked the local mental health team for counselling but been told that the resources are simply not available. Eventually, a sympathetic member of staff mentions the CASSEL Centre, where Lorraine at last finds the help she is seeking. The difficulties involved in gaining access to counselling and psycho-therapy are a matter of serious concern and will be discussed further in Chapter 12.

'Clare', the counsellor who undertook the work with Lorraine, is a psychodynamic counsellor registered with the British Association for Counselling and Psychotherapy. During the period in question, she worked at the CASSEL Centre, a voluntary organisation offering counselling in the London Borough of Lewisham and I was her external supervisor. The following information is recorded on Lorraine's referral report:

> Lorraine phoned to refer herself for counselling. She said that she had attempted suicide by slitting her wrists ten months earlier. Following a night in hospital, she had been referred to local mental health services who could not offer counselling and advised her to contact the CASSEL Centre. Lorraine gave a brief history over the telephone, saying that she had first attempted suicide when she was nine years old and that since that time she had harmed herself 'on and off for years'. Self-harm helped her with the anger she felt – when she cut herself she could see the anger pouring out. However she really wanted to stop and was embarrassed about the appearance of her arms.
>
> In talking about this, I asked Lorraine if she knew why this had started from such a young age. She said it was because she was sexually abused by her step-father.

Lorraine arrives promptly for her first session and seems able to make a connection with Clare. A period of counselling lasting approximately one year is envisaged. In the event, this is extended by a further six months, giving Lorraine the opportunity to negotiate her own ending. This negotiation turns out to be an important aspect of the work. Lorraine is able to articulate her needs and exercise control over her life in a thought-through way, a process that serves to increase her confidence in her newly discovered capacities.

Towards the end of the year, Clare asks the client and the CASSEL Centre on my behalf for permission to publish an account of the work undertaken. Lorraine seems pleased to be asked and agrees, saying that she would like to help other people 'to know how it really is'. In writing this account, I have been fortunate in being able to draw on client case notes as well as on regular discussions of the counselling process in supervision. As I did not undertake the work myself, I have included few verbatim exchanges in this particular case.

Early on, Lorraine describes feeling 'very bad' and suicidal and turning to self-harm in a desperate bid to cope and keep going. Gardner notes that

> attacking the body is essentially a paradoxical gesture in that the apparently destructive act reflects a desire to continue to live and get on with life. Cutting can function as a way of cutting off from internal pain by providing a distraction. (Gardner 2001, p.25)

Clare and I soon learn that Lorraine's history is similar to that of many people who harm themselves through self-cutting. The 76 women who took part in the Bristol Survey reported incidents of childhood sexual abuse (49%), neglect (49%), emotional abuse (43%), lack of communication (27%), physical abuse (25%), loss/separation (25%) and parent ill/alcoholic (17%). Lorraine has suffered *all* of the above. She describes a family life that was chaotic due to her mother's alcoholism, frequent changes of sexual partner and probable (though undiagnosed) mental health problems. As well as suffering from emotional neglect and abuse, Lorraine was sexually abused by one of her step-fathers. She had several periods in local authority care, as did all of the children in the family, and the family is well known to the local Social Services Department.

In the early stages of the work, much time is given over to the exploration of this very difficult and chaotic family background. Clare learns that Lorraine is the second-born of her mother's nine children. She has one brother and two sisters; also three half-brothers and three half-sisters. Other teenage and adult offspring are mentioned, who turn out not to be related by blood but to be other sons and daughters of her mother's various partners. One of Lorraine's step-brothers has the same name as one of her step-fathers. Clare finds herself feeling confused as Lorraine talks about the different people in her family. The information seems overwhelming and impossible to put in order.

Reflecting on her own confusion, Clare recognises the operation of the mechanism of projective identification. When this term was introduced (Klein 1946), the emphasis was on the client's need to get rid of or 'evacuate' unbearable feelings and states of mind by pushing them into the other. In Bion's later work (1962), more emphasis is placed on projective identification as a primitive but meaningful form of communication. Clare feels that Lorraine is communicating a particular state of mind that cannot yet be put into words, by stirring up feelings that she herself has experienced during her chaotic and unpredictable childhood. She responds to the challenge by producing a pencil and a large sheet of paper and helping Lorraine to draw a family tree. This clarifies the situation – although it takes some time – and, more importantly, gives Lorraine an early opportunity to recognise and begin to internalise Clare's capacity to remain thoughtful in the face of chaos and confusion.

Lorraine describes her mother as 'having an alcohol problem' and says that she herself did much of the looking after of the younger children, which was 'not right'. She was sexually abused by one of her step-fathers. She spent various periods of time in care – she thinks the first of these might have been when she was about six. Lorraine is unclear about many things – her age when she was sexually abused, the duration of the abuse and the time she spent in care – and this adds to the overall impression of a childhood marked by repeated impingements and unpredictable turns of events.

From these unpromising beginnings, Lorraine has managed to fashion a life that has a surprising degree of order and coherence. She has her own flat, which is a source of great pride, and she has sustained a seven-year relationship with a man, 'Mike'. Prior to this relationship, Lorraine lived with Mike's family for a year and this was very important for her. She was wrenched away from this 'oasis of sanity' when new difficulties blew up in her own family. However, her relationship with Mike survived and they were eventually able to get a place of their own. Mike and his family seem to have offered both continuity and containment over the years and this has helped Lorraine to keep going.

Hearing all this, it is difficult to believe that Lorraine is still only 23 years old! She is the only one among the adult siblings in the family not yet to have children herself. This reflects a very definite decision and Lorraine emphasises to Clare that she is 'not ready to be a mother'. Lorraine is not working and Clare suggests that, here too, she feels 'not ready'. This is confirmed, with Lorraine saying that she has to concentrate on getting to grips with her difficulties. In particular, she very much wants to stop cutting herself. In these early communications, there are hints of a determination and strength of character that counter the sense of chaos and impossibility also present in the sessions.

An issue that is apparent from early sessions onwards is Lorraine's general level of agitation. She seems enormously anxious and is constantly fidgeting, kicking her feet and playing with her hands. She refers to events occurring between sessions that also suggest difficulties with self-soothing. In physiological terms, we could say that her levels of arousal appear to be chronically raised. Lorraine describes herself as very house-proud and admits that she can become obsessive about cleaning and tidying. She spends a lot of time decorating and redecorating her flat. Lorraine tells Clare about going with Mike to their regular pub, collecting up all the ashtrays, washing them and returning them to the table. This has been commented on in the pub on a number of occasions. Although she feels embarrassed when the other locals raise their eyebrows and tease her, Lorraine finds it impossible to sit and relax.

As recommended by the British Association for Counselling and Psychotherapy (BACP), I sometimes take my supervision work to supervision, in my case to a peer supervision group. Supervision of the supervisor provides a third level of containment, complementing the containment provided by the counsellor for the client and by the supervisor for the counsellor. (Naturally the same strict rules of confidentiality apply in all of these situations.) When I tell my group about Lorraine, one colleague is reminded of a television programme revolving around the psychological problems of household pets. Following a house move, a cat became very unhappy and agitated. It groomed itself constantly and with excessive vigour, until patches of fur disappeared, leaving only bare skin. It seemed that the cat was hurting itself in an attempt to soothe itself. We wonder in the group, as I later wonder with Clare, whether Lorraine's constant cleaning and tidying are desperate attempts at self-soothing and whether, when things are particularly bad, self-cutting serves this same purpose.

Lorraine confirms that cutting helps her to feel calmer and that this in turn enables her to carry on. She also derives comfort from tending her wounds. When Clare tells me this, I am reminded of the poignant words of one of the women taking part in the Bristol Survey:

> When I was a child cutting was safe, reassuring, consistent, something that would be there for me whatever happened. Now once I have cut myself I go into 'nurse mode' and can enjoy taking care of my wounds. (Arnold 1995, p.16)

Without consistent mothering, somebody to understand her states of mind and to soothe her emotionally and calm her physically, Lorraine would have been obliged from early on to hold herself together as best she might. Referring back to Bick's work, described in Chapter 4, we can imagine that she may have felt held together through her own intense concentration on a detail of the environment, perhaps a patch of light or a moving curtain. At other times, she may have relied on the sensation derived from constant movement, from the exercise of her 'muscularity' to maintain her sense of bodily integrity. In adult life, Lorraine's inability to sit still and her obsession with the small details of dirty ashtrays and dust on the carpet convey a quality of intense agitation and a desperate need for soothing. It seems possible that self-cutting is also a form of 'self-handling' that soothes Lorraine and helps her not to 'fall apart'.

We know from the writing of Krystal (1978, 1988) and others that any physical handling, even if rough and insensitive, is preferable to no handling at all. Even distorted and insulting forms of handling seem to have some value in warding off the danger of psychogenic death, as described by Krystal and as witnessed by Spitz (1945) in his observations of very touch-deprived infants in institutional settings. *Thus, we might see self-harm as a kind of self-attention to the need for handling in order to stay alive.*

However, the price of regaining a feeling of aliveness and reality is very high, in terms of the negative experiences, both internal and external, which follow in the wake of self-harm. (Turp 1999a, p.317)

Face to face with Lorraine's fidgeting and agitation, Clare herself is aware of becoming anxious. In the matrix of unconscious communication, we discern silent and unconscious requests for help. Clare takes such opportunities as arise to discuss with Lorraine how she might address her legitimate need for self-handling in more helpful, less damaging ways. In line with a 'body storylines' approach (Turp 1999c), Clare does not make suggestions but works with Lorraine to identify and build on activities that she can identify with and that feel helpful. Glass-painting, something that Lorraine already does, is one of the activities discussed. It requires close and detailed attention and offers the possibility of artistic self-expression while at the same time calling for physical stillness and intense concentration. Lorraine likes to walk and recognises that one reason for this is that it makes her feel calmer. She also identifies swimming as something she would like to do. During the period of counselling, she is unable to follow up her wish to swim because she is too embarrassed about the scars on her arms, but it remains a possibility for the future. By taking an interest in these matters, Clare confirms their importance and their value as an expression of self-caring tendencies.

As the work proceeds, details of a succession of traumatic impingements emerge. It seems probable that, to use Winnicott's term, Lorraine's 'continuity of being' has been under attack from the moment she emerged from the womb. Perhaps we might even say that her problems began *in utero*, in view of her mother's alcoholism and mental health issues. At home, Lorraine received very little mothering and was obliged to 'mother' her siblings from an early age. She remembers her mother going out and leaving her and her brother alone at home, there being no food in the house and her mother returning in a drunken state. The sexual abuse she suffered trampled her personal boundaries. When she was taken into care, she lost even such containment as she was able to glean from the familiar physical space of her home and from other family members. She frequently had to change schools and, as a consequence of this and of the chaos of family life, her attendance was erratic and she did not gain any qualifications.

Not surprisingly, pain and confusion dominate Lorraine's feelings about herself and her past. She has experienced very little containment during her childhood. It is not surprising, therefore, that she finds it difficult to remember, articulate and think about her experiences and emotions and that they have a tendency to spill over into action. She cuts herself when she feels 'angry', 'really bad' or 'full of badness'. As she cuts, she feels physically numb, experiencing no pain. As she puts it, 'Something else takes over.' At the moment of the self-injury, it seems that her feelings have risen to an unbearable pitch. Unable to manage them by thinking and speaking about them, Lorraine lets them spill out, a spilling out that is graphically symbolised by the flow of blood. Like many individuals who cut themselves, Lorraine feels relieved when she sees blood flowing from her wound.

In supervision, Clare and I share feelings of sadness and outrage about the sufferings of a child who was so little loved and so poorly protected. In the consulting room, Clare is able to offer containment of Lorraine's feelings by recognising and speaking about what is going on in the here and now of the therapeutic encounter. Lorraine has the benefit not only of Clare's concerned and thoughtful presence but of a role model, who suggests through her own behaviour that it is possible to put very painful experiences into words and that this in itself affords some relief. It is this quality of containment, I believe, along with the identification of safe self-handling activities, that enables Lorraine to substantially reduce her level of self-cutting within a month or two of starting counselling.

Lorraine spends a lot of time in her sessions talking about what is going on in the lives of various members of her family. There are always family dramas and crises in play. On one occasion, Lorraine says of her family: 'We could have been on the Jerry Springer show – we are all mad!' Clare reminds Lorraine that the counselling space is for her alone and comments on how easily it becomes invaded by other people's problems. Lorraine suddenly reaches into her handbag and pulls out a cigarette lighter. She flicks it on and uses the flame to burn off a loose thread hanging from her trousers. Clare is aware only of a sudden flame and a feeling of shock and dismay. A question flashes into her mind regarding the flame-retardant quality (or otherwise) of the client's chair. Things seem alarming and unpredictable. Recovering a degree of equanimity, Clare says to Lorraine: 'Can you tell me what happened there?' Lorraine giggles and says 'I've shocked you', and Clare responds by saying, 'Yes!' Lorraine then explains her action in a matter-of-fact tone, saying that she needed to burn the thread to seal it so that it would not unravel.

Clare feels unable to say more at this point but is keen to discuss the matter in supervision. Something about the swiftness and unpredictable nature of the action with the lighter feels significant. We wonder about Clare's concern regarding the flame-retardant quality of the chair. Perhaps the intrusion of this detail represents an 'attack on linking' (Bion 1967a) which has temporarily immobilised Clare's capacity to think coherently. Certainly, attacks on thinking and linking will have been something that Lorraine herself has experienced during her childhood, for how is a child to make sense of being hurt, sexually abused, sent away to foster parents, then brought home, only to be sent away again?

We reflect that there may be meaning also in Clare's apparent fear that her client, symbolised by the chair, might 'explode' or 'ignite'. Lorraine often speaks of being 'depressed' and of 'feeling bad'. A flame seems more associated with anger – we speak sometimes of a 'fiery rage' – and we note in supervision the importance of bringing anger in view and acknowledging that anger is a legitimate response to intolerable impingements.

We also wonder about the meaning of Lorraine's giggling and consider what, apart from the literal thread woven into the trousers, might be at risk of 'unravelling' if the end is not burned and sealed. Lorraine has put together a life that, at a certain level, works for her. When Clare challenges her continuing entanglement with her family and suggests a shift of focus on to Lorraine's inner world, Lorraine may feel that her way of coping will unravel. As she has no idea what might become possible in its place, the intrusion of fear and alarm into the session makes a great deal of sense. In the next session, Clare feels able to return to the subject of the thread-burning. She says that she thinks Lorraine wanted her to know what it was like to feel alarmed, to be put on a spot and not to know what to think. Lorraine at first insists that it was a purely practical matter but later says that she can see the sense of what Clare is saying.

This dynamic is played out again in a number of different ways in later sessions. In supervision, we become more confident that our understanding is along the right lines. Lorraine is, it seems, involved in a process of dramatic repetition, unconsciously creating situations that re-evoke earlier traumas and associated states of mind. A couple of months on, Lorraine tells Clare that her sister has moved into her flat, along with her two young sons, following the break-up of her marriage. Clare expresses concern at the breaching of the boundary offered by the client's flat, which has seemed in a way to symbolise the boundary between the island of sanity that Lorraine has created in her own life and the craziness of her family which is literally 'just around the corner'. Lorraine responds by saying, 'I can't say no. They are my family.' Two small boys in small flat cause a fair amount of mess and Lorraine redoubles her house-cleaning efforts.

There have been intimations from the start that Lorraine feels very entangled with other family members. Lorraine's mother makes the first approach to the CASSEL Centre on her daughter's behalf. The person who takes the call has to insist on Lorraine phoning herself. It is Lorraine's mother, or partner Mike, who phones in to say, on the rare occasions she is unwell, that Lorraine will be missing her session. As Clare says, 'She doesn't seem to be sure where she ends and they begin.'

Through all of this, Lorraine's flat has been very important to her, has been her sanctuary. We are concerned about the breaching of the boundary that has taken place and feel that Lorraine's actions reflect a lack of concern for her own well-being and are in this sense a worrying lapse of self-care, although we recognise her good intentions. Our concerns are not, it seems, without foundation for, with her sister in residence, Lorraine again resorts to cutting herself. Her injuries require medical attention and Lorraine speaks of being 'ignored', 'looked down upon' and 'callously treated' at her local Accident and Emergency Unit. This treatment makes her feel worse and threatens to set in train another round of self-cutting:

> By far the most commonly reported issue for women in their contacts with services was the attitudes of staff. Over and over again women told us of being criticised, ignored, told off, dismissed as 'attention-seeking', 'a nuisance' or 'wasting time'…
>
> Some felt they were punished for being a 'self-harmer', sometimes being made to wait far longer than other patients for treatment, refused treatment altogether or treated cruelly, for example being treated without local anaesthetic. These attitudes were encountered in at least some individual staff in all types of service, and caused women terrible distress, sometimes deterring them from seeking help, at other times reinforcing the self-hatred and desperation which contributed to their need to self-injure. (Arnold 1995, p.18)

This is a difficult situation, damaging to the client and unsatisfactory for the practitioner, who is not providing an acceptable standard of care. Many practitioners called upon to work with self-harm do so without the benefit of supportive supervision or appropriate training.

> When a person has cut, bruised, burned or poisoned herself, or interfered with wound healing or brought injury upon herself through reckless behaviour, it can be difficult not to react in a judgmental or even punitive manner. The action seems so wasteful, so shocking. Unless we are well supported in our work, we will tend to defend ourselves against the levels of distress involved and such defensiveness will inevitably interfere with our ability to remain thoughtful in the face of self-harming behaviour. When incidents of self-harm impinge upon a practitioner who is inadequately supported and supervised, we have the makings of a situation where treatment is unlikely to be therapeutic and may be less than humane. (Turp 1999a: 310)

Shortly after her negative experience at Accident and Emergency, Lorraine describes in her session what we come to think of as 'the bathroom incident'. She tells Clare, as if it were nothing special, that on the previous evening she locked herself in the bathroom and that Mike and her sister had to break down the door. Clare asks how things came to this point. Lorraine replies that Mike and her sister were worried. She then shrugs and says: 'Actually, I was just wanting a bit of peace and quiet.' This story makes very little sense and as with the thread-burning incident, Clare feels in the presence of something quite bizarre. She asks Lorraine why she didn't forestall this drama by communicating with Mike and her sister, a question that seems to completely stump Lorraine. In supervision, we question whether 'peace and quiet' is really what Lorraine wanted. The material suggests that she is still unconsciously choosing to provoke chaos and drama.

Clare and I consider the possibility that Lorraine has been through so many traumatic experiences that her responses have become deadened. She seems genuinely surprised by Clare's reaction to the lighter incident and the bathroom incident, as if she really can't see what all the fuss is about. This lack of a reaction suggests the operation of defensive dissociation. Through dissociation, the thinking part of an individual is split off from emotions and bodily sensations. The client is perhaps able to imagine that she is not really present, that the things that are happening are not really happening to her. This phenomenon is described by Winnicott as 'depersonalisation':

> The ego is based on a body ego, but it is only when all goes well that the person of the baby starts to be linked with the body and the body functions, with the skin as a limiting membrane. I have used the term personalisation to describe this process, because the term depersonalisation seems at basis to mean *a loss of firm union between ego and body*. (Winnicott 1962b, p.59, my italics).

Orbach builds on this work, writing with particular reference to the situation of women:

> For many women a body that is theirs and stable, that they live in, is a fiction. They have rather a crisis relationship to their bodies and their selves, as though this is a way in which a sense of self can be maintained. (Orbach 1978, 1982, 1986) To quote Winnicott:
>
>> Survival is sought in the management of crises. In other words the person has no real sense of continuity of being an ongoing proposition themselves. They provide this continuity for themselves through the creation, management and survival of crises...in extreme cases the infant exists only on the basis of a continuity of

reactions to impingement and of recoveries from such reactions. (Winnicott 1960)

The somatic self or body self, like Winnicott's False Self, may be fash-ioned defensively on a crisis basis. The body self finds itself through crises which have to be managed and survived. (Orbach 1995, pp.4–5)

Having identified this reactive pattern, Clare becomes more confident in her management of the 'crises' that are evoked in the consulting room. Schafer (1992) writes of actions that take the form of 'showings' and actions that take the form of 'tellings' and these are both in evidence. Crisis-laden 'showings' include burning a thread and taking a telephone call during a session (see below). Crisis-laden 'tellings' involve descriptions of a door being broken down, of nephews at risk and of a sister in the grip of suicidal tendencies. Clare does her best to contain the situation by listening carefully and encouraging Lorraine to think about the dynamics beneath the surface of her actions.

By this time, it is clear to everybody that Lorraine is especially likely to cut herself when she has been in contact with her mother, whether face to face or on the telephone. Typically, Lorraine's mother telephones and insists that Lorraine should sort out the latest family row or bring somebody into line who is acting against the mother's wishes. Lorraine comes in to one session having cut herself the previous day and speaks of 'impossible demands' and 'a hopeless muddle'. She describes the anger and distress that she feels. I am reminded of Welldon's work (1988), which refers to the plight of the female child who is unwanted and who is not permitted to enjoy a sense of her own development as a separate individual. Instead, she is treated as a part-object, as an extension of the mother. One of the points noted in the CASSEL Centre's closing report on Lorraine is: 'She has been used by her mother for her own needs.' Lorraine is beginning to acknowledge that she should stay away from her mother. She tells Clare: 'Seeing my mother *is* my self-harm. It does me harm. It's no good for me.'

In the next session, Clare returns to Lorraine's comments on the connection between her involvement with her mother and her self-harm and asks Lorraine why she continues to have so much contact. Lorraine emphasises her love and concern for her two nephews. It is her wish and, she feels, her responsibility to ensure that what happened to her does not happen to them. Her mother uses her knowledge of this situation to manipulate Lorraine into having contact with her and into becoming involved in family battles. By now, Lorraine recognises this and is able to talk about it, although she has not found a way to resolve the situation. As she becomes more able to 'mentalise' (Fonagy 1991), to manage her feelings by putting them into words and thinking about them, her need for self-harm is abating.

Throughout the period of counselling, Lorraine remains closely involved with her sister and nephews. In one way, this is a repetition of the mothering role she has occupied in relation to her siblings since she herself was a young girl. In other ways, it is a matter of emotional self-care. Lorraine needs to feel that she can make some kind of positive contribution. She gives her nephews important and substantial support and in doing so is able to feel that her childhood suffering has not been in vain. Her relationship with her sister has this particularly valuable aspect, that Lorraine herself feels helped and comforted by being able to protect her nephews from the kind of experiences she went through as a child. Her care and generosity is healing for them and also self-healing.

At the same time, these relationships continue to be a source of complications that can suddenly erupt into Lorraine's life and into her counselling sessions. On one occasion, Lorraine's mobile phone rings in the middle of a session. Clare finds herself feeling angry when Lorraine answers the telephone and has a long conversation with the caller. Subsequently, Clare speaks of the intrusion of the external world into the session and the way in which boundaries are again being breached. Reflecting on her anger, Clare senses that Lorraine wants her to know how infuriating and unfair it feels to be repeatedly disturbed and disrupted. She offers this interpretation, which is met with silence. Clare adds that it is her responsibility to ensure that the boundaries around Lorraine's counselling space remain intact and asks Lorraine to turn off her mobile phone and to ensure that it is turned off in future sessions.

Lorraine replies that she has to have the telephone turned on because she is worried about her sister, who recently harmed herself through taking an overdose. There is a fine line between involvement and over-involvement and Lorraine is still experiencing difficulties in this area. She does not feel well equipped for the task of balancing her rights as an individual, separate from her family, against her concern for her sister and nephews. It is clear, however, that she is increasingly able to take Clare's comments on board. A few weeks later she describes a row with her sister, painful at the time but leading to a good outcome, in that her sister is now seeking her own counselling.

The period of counselling is entering its final phase. It feels significant when Lorraine lets Clare see her arms, having previously worn long-sleeved clothes throughout her sessions. Clare tells me that the scars weren't all that noticeable, not nearly as bad as she had imagined. At this time too, Lorraine's hair, which has always been tightly tied back, is allowed to escape from its band and hang more softly. Her style of dress becomes less severe and, overall, she looks less tense and guarded. Lorraine decides to cut off all contact with her mother and is able to stick to this decision. In supervision, we feel that this is right for her and are filled with admiration for her very considerable achievement.

The previous agitation and fidgeting are by now less in evidence. Lorraine is still strongly affected by her sister's problems but has managed to establish a better boundary. It is now several months since she last cut herself. However, the approaching end of counselling stirs up old and new anxieties. These are first expressed in a physical way when she starts to regularly bring in a bottle of 'Red Rock' (a soft drink with a high caffeine content) and to sip at and suck on it during the sessions. In supervision, we wonder whether the bottle is a 'transitional object' (Winnicott 1971), representing the maternal breast and the maternal care enjoyed by Lorraine during the period of counselling, which must now be relinquished. Clare asks Lorraine why she needs to bring a bottle of drink and Lorraine says that she is beginning to doubt her capacity to stop self-harming completely. She wonders aloud, 'Can I really manage without it?', which Clare interprets as meaning, 'Can I really manage without you?' This is a helpful exchange, at the end of which Lorraine reiterates her desire to 'get out there and do it on my own'.

Increasingly, Lorraine's thoughts turn towards the future and the last few sessions are spent considering her plans. In seven years of being together, she and Mike have never taken a holiday. Now they are planning to do so. Lorraine is keen to discuss the possibilities with Clare, who acknowledges in this development another significant step in the direction of good self-care. Lorraine is no longer in reactive 'survival' mode but is able to look towards and think about the future. In the last few sessions, Lorraine talks again about artistic leanings. She is beginning to think in terms of translating her talents into gainful employment. Her sessions with Clare are due to finish in June (which is Lorraine's choice) and she talks of possibly going to college in October. Clare enquires whether this plan stems, in part, from Lorraine's concerns about how she will manage without counselling. Lorraine acknowledges that she will miss Clare very much, but also expresses optimism about the future.

Clare has asked me to highlight the importance of the supervision process, the sense, in her words, of 'three of us being involved', and I hope that I have done so. I will conclude this chapter by acknowledging that some practitioners are sceptical about the usefulness of psychotherapy for people who harm themselves. It is partly for this reason that verbal therapies are so seldom made available to this client group. I hope that the good outcome in this case will contribute in a small way towards combating such scepticism. Lorraine has made very considerable gains, among them the cessation of self-harm. In many ways, her experience of life has been transformed. Her good recovery is not an isolated instance but is echoed in other accounts of object-relations based psychotherapy, most recently in Gardner (2001).

7

The Skin in Question:
Working with Ellen May

> The need for a containing object would seem, in the infantile unintegrated state, to produce a frantic search for an object – a light, a voice, a smell, or other sensual object – which can hold the attention and thereby be experienced, momentarily at least, as holding the parts of the personality together. (Bick 1968, p.484)

Lorraine's self-harm, described in the previous chapter, involved physical attacks on the skin through self-cutting. Self-cutting had many functions for Lorraine, among them the translation of a sense of a damaged 'psychic skin' into a visible external reality. An eating disorder – the crucial issue for Ellen May – can be viewed from a number of different theoretical perspectives, all of which may be helpful in particular circumstances. When I started working with Ellen May, Bick's work quickly came to mind. Ellen May conveyed a sense of enormous agitation and internal disruption, reminiscent of the 'frantic search for an object' referred to above. Later, she told me that she had also physically damaged her skin internally through repeated vomiting, which had left her throat sore and bleeding, and that she could not bear to look at her skin, for example when she undressed to take a shower.

The way in which Ellen May reaches me reflects the increasing penetration of the world of e-mail and the internet into the world of counselling and psychotherapy. I receive an e-mail from her father in America stating that his daughter is living in London for a period of six months while she completes an 'internship'. (I later learn that this term refers in the USA to a period of study undertaken abroad that counts towards a student's undergraduate degree.) Ellen May has a history of depression and is receiving medication from a private doctor in London. Her history includes inpatient admissions for an eating disorder. The e-mail concludes with a request for details of my qualifications and experience and an enquiry as to whether I would be willing to work with Ellen May during the six months in which she is based in London. I reply with the details requested and add that I would be interested in working with Ellen May but that she will need to make contact with me directly.

Ellen May telephones me a few days later and I invite her to come along for an initial session so that we can decide whether useful work can be done in the six months available. She asks how soon she can see me and conveys a sense of extreme urgency. She has time free during the day, when I myself tend to be less busy, and so I am able to offer her an appointment for two days later. On the morning of the appointment, Ellen May telephones to say that she will not be coming as she is due to see a previous therapist, who is going to charge her for the appointment whether she goes along or not. This is the first of many experiences where I feel whirled around and, in spite of my best efforts, am unable to clarify with Ellen May exactly what is going on. It is the first I have heard of the involvement of another therapist. I advise Ellen May to work out her difficulties with her current therapist, emphasising that it is most inadvisable to chop and change.

A week later, I receive another phone call from Ellen May. She says she has now finished with the previous therapist, 'Lesley', and asks me to give her another appointment. Very much in two minds, I agree. I do not respond to Ellen May's plea to see her on that same day but am again able to offer her an appointment a few days hence. This time she comes along, although she is nearly fifteen minutes late. I am immediately struck by her well-groomed appearance, quite different from what I had expected and quite unlike any other student I have ever seen. She is an attractive young woman with long dark hair and is immaculately turned out in a black coat, elegant shoes and a designer sweater and trousers.

As soon as she is seated, Ellen May begins to talk rapidly, jumping from one topic to another. I try to slow things down, interrupting at various points to ask for clarification. Such is the chaotic quality of the communication that I find it difficult to establish even the most basic details, such as how long Ellen May has been in London and when she is due to depart. (After the session, I realise that this is still not clear. She has spoken of remaining 'until May or possibly until August'.) I bring up the subject of Ellen May's recently terminated period of therapy. She says that she saw Lesley for a time, but found it objectionable when she was asked about her dreams and her childhood.

Ellen May: I just want a space to burble on. I have a therapist back in the US to do that other kind of thing with.

This statement confirms my impression that Ellen May is talking 'at me' and is not interested in taking in anything I have to say. She continues with a stream of negative comments about Lesley and about her private doctor.

Maggie: I wonder if you would like to think it over for a few days before you decide whether you want to commit yourself to seeing me regularly. You found your last experience with a therapist unsatisfactory and you are none too pleased with your doctor either. I could understand it if you felt wary about getting involved with me.

Ellen May: No, it will be all right. I'll be able to talk to you. Maybe Lesley was a bit old or something. I didn't feel she was on my wavelength.

In this disparaging tone, I hear quite clearly Ellen May's demand that I should simply allow myself to be used as a prop, an inanimate object. I am not to be allowed to have thoughts, feelings or opinions of my own. I suspect also that I will be the next female practitioner to be disparaged and held in contempt. It is Ellen May's account of her eating disorder that tips the balance and persuades me to carry on working with her. She tells me that she has had three periods of inpatient treatment, all in the United States, precipitated by her dangerously low weight. She has come very close to dying. I ask her to tell me about her eating disorder and she says 'anorexia and bulimia'.

Maggie:	You both restricted your food intake and vomited in order to keep your weight low?
Ellen May:	Yes. The last time I was in, I had vomited so much that my throat was bleeding. Every time I eat now, I want to vomit. But I know if I do it once, I'll be back where I was. I won't be able to stop.
Maggie:	Your most important aim, and it sounds like not an easy one to achieve, is to resist the urge to vomit?
Ellen May:	My throat was badly damaged but it's healed now. But I worry all the time that I'm getting fatter… You see these trousers? Well, I think they're a bit tighter than last time I wore them. But I asked a friend and he said, 'No, you don't look any bigger at all', and then I wondered if maybe I had different underwear on. And so I phoned another friend and asked her if that could be the reason, if I was wearing different underwear, and she said it could be and she was sure that's what it was.

Before I can speak, or even think, Ellen May starts talking about what she has eaten that day and what she thinks she should eat and what prevents her from buying some nice bread. She tells me she will probably have turkey burgers again tonight but instead of two she wants to eat just one and that will be quite enough even though her flatmates will have two and that two is too much. Her speech is rapid and I find myself feeling quite dizzy.

The first session is almost at an end and I interrupt in order to negotiate some kind of contract. Although I do not have high hopes of a good outcome, I feel that Ellen May could be on the brink of another hospital admission and I cannot bring myself to turn her away. Ellen May has made clear her objection to talking about her childhood experiences. On the one hand, this is very limiting. On the other hand, I would in any case be wary of doing too much 'uncovering' psychotherapy with a vulnerable client who will be seeing me for a maximum of six months. I decide that it may be possible to manage a holding operation, staying with Ellen May's chosen agenda, namely her day-to-day struggles to get by.

Maggie:	I will continue to see you, if that is what you would like. But I will need your permission to liaise with your doctor and also a commitment from you to come along twice a week.

Ellen May says that she cannot afford to come twice a week. I offer her a reduced fee but insist that, since she feels so on the edge, coming twice a week is absolutely necessary. Ellen May says rather sulkily that she will ask for more financial help from her father and we book in our appointments.

After Ellen May leaves, I decide to note down examples of verbatim exchanges, both for supervision purposes and with a view to writing a case study – if it feels appropriate to ask for permission to publish and if permission is given. At this early stage, I have a first taste of how difficult this may prove. I have had little opportunity to speak during the session and Ellen May's monologue has been chaotic and fragmented. Feeling invaded by this chaos and fragmentation, I struggle to remember details and to put them into some kind of order. Thinking about Ellen May's carefully groomed exterior, I wonder whether her beautiful and carefully selected clothes might be a 'skin of clothing', a substitute for a living skin capable of offering a sense of cohesion and a boundary between a private internal world and the world of others.

I will digress here to discuss the question of whether or not eating disorders 'count' as self-harm. Most of the practitioners I have spoken to regard eating disorders as a form of internal self-harm, albeit a specialised form with significant features of its own. In the supervision groups where some of the clinical vignettes were generated, anorexia, bulimia and over-eating were often mentioned as examples of self-harm. All the practitioners who discussed the vignette of 'Ellen May' in preliminary research saw her behaviour as self-harm. This perception is in marked contrast to the formal definitions of self-harm to be found in the manuals of psychiatric diagnosis, DSM IV and ICD 10. Neither of these volumes includes eating disorders in its list of self-harming behaviours. There is no reference either to accident-proneness, as described in Chapter 9, or to harm that results from failures of self-care, as described in Chapter 10. To summarise, the official diagnostic manuals define self-harm in a narrow way, whereas most practitioners working in the community define it in a much broader way.

Self-harm is essentially a psychosomatic phenomenon, in the sense that psychological disturbance is finding a physical form of expression. This expression may take the route of conscious behaviour, although the behaviour in question is often not experienced as 'voluntary' in the sense of being under the client's control, or it may take the unconscious route of physical symptoms with no apparent organic underlay. Buckroyd (1989, 1994) argues that an eating disorder can usefully be thought of as a particular kind of psychosomatic illness:

> This paper describes a body of theory which points to the possibility that eating disorders can be seen as psychosomatic illness, which is to say a symbolization of affect via the body rather than with words. (Buckroyd 1994, p.106)

My supervisor and I discuss the psychosomatic nature of Ellen May's difficulties. The contrast between her carefully groomed exterior and her chaotic internal world is striking. Winnicott identifies 'joining up' of physical and psychological aspects of experience as one of the key maternal functions (Turp 2001, Winnicott 1970). Might Ellen May's self-presentation be in part a mute and unconscious plea for help in this area of experience? Ellen May misses her next session, phoning on the day to say that her parents are over for a visit. When she returns, she is feeling resentful and injured about her father's behaviour. I am reminded of Young and Gibb's writing (1998) on the sense of grievance that pervades the perceptions of many victims of childhood trauma.

Ellen May:	My father said something like, 'Well, we're not too worried about you because you're not looking any thinner.' I couldn't believe it! My mother always says crap things like that but my father should know better.
Maggie:	You felt patronised?
Ellen May:	(*in an exasperated tone*) Everybody knows you can't talk to somebody with an eating disorder in that way. It just makes it worse.

| Maggie: | It is very important that your parents do things the way you want them to. Your father gets it right for you more often than your mother, but on this occasion you felt wounded by what he said. |

Ellen May bursts into tears. The feeling communicated is one of frustration and rage rather than of sadness. She cancels the two following appointments, citing a deadline for unfinished class work. Then she telephones me one morning pleading to be seen the same day, a request that I resist but that leaves me feeling very anxious. Again I take the work to supervision, where we note Ellen May's apparent terror of compliance, of giving her parents/therapists what they want, which seems to her to mean that they have won. A contest seems to be being played out, which takes another turn when Ellen May arrives for her next appointment, owing me for two missed sessions, with no money. She says that her bank account is empty but that money is on its way from her parents. I feel furious when she tells me this. I stress the importance of a regular pattern of appointments and of avoiding last minute changes. Ellen May spends much of this particular session complaining about her doctor.

| Ellen May: | My parents have insisted I go along to see her. I have to go every two weeks and all she does is weighs me and give me my Prozac. She charges £50 per session, but my parents are paying and I go just to keep them off my back. What I can't stand is that she tries to talk to me about eating disorders. She thinks she knows something but she really hasn't got a clue. |

There is no mistaking the triumphant tone in which this is said. I have substantially reduced my fee because of Ellen May's pleas of poverty and feel now that I have been 'taken for a ride'. I wonder whether Ellen May is also seeing me because her parents have ordered it – 'just to keep them off my back' – or at least that she wants me to think this is the case. The thought comes to mind that her parents have probably handed over the money for the sessions she has missed and that she has kept it for herself! In fact, there is no evidence that I am being 'robbed' in this literal sense. I am aware of

my vindictiveness, my wish to retaliate. I am reminded of Klein's account
of primitive aspects of the mother–infant relationship:

> Klein's vision of infancy had always involved the idea of acquisitive, ter-
> ritorial urges towards the maternal body, but jealousy and envy went only
> some way in accounting for these. This now led her to suggest a further
> element that could be identified in early sadistic attacks, and this was
> greed. Klein underscored greed as the particular form of sadism impli-
> cated in human acquisitive and territorial instincts. She felt that unlike
> envy and jealousy, greed accounts specifically for ferocious phantasies of
> 'scooping out' the contents of the breast and ruthlessly extracting all the
> goodness from the object. As a form of aggression, greed is an exploit-
> ative tendency that underpins urges to plunder and rob. It was immedi-
> ately apparent that greed, though different from envy, could be stimu-
> lated by it. One response to envy is to steal what is good from the object
> and so deprive it. (Likierman 2001, pp.175–176).

Ellen May's unconscious attacks have succeeded temporarily in 'extracting
all the goodness from the object', from me, leaving me feeling sour and
resentful. Ellen May continues undaunted, talking about her flatmates and
what a strain they are on her, particularly one of them who cuts herself and
who apparently turns to Ellen May for help.

Again, I am fortunate to have a supervision session booked in for the
next day. We discuss my feelings of being manipulated and controlled. We
wonder whether Ellen May herself has felt manipulated and controlled in
the past but there is little to go on. In view of Ellen May's resistance to
talking about her childhood, this may well continue to be the case. My
supervisor emphasises the difficulties of doing interpretative,
insight-oriented work with Ellen May, although at this stage I am reluctant
to give up on the possibility. Whether or not interpretations are made, our
efforts to reach towards an understanding of the internal dynamics that
fuel Ellen May's behaviour will continue, a process that will support my
efforts to contain my own feelings and sustain a therapeutic presence. My
attempts to make a record of the work operate as an additional 'internal
supervisor' (Casement 1985) and help me to manage the situation.
Although we are rightly concerned with the potential harm that may result
from writing about our clients, it is also relevant to note the benefits to the
client of the recording process and the extra thinking time involved.

An urgent decision needs to be made about what to do if Ellen May again comes along without any money. By this point, I am ready if necessary to interrupt the sessions until the debt has been paid. This is perhaps unconsciously communicated, for, in the event, Ellen May brings the money she owes me with her to the next session. At this session, she is again very driven and agitated and bombards me with fast talk. Some of what she says relates to her desire to vomit and I feel that, symbolically, she is vomiting all over me. This impression is heightened when she begins to talk about food in an obsessive way, about what she has eaten and what she plans to eat. What she has eaten is bread and chocolate spread and (again!) turkey burgers, the kind of food that I do not eat and find it unpleasant to think about. My supervisor suggests that Ellen May has perhaps intuited my wholefood–vegetarian inclinations and is unconsciously stirring up in me her own feeling of wanting to vomit! I laugh, only realising later that what she has said rings absolutely true.

At her next session Ellen May talks about going shopping for the pair of trousers that she is wearing.

Ellen May: They were expensive but my mother always said, even if you're just going to the shops, why not look smart? So I would never wear casual shoes or a casual pair of trousers.

At this point I feel I am being openly mocked, both for conceding the reduced fee and for my style of dress, which is more casual than Ellen May's. Spiked comments, together with bitter complaints about the various practitioners with whom she has been involved, seem to serve as a 'toughened second skin', an impermeable barrier of harsh words defending against the threat of psychic disintegration. Is this Ellen May's way of surviving, of holding herself together? The situation is reminiscent of Bick's description of a 'hippopotamus' experience of self: 'In the "hippopotamus" state, the patient was aggressive, tyrannical, scathing and relentless in following his own way' (Bick 1968, p.485). Ellen May's touchiness and vanity – expressed in the way she dresses and shows off her clothes, in the offence she takes at her father's comments and in her disdain for her previous therapist, her private doctor and me – fit with Bick's description of a 'sack of apples' experience of self: 'In the "sack of apples" state, the patient was touchy, vain, in need of constant attention and praise, easily bruised and constantly expecting catastrophe, such as a collapse when getting up from the couch' (Bick 1968, p.485).

At almost every session, Ellen May tells me she is on the brink of losing the battle against her urge to resume vomiting. Sensing a real risk, I create opportunities to bring her immediate coping strategies and overall self-care into the conversation.

Maggie: How do you manage to stop yourself? Do you have particular strategies that work for you?

Ellen May: (*after a long pause*) I think of the other girls in the hospital and about how they would not want me to do it.

Maggie: It sounds as if they are the people you care about the most.

Ellen May: Oh, yes! We are the only people who know anything about it. But when I think of those poor girls, still in there… I write letters to them, you know, to try to keep them going.

On another occasion, Ellen May tells me how fond she is of her grandmother, who lives in a retirement home.

Ellen May: I'm the only one who goes to see her, you know. The others are too busy to bother but I always go along, whenever I'm home.

In these and similar comments, Ellen May indicates that she is the one who can give care and advice. While others are neglectful and fail to understand, she can be relied upon. By this time, I know that Ellen May has chosen to live with housemates who include a compulsive eater, a continuous dieter and, as mentioned above, a woman who cuts herself. She often complains about their neediness and their demands, while at the same time preening herself and emanating a sense of kindly superiority. In view of her extreme fragility, Ellen May's illusions about herself are almost laughably grandiose. Communications of this kind seem to reflect a desire to control me, not to allow me to permeate her in any way, not to be affected by me. They also convey a feeling of envy. It may be that my position – as a therapist with a legitimate platform for offering help to others and as a woman whose life is not marred by the difficulties Ellen May herself is experiencing – is in itself experienced as provocative. I venture a modest interpretation along these lines:

Maggie: I imagine it might be difficult for you, because you want to help others, to be in need of help yourself.

(Ellen May quickly 'cuts me down to size'.)

Ellen May: No, you are wrong. People with eating disorders are the best people to help others with that kind of problem. They are the only people who understand.

Ellen May cancels her next two sessions, at very short notice, citing unmet college deadlines and saying that she has been working through the night.

In supervision, I reflect on my interpretation, which has been unhelpful and has, I am sure, contributed to Ellen May's decision to stay away. We also discuss what we know of Ellen May's mother. Ellen May has described her as rich, ambitious, well-dressed and as travelling a great deal. We wonder whether she spent very little time with her daughter when she was younger. Is trauma in the form of a deep narcissistic wound the source of Ellen May's difficulties? If it is so, then we could perhaps say that she is now paying her mother back with interest. She snubs her mother by preferring her grandmother and causes a great deal of worry, trouble and expense through her eating disorder. Now her mother *has* to pay attention and is, in a way, being publicly shamed by her daughter.

Whatever the source of the difficulty, it is Ellen May who pays the higher price, for her life is in many ways in ruins. And it does not escape my notice that Ellen May is in some ways very like her mother, for example in her love of expensive clothes and in her ambition to work in politics – in the White House specifically. Unfortunately, we do not have the kind of therapeutic alliance that makes it possible for these matters to be brought into the open and talked about. Ellen May resists at all costs the experience of being helped by me. To feel that she could be helped by another person would be to abandon her position of assumed superiority and thus to feel humiliated.

Sensing the underlying misery, I feel considerable compassion for this young woman, caught in a self-sustaining and self-sabotaging cycle of behaviour. Compassion and goodwill do not, unfortunately, resolve the question of how the situation might best be addressed. Putting words to unconscious enactments as they are played out in the transference and countertransference is the usual procedure in psychoanalytic psychotherapy, one that has a good prospect of success where the client's ego strength is sufficient. I have by now conceded, however, that Ellen May is unable to make use of interpretations. Those I have offered have led either to missed sessions or to a bombardment of words that leaves me no room to speak at all.

This state of affairs leads me, rather reluctantly, to think about Ellen May as a 'borderline' client. My reluctance stems from the tendency for the psychiatric diagnosis of 'borderline personality disorder' to be used far too freely with reference to clients who harm themselves. The word 'borderline' is used by psychotherapists descriptively and not as a formal diagnosis. As such, it does not form part of an official record and so is less pernicious, less likely to deny the client access to psychological therapies or to harm his or her prospects of employment or promotion.

Nevertheless, I remain somewhat uncomfortable about the close link between the word 'borderline' and the psychiatric term 'borderline personality disorder'. Giovacchini refers to 'patients whose egos are fragmented' and perhaps 'fragmented ego' clients could be considered as an alternative description, but for now I will remain with the most commonly used terminology. I want to emphasise that, in my experience, this description *does not,* in fact, apply to most clients who harm themselves. It does seem relevant, however, to Ellen May at the time of our therapeutic encounter.

Giovacchini notes that borderline clients 'frequently suffer from psychosomatic problems' (Giovacchini 1993, p.81). Zalidis also makes a connection between 'borderline' features and psychosomatic disturbance:

Within the fields of psychoanalysis and psychosomatic medicine, clinicians have observed that certain patients have difficulty identifying and describing subjective feelings, and show an associated limited capacity for fantasy and imaginative play, presumably because their emotions are poorly represented mentally...

Although this emotion is often poorly differentiated, it is frequently used by these individuals to coerce others, including physicians into meeting their dependent needs. (Zalidis 2001, p.xiv)

Many readers will have a good sense of the difficulties likely to be associated with a 'borderline' description. A counsellor in supervision with me recently used the word 'borderline' in relation to a client she is seeing at the GP practice where she works. I asked her to define what she meant and she said the client seemed unable to make a relationship with her, that she was in a world of her own. She added that she supposed she was also concerned that the client might become psychotic, that her connection to the shared reality that enables us to communicate with each other was unusually fragile.

In addition to the other difficulties mentioned, Zalidis's reference to the limited capacity for fantasy and imaginative play is apposite. Ellen May's inability to make use of the 'as if' quality of the therapeutic encounter is striking, although she is clearly a very intelligent young woman. Opposing the view of some psychoanalysts, who have suggested that it is impossible to do useful work with borderline clients, Giovacchini suggests that it is time to 'clean our house':

It is not enough to smugly isolate ourselves and state that what we have to offer is just for an elite, select few. Patients need and want help, and if we denigrate them by implying they are not good enough for our esoteric type of treatment, they will turn elsewhere, as indeed many have done. (Giovacchini 1993, p.2)

He goes on to note:

The treatment of borderline patients has caused clinicians to revise their views about the therapeutic process. In many instances, the formation of a holding environment is more important than insight-producing interpretations. (*ibid.* p.5)

There are interesting echoes here of Winnicott's emphasis on the pre-eminent importance of the regular and reliable setting and of emotional holding in the therapeutic process. I am beginning to accept that my role as a psychotherapist in this case may be limited to the provision of a holding environment.

Apparently reading my thoughts, Ellen May herself gives what I understand to be an indication of how she would like me to proceed. She speaks about her boyfriend in the US, who is due to come over and to take her on holiday to Tuscany for a week. Prior to this, Ellen May has told me that she is very bad at taking her medication, although she acknowledges that she feels much worse when she fails to do so. It is at these times – when she misses her Prozac – that she feels most agitated and most desperate to make herself vomit. Her boyfriend apparently 'spoon-feeds' her and does not challenge her to take responsibility for herself:

Ellen May: He will make sure that I take my meds. He will put
               them out for me. He will ask me in the morning
               whether I have taken them, and then again in the
               evening. But he does it in such a nice way. I don't think
               I would let anyone else do it.

Maggie: He does his best to take care of you and doesn't expect
               too much. I think that's probably what you want from
               me as well…

Ellen May does not confirm my comment but at least does not retaliate against it. From here on, I concentrate on supporting Ellen May's attempts to soothe herself, with the explicit aim of helping her avoid another hospital admission. We return on a number of occasions to the 'strategies' she has available when she feels desperate to make herself vomit.

Ellen May: I have a scrapbook and sometimes I cut out phrases and
               pictures from a magazine and stick them in. You see, I
               can't write things because I get obsessed with my
               handwriting. It's never good enough for me and I have
               to do it over and over again. But if I cut out something
               printed then I get around that. The only trouble is, if I

	spend too long with the scissors, I start to want to cut myself.
Maggie:	Do you actually cut yourself?
Ellen May:	Not here, no. I did in the hospital. Everybody does. Most people don't know that. When I was in there, there wasn't a single girl who didn't cut herself.
Maggie:	It is good that you have managed to stop now that you are no longer an inpatient. Tell me some more about your scrapbook…
Ellen May:	When I feel bad, I look at the things I have stuck in. Phrases like 'getting better', 'you can do it' or 'stay strong'. Or just words like 'beautiful' or 'happy'.
Maggie:	It sounds quite soothing, finding these small things, these small words and phrases and cutting them out and sticking them down. It helps you to feel calmer, to feel better. Tell me more about the things you choose and the places you find them.

I am aware of adopting a soothing tone of voice myself and offering a narrative that echoes those contained in the phrases Ellen May selects for herself. Now the observation of Esther comes to mind and I remember how her mother Helen told her: 'Earlier you did this, now that is happening and later on we will do something else.' It was, of course, the rhythm and tone of voice that was important, not the meaning of the words themselves. She was offering what I have called a 'narrative skin', including a sequencing element that conveyed the orderly progression from one part of the day or one activity to another. Now I find myself offering a similar web of words for Ellen May.

When she returns from her holiday in Tuscany, Ellen May tells me that she spent a lot of time reading, something that she used to love to do but now rarely manages. I wonder whether her ability to reconnect to the 'web of words' that a novel can provide is linked to our work together in therapy. Experience has taught me that, with Ellen May, putting this thought into words is unlikely to be helpful. If I do so, she will feel that something she has found for herself is being appropriated by me, that she is being upstaged, and this is something she cannot bear. Choosing my words carefully, I say that she seems calmer than when she left and that she has identified reading another thing that is helpful to her. Reading fiction is now added to 'our' list of the strategies available to Ellen May for keeping self-harming tendencies at bay.

This incident recalls to me both my own love of reading and the excellent work of Michael and Margaret Rustin on the layers of meaning present in certain examples of children's fiction. As I write, the Harry Potter phenomenon is at its height, with J. K. Rowling's books (1997, 1998, 1999, 2000) selling in huge numbers and the film of the first book in the series drawing in record audiences. Fiction, whether for children or adults, can provide its own form of containment. In *Narratives of Love and Loss*, Rustin and Rustin (2001) highlight the way in which fiction can help a child who feels deprived and unloved to conjure up and imaginatively connect to a different version of events.

Harry Potter is a fictional character who does exactly that. Following the untimely death of his birth parents, his aunt and uncle reluctantly adopt him. He is neglected and abused at home and made to live in the cupboard under the stairs. Rescue comes at the age of eleven, when, with help, he is able to take up his place at 'Hogwarts', the school for magicians. His way of conducting himself speaks of the survival of creativity and hopefulness in his inner world. He earns the respect of his peers and is discerning in his choice of friends:

> How does Harry have such a nose for a nice family (the Weasleys) and such good friends? His life from one to eleven years appears to have offered him virtually no opportunity to have good qualities in himself recognized or to be offered experiences imbued with love. Yet the idea that other relations might rescue him represents Harry's belief that there is a different life beyond Privet Drive, and this seems to spring from an awareness of human feeling (warmth, fun, friendship, appreciation, generosity, etc.) which Harry can imagine. These are the preconceptions of the hopeful child whose adverse early years have not crushed an expectation that the world contains beauty and good feelings. At depth, this is the baby's belief that there will be a good mother out there, a mother who will answer his questions (in contrast with Aunt Petunia, who never does

so) and will be interested in getting to know him. (Rustin and Rustin 2001, p.277).

My work with Ellen May was slightly in advance of the Harry Potter phenomenon and I do not know if she found her way to the books. I hope she did, for I feel that they would serve as a helpful resource, both with regard to the themes outlined above and in their invitation to enter into a conjured up 'as if' world.

In adult life, an important aspect of 'second skin' phenomena is the rigidity of the individual's self-narrative. The skin function of preventing intrusions has become dominant and the consequent toughening reduces the individual's capacity to accommodate change. With Ellen May, I have no sense of elasticity. Instead, I have an image of a great gash in the skin. A mass of unsorted, chaotic material spills out. The bombardment, the torrent of words, uses up all the space and in this way Ellen May unconsciously ensures that she takes nothing in from me. Fiction, and also film and drama, can play a useful role in addressing this situation. A book is very much under Ellen May's control. She can pick it up and put it down at will. By identifying with the different characters, she is perhaps developing within herself different self-narrative possibilities, with, it is hoped, a consequent reduction in rigidity.

At around this time, I ask Ellen May whether there are other hobbies or physical activities that she enjoys or has enjoyed in the past but that she hasn't thought to mention. To my surprise, she begins to talk about playing volleyball at college in the USA. She becomes animated as she realises that she misses playing and that when she goes home she will be able to play again.

Maggie: This is really important to you. I don't think I've seen you looking so happy and excited.

Ellen May: Wow. Yeah. I'd really forgotten. Thank you!

I am touched by this first ever expression of appreciation. Perhaps Ellen May's narcissistic world view and the sense of grievance that sustains it is beginning to change? Further therapeutic progress lends support to this suggestion. From the start, a major area of difficulty for Ellen May has been her management of college assignments. Because she cannot organise her time, she misses crucial deadlines. She sometimes works all night and then misses her appointment with me or fails to turn up at her workplace. I learn that she has extra assignments to complete because she failed some course modules when her eating disorder was at its most serious. She has promised her father that she will 'catch up' and this promise is informally written into his agreement to provide continued financial support. Feeling genuinely sympathetic, I suggest to Ellen May that she is now finding herself in an impossible situation. With my support, she manages to negotiate a different arrangement with her father and so to reduce her workload.

Following these small but significant steps forward, Ellen May arrives one day in her usual state of agitation. She speaks non-stop for five minutes about her flat-mate's diet and how this 'winds her up', then suddenly stops in mid-sentence and looks at me directly:

Ellen May: Do I smell today?

Maggie: (*taken aback*) You're afraid that you might smell?

Ellen May: It's just that I haven't had a shower for two days.

Maggie: Can you say some more? This sounds important but I'm not sure what you're trying to tell me…

Ellen May: I hate to catch sight of my skin. I have to cover up all the mirrors in the bathroom so that I don't catch sight of myself. Then it takes me ages to take my clothes off. I try not to catch sight of myself. But when I wash myself, I have to look at my skin and that's really hard. Sometimes it takes me two hours to have a shower, so you see sometimes I don't manage to have one every day.

Maggie: Can you tell me what is so terrible about seeing your skin? I mean, do you suffer from eczema or something like that?

Ellen May: No. I think it's that I'm getting fat… But, well, I suppose I don't really know.

I feel a wave of sadness sweep over me and say to Ellen May that what she has described has made me feel very sad for her. I ask her whether it is sometimes easier to look at herself, and whether she imagines other people share her disgust for her own body. I see her soften a little and she looks quite tearful, quite bereft.

Ellen May: It's funny you should say that because, actually, when I'm with my boyfriend, I feel much more OK about myself.

Maggie: When you are with him you are able to keep this feeling of self-loathing at bay, but once he is gone it comes back again.

Ellen May nods sadly and is unusually quiet and thoughtful. She ends the session in a much calmer frame of mind.

Although some progress is being made, there is a real cost attached to working in this way and I do not want to present too rosy a picture. Normally in psychoanalytic work, the harsh and primitive quality of projections is modified as they are identified in the transference–countertransference matrix, spoken about and gradually defused. As a result, the client's internal world comes to be experienced as a more benign and less dangerous place. When interpretation is not possible, underlying issues are not addressed and communication by means of projective identification continues unabated. The projections retain their original harshness, as is evident in the following examples, taken from my last few sessions with Ellen May.

Three months into the work, Ellen May talks about going home in May rather than in July. I encourage her to discuss the pros and cons, taking care not to consciously attempt to sway her in one direction or another. My underlying feeling is that returning to the US, where she has a familiar environment and some kind of support network, is the better option for her. At the next session, Ellen says that she has reached a decision and then conveys it in a provocative manner, as if it has been made in the face of objections from me. She tells me that, despite my advice to the contrary, she has decided to go home early!

Two weeks later, I raise with Ellen May the suggestion that I might write a piece for publication based on our work together. I ask her to think about it during the next week and to ask me any questions that come to mind before making a decision. She says immediately: 'Oh, I don't care. You can write what you like.' I feel she is saying 'You and your actions make absolutely no difference to me', and by implication, 'The time I have spent with you makes absolutely no difference. You are nothing to me.' At the next session, I ask her whether she has thought some more about the question of publication and she says again: 'It's not a problem. Write what you like.' We continue for two more weeks, talking mainly about Ellen May's plans for the future. Ellen May cancels her last appointment and leaves therapy, and presumably the country, owing me a small amount of money.

I think it is clear from this account that the value of the work described was limited. The most tangible achievement was that Ellen May did not again become bulimic while she was seeing me. Her weight remained within tolerable limits and another hospital admission was avoided. It is impossible to know what would have happened but for the therapy. My reflections conclude with some thoughts on a quotation that follows on from the one cited at the very beginning of the chapter. Referring to the 'containing object', Bick continues:

> Material will show how this containing object is experienced concretely as a skin. Faulty development of this primal skin function can be seen to result either from defects in the adequacy of the actual object or from fantasy attacks on it, which impair introjection. (Bick 1968, p.484).

Since Ellen May has declined to speak about her childhood experience, I cannot know whether her difficulties emanate primarily from 'defects in the adequacy of the actual object' or from 'fantasy attacks upon it'. Was Ellen May's parenting in one or another respect inadequate? And/or was the potential availability of her parents as good objects spoiled by primitive unconscious attacks, where greed and envy were the dominant emotions?

What is clear, I think, is the impairment of psychic skin function. As the literal skin outlines and defines the body, giving it visual coherence, so the psychic skin outlines and defines experience, giving it a recognisable shape and defending against internal chaos. In health, the psychic skin has similar qualities to the physical equivalent – flexibility, elasticity and the capacity to form a boundary between inner and outer worlds. The boundary is permeable, though not too permeable, and allows an exchange. Something is allowed out of the inner world and taken in from the external world, an exchange that is at the heart of fruitful relating. In the course of my work with Ellen May, this kind of relating often felt impossible. There were moments, nevertheless, when real contact was made and at these times Ellen May was able to take small but significant steps forward.

8

Acting, Feeling and Thinking: Working with Tracey

> The life of a healthy individual is characterised by fears, conflicting feelings, doubts, frustrations, as well as by the positive features. The main thing is that the man or woman feels he or she *is living his or her own life*, taking responsibility for action or inaction, and able to take credit for success and blame for failure. (Winnicott 1986, p.27)

In this chapter I describe work undertaken over a period of two years with a client, 'Tracey'. Her self-harming behaviour takes the form of self-hitting. This is not what brings her along to therapy and the self-harm is not mentioned until several weeks into the work.

'Tracey' finds my name in the BACP directory. We arrange an introductory session, at which she decides that she would like to come along to see me regularly. This wish is expressed in the words 'I need to do something and I suppose you're as good as anybody', a communication that leaves me feeling 'dismissed', although I am in fact being 'engaged'. Tracey tells me she feels stuck in a relationship that is going nowhere and that the same is true of her job. She also thinks it is maybe time she moved out of her family home, as she is now 25. I suggest that it may be helpful to meet more than once a week, at least at the beginning of the therapy, but Tracey says she cannot afford more than a weekly session.

My initial impression is of a slim but muscular young woman with short blond hair and a working-class accent, wearing a smart sweater and jeans. I am struck by the fact that Tracey is wearing a lot of make-up, including bright red lipstick, perhaps because this is somewhat at odds with the rest of her image. Tracey speaks in a blunt way, swearing a lot, and there is a grating coarseness about many of her communications. She has a particular way of looking at me, with which I am to become very familiar. Her gaze conveys a complex mixture of wariness, defiance and contempt.

I have introduced elsewhere (Turp 1999, 2001) the concept of 'body storylines', narratives that are physically inscribed, written into the body, by the individual's lived experience. Body storylines find expression in many different ways, for example in characteristic postures, gestures and facial expressions and in a general tendency towards liveliness or inertia. Some of these elements serve as markers of social standing or of identification with particular cultural or sub-cultural groups. They are matters of 'habitas', as described by Bourdieu (1984). Others are embodiments of personal experience over the years and it is these individual elements that are of more interest in the current context. The client's physically inscribed body storyline, silently telling the story of his or her experience and state of mind, has a physical impact on the therapist. In the presence of a person who is slumped, for example, who stares at the floor, whose speech is slow and monotonous, any one of us may feel our own energy level plummeting. There is a quasi-physical contact involved in these unconscious communications, which I have described elsewhere as a symbolic equivalent of physical touch (Turp 2001, p.69).

When Tracey's gaze meets mine, there is a quality of symbolic touching. Her gaze is part of a 'body storyline', an ingrained style of physical communication shaped by past experience and future expectation. It exerts a powerful effect on me. In the words of a popular phrase, it 'speaks volumes', conveying fear, an expectation of disappointment and an angry determination 'not to care'.

A few weeks into the work, Tracey tells me about a man with whom she is having a sexual relationship, a man who is married and living with his family. According to Tracey, all of her problems stem from 'the rotten bloody cards I've been dealt'. A picture builds of seething fury, reluctantly held in check for fear of its potential consequences. Tracey speaks in an angry and resentful tone of voice. The following week, it becomes apparent that anger is taking the form of physical violence as well, with self-harm emerging as another well-established body storyline. Tracey arrives and holds up her hand to show me her bandages. I ask her what has happened and she tells me that she has been punching the wall in her room at home. She looks at me in a challenging, almost triumphant way, as if to say, 'Well, what are you going to do about it then?'

I ask Tracey how long she has been harming herself. She says she has been punching walls since she was twelve. She has never needed medical attention and nobody else knows what she does.

Maggie:	I'm really surprised to hear that you've managed to keep this hidden for such a long time.
Tracey:	The stuff I do covers it up. Anyway, nobody takes that much notice of me.
Maggie:	The stuff you do?
Tracey:	Yeah, hockey and army games. You know, with paint pellets. You get lots of bruises.
Maggie:	And nobody takes much notice of you… Is that why you put the bandages on? Were you afraid that I wouldn't take much notice of you?
Tracey:	Well, I should hope you would. I'm paying you, aren't I?

I have referred in my writing to the psychologically beneficial potential of sport and physical activity, citing a number of examples from client work (Turp 1997, 1999c, 2000b, 2001). Physical activities also have a negative psychological potential and it is this that is to the fore in Tracey's case. Hockey and 'paint-balling' seem to serve as little more than avenues for the discharge of aggression, which is being acted out rather than being experienced emotionally and reflected upon. They are part of her toughening of herself and serve to disguise her self-harming behaviour. This impression is strengthened when I encourage Tracey to associate to these activities, to tell me what they mean to her and how she feels when she is engaged in them. With other clients, such enquiries tend to lead to the discovery of a whole range of emotions, memories and personal meanings. With Tracey, however, they draw a blank.

From early on, Tracey recounts a litany of woes, all of which refer in one way or another to what she sees as the essential unfairness of life. She feels she should be married and settled but is 'caught up' in a relationship with a married man. She feels that she is intelligent and should not be in the secretarial position that she occupies but should have gone to university. Therapy comes into this equation, with Tracey complaining that she has to spend her money on therapy, while other people can go out and have a good time. Listening to this stream of complaints, I am reminded as with Ellen May, of Young and Gibb's work (1998), which explores the issue of grievance and suggests a link to childhood trauma. I try to explore these possibilities but Tracey is reluctant to talk about her childhood. She responds by saying that she doesn't know what I want her to say and that her childhood was 'nothing special'.

Arriving for a session a few weeks later, Tracey sits down and holds up her fist for me to see the new bandages on her hand. I feel rather threatened and notice that her posture is indeed threatening, as if she might punch me.

Tracey: Look at this! I've been punching the bloody wall again, haven't I? There's a big dent where I punched it.

Maggie: Can you tell me more about what you did and why?

Tracey: Well, I don't fucking well know, do I?

Tracey experiences herself as the victim both of external events and of her own internal states. She genuinely has no idea what she feels or why she does the things she does. Sadness, like anger, is an event experienced as if coming in from the external world.

Tracey: I've had three attacks of sobbing this week.

Maggie: The way you put it, it's as if a black cloud comes over and tears fall out of it. As if, in a way, it's nothing to do with you personally…

(Tracey sits in a resentful silence.)

Maggie: Can you say anything about how you felt when you began to sob?

Tracey: I suppose I must have felt miserable, otherwise I wouldn't bloody well do it, would I?

On another occasion, Tracey tells me that she has a car but cannot bring herself to drive it, because she feels afraid that she will panic. We talk about this at some length, trying to understand the nature of the difficulty. What emerges is that Tracey is paranoid about the imagined thoughts and judgements of other drivers. For example, she is convinced that the driver behind her will be watching her and waiting for her to stall the engine or crunch a gear or put on the wrong indicator. Her frustration about this is sometimes vented on the car itself.

Tracey: That damned car just stands there and soon it's going to need its MOT.

Maggie: You're still not driving it?

Tracey: I get in it every night and start the engine but I don't go anywhere. A few days ago the bloody thing needed petrol and I had to get my brother to drive it to the garage and fill it up. *(Pause.)* Then last night I gave it a good kick, which didn't do my foot a whole lot of good. *(Pause.)* Oh Maggie, I don't know…

In this last statement, there is a sense of yielding and with it a feeling of suffering and defeat, hinting at the despairing feelings hidden behind Tracey's tough and aggressive self-presentation.

Another symptom that comes to light involves what Tracey describes as 'the shakes'. She cannot have a drink – alcoholic or otherwise – in a social situation because her hand shakes so violently that the drink spills. On one occasion, Tracey describes one of her 'paint-balling' weekends, spent with male work colleagues. She complains, not for the first time, that all her work colleagues are married.

Tracey: I would try and find an unmarried bloke, maybe, if it weren't for the shakes.

Maggie: The shakes?

Tracey: Yes, I can't go to the pub and have a drink because I'm afraid I'll start shaking and I'll spill it everywhere. So you see, I can't go and find myself another man.

Tracey goes on to fantasise about finding another relationship. I discover that under such circumstances she plans to continue her sexual relationship with Pete. I express surprise and Tracey becomes angry with me, telling me that I can't expect her to give him up. She will have to hang on to him as an 'insurance policy'. Somewhat bemused, I say to Tracey that she seems to regard men as inanimate objects, impervious sources of sexual gratification. Tracey sulks and I realise that my intervention was prompted more by feelings of sympathy for the hypothetical man involved than by concern for my client! No doubt Tracey's lack of concern, echoed in mine, reflects a particular form of psychosomatic splitting. For Tracey, the physical sensation of sexual intercourse seems entirely split off from her sense of herself as a person who might have an emotional effect on others.

Some of the difficulties involved in an inadequate or damaged 'capacity to mentalize' (Fonagy and Target 1995) are illustrated in the above exchanges. Tracey does not see Pete or her imagined new lover as people capable of suffering, people with feelings of their own. This imaginative failure seems to be rooted in Tracey's difficulties in identifying her own feelings. As she experiences it, physical markers of emotional states – 'attacks of sobbing' or 'the shakes' – come out of the blue. When asked, Tracey tries to identify the underlying emotion on the basis of her behaviour: 'I suppose I must have felt miserable, otherwise I wouldn't bloody well do it, would I?' Her answer suggests frustration, perhaps linked to an embryonic awareness that this method of working out how she feels is far from satisfactory.

Fonagy describes how early trauma and deprivation undermine the development of a primary attachment and so inhibit the growth of the all-important 'capacity to mentalize'. Fonagy and Target (1995) suggest that, in extreme cases, an inability to reflect on the mental states of others is linked to acts of criminal violence, with the perpetrator having no sense of the suffering of the victim. In the case of self-harm, the situation is complicated, since the perpetrator and the victim are one and the same. In a situation made possible by psychosomatic splitting and dissociation, the 'self' that executes the action is not experienced as identical with the 'self' or the 'body' that is the victim of the action.

> We suggest that both *self-harm and mindless assaults on others* may reflect an inadequate capacity to mentalize. Poor functioning of this capacity tends to lead to mental states being experienced as physical, in both the self and others, and violence is seen as an attempt to obliterate intolerable psychic experience. (Fonagy and Target 1995, p.487)

I admit that I sometimes find it difficult to be with Tracey. At a conscious level, I catch my thoughts drifting towards what to eat for dinner or the clients I am scheduled to see later in the day. Physically, I notice that I feel strangely empty and low in energy at the end of each session. I suffer various physical symptoms that thankfully disappear within an hour or so of Tracey's departure, including vicious headaches and, strangely, 'pins and needles' in my arms and legs. When I reflect on the latter, I recognise a feeling of numbness and of a limb 'not belonging', which seems informative. My understanding of these physical states is that they are in some way connected to how Tracey herself feels or has felt in the past. It seems therapeutically significant therefore (as well as a personal relief) when my symptoms abate during the second year of our meetings. What changes is that Tracey now seems to recognise me as a second person in the room, somebody who might possibly have something useful to say. My survival of her psychological attacks has perhaps mitigated the violent and primitive quality of her internal world and reduced the harshness of her projections.

During our more difficult sessions, I experience myself as wanting to make contact with Tracey but being kept at bay, and as weak and useless. Ogden (1997) describes how the apparently random images that come to mind during sessions can be surprisingly illuminating. During one such session, I recall a very old television advert for Michelin tyres, something that I have not thought about for years, that featured a 'steel man' in the shape of a tyre flexing his 'bands of steel'. This is a telling image in relation to my feelings when I am with Tracey, speaking of a sense of physical toughness and muscularity that holds her together and keeps me out. I see myself moving towards her and bouncing off again. These images and responses in turn call to mind the work of Bick (1968), already referred to in relation to the infant observations, on the development of a 'toughened second skin', a defensive psychic structure that succeeds in holding the individual together but reduces permeability and capacity for relationship.

At an emotional level, Tracey does not recognise and own the angry feelings that are expressed in her actions and words. Split off and denied, her destructive impulses emerge in self-hitting and in projections onto the external world, which is experienced as harsh, vindictive and unfair. Tracey sees herself not as angry or attacking but as a victim. Her feelings of fury and envy are not available to be thought about. Instead, they 'haunt' her, making their presence felt in paranoid fantasies and physical symptoms such as self-hitting, physical shaking and driving-related panic attacks. I remain alert for occasions when Tracey's destructive feelings are directed towards me and can be spoken about in the context of our relationship. Such situations occur often enough. At times I feel threatened, usually verbally but sometimes physically as well. When I try to name and describe what I think might be happening, however, I feel that my words become 'lost in space'.

Tracey:	I'm not blooming well getting anywhere here. How long is this going to take?
Maggie:	You're not satisfied with the therapy and you sound really angry with me.
Tracey:	Angry? No, I'm not angry. I'm more, well, upset, that things go so badly for me. I had three attacks of sobbing this week.

On this occasion, my intervention is brushed off by Tracey, suggesting that it was either inaccurate or premature. Shortly before Christmas a similar intervention meets with greater success. Tracey complains again that all her colleagues at work are married and that she 'never meets anyone'. Gradually, her mood becomes more vindictive.

Tracey:	It's all right for that lot, isn't it, looking forward to Christmas. They've all got wives and husbands and children and everything. *(A long pause.)* Sometimes I wish something would happen to them – one of the wives would die or something.

Maggie:	I think you're saying not just that 'it's all right for that lot' but that 'it's all right for you, Maggie'…
Tracey:	Yes, well, OK. I suppose I do feel a bit like that. You're not on your own like me, are you? (*Pause.*) I could go out and get myself a husband as well, you know, but I can't drag myself away from Pete and he's blooming-well married.
Maggie:	You feel very short-changed, very hard done by. Everybody seems to be luckier than you.
Tracey:	Well, it's not fair, is it? They've all met somebody but the person I've met is already married.
Maggie:	When you talk about Pete, I have the impression of somebody stuck in the middle of a desert and glued to a tap that drips very, very slowly. You're not satisfied with what you get but you can't bear to take the risk of moving away to look for something better.

On this occasion, I sense some sadness behind Tracey's anger and feel unusually compassionate towards her. This seems to be unconsciously communicated. Tracey begins to cry and there is a feeling of real under-standing between us. As happens from time to time, I feel that good work has been done and that Tracey has taken something useful in. Envious attacks on the work follow, however, countering much of the progress that has been made.

At a conscious level, Tracey comes along to her sessions for help. At an unconscious level, it seems that she so envies my 'satisfaction', including my phantasised sexual satisfaction, that she would rather spoil the sessions than receive something from me and allow me the additional satisfaction of having been able to help her. By the beginning of the second year, these dynamics are being more obviously played out in relation to me. In principle, I regard this as a helpful development presenting additional opportunities to bring the conversation around to the 'here and now' of transactions between us in the consulting room. In practice, I often find it difficult to think coherently in the face of Tracey's unconscious attacks. Perhaps it is indicative of the atmosphere in the room and of my own difficulties in holding my thoughts together that I do not remember the exact circumstances leading up to the following exchange. Ten minutes into the session, Tracey scowls at me, then rises from her chair.

Tracey: If I was to pick up this chair and throw it through your window, would you be insured for that?

At this time, I am working from an upstairs consulting room in my home. I can hear neighbours in the garden and have an image of the chair flying down through the air. It is an enormous struggle to find any words. Eventually, I do:

Maggie: Let's think for a moment about what you are saying. Last week, I think you felt you were beginning to make some progress. You remembered an image from an earlier session, of a person bound to a dripping tap in the middle of a desert, an image that spoke to you in some way. Today you feel like destroying everything. You want to spoil the room, to spoil our work together. There's a real problem with holding on to anything good.

(Tracey laughs derisively and looks out of the window.)

Maggie: There's a part of you that wants to spoil things and a part of you that wants to come through. I can see the sense of both of them but I know which side I'm on.

To my relief, Tracey sits back down in her chair.

Looking back on this session, I have a sense of having felt profoundly disrupted and almost entirely unable to think. In his development of Klein's work on projective identification, Bion describes the way in which the projections of intolerable states of mind into the therapist amount to 'attacks on linking' (Bion 1967a) that disrupt the therapist's thought processes. Referring to this work, Rhode comments: 'Bion writes with a pioneer's courage about sessions in which the patient's psychopathology knocks all meaning out of the therapist's mind' (Rhode 1993, p.504). Some of Tracey's statements and actions do indeed seem to knock all the meaning out of my mind. Tracey inhabits a concrete world of action and reaction, dominated by anger and resentment. There is much paranoia and much confusion with regard to what is external and what is internal. Readers will recognise how difficult it is to begin to make sense of self-harming behaviour in the situation described. The basis for insight – the idea of an internal world that shapes perceptions and behaviour – seems to be almost entirely missing. Tracey apparently sees her problems as caused by external circumstances, in particular by 'bad luck', by the cruel unfairness of fate.

Nevertheless, Tracey attends all her sessions and pays a full fee, a commitment that suggests she is at some level aware of the part she plays in her difficulties. She also shows a certain degree of ego strength. Her external life is not chaotic, insofar as she holds down a job and manages to more or less function in the outside world. I say 'more or less' because Tracey's activities are curtailed by not being able to drive, by not being able to drink in the company of others for fear of 'the shakes' and by her attachment to Pete. In supervision, I reflect regularly on Tracey's unconscious positioning of me in the relationship between us. With the passing of time, it becomes ever clearer that I am the one now being blamed for her difficulties.

Projective identification is a marked feature of Tracey's communications to me and her projections have a very harsh feel. Unconscious attacks are mounted on me and on our work and I sometimes find myself feeling hopeless, useless and utterly stumped. Having no conscious knowledge of these matters, Tracey does not refer to them in a direct way. They are really body-to-body matters, finding expression in sequences of harsh words followed by silences, in action and gesture and in my feelings of foreboding, exhaustion and physical tension. By now, I am seeing the harshness of Tracey's speech as another version of the 'Michelin Man' scenario, a toughened 'second skin' (Bick 1968) expressed in verbal muscularity as well as in 'tough' activities such as hockey, paint-balling and self-hitting.

The charged, sometimes hostile atmosphere makes it difficult to work in an interpretive way. When little else seems possible, I endeavour to take in and reflect on what is happening and to sustain and communicate the idea that thinking is possible, even in the most difficult of situations. Nevertheless, many of the sessions are dominated by raw and primitive emotions communicated primarily through non-verbal channels.

(Tracey comes in and sits down. She looks down at her hands for a minute, then looks up and over towards me, her face absolutely furious.)

Tracey: I've been coming here for over a year, and I'm still no better. I've stopped doing the punching, but I still haven't got a proper relationship. I'm still stuck in the same dead-end job! What good is this doing me? I don't know why I bother!

This attack on my competence is very effective. I feel myself slump. I am inadequate, worthless, a complete fraud. After a while, I remind myself that Tracey's assessment is not entirely accurate and that there have, in fact, been changes. For example, Tracey has moved out of the family home and is buying a flat of her own. These changes have been recognised by both of us, in happier moments, as significant achievements. I decide to speak directly about the projective identification in play.

Maggie: I think you want me to know how it feels when all your efforts are for nothing, when no matter how hard you try, it simply makes no difference. You are just seen as a worthless drain on others.

At this, Tracey begins to cry. I notice that my own feelings change. My anxiety dissipates and I begin to feel warm and sympathetic. The rest of the session has a quiet and thoughtful feel, reflecting the connection that has been established between us. This development brings the possibility of returning to the matter of Tracey's childhood. So far my enquiries have yielded very little. I have listened for references to any particular events or circumstances that might account for her enraged state and her pervasive sense of having been cheated. Nothing particular has emerged. The most Tracey has said is: 'I wasn't abused, or anything like that.'

In the following exchanges, it emerges that Tracey is disappointed in and resentful towards her mother. However, she is clearly very fond of her father.

Tracey: If I had a child, I would take her to Kew and tell her the names of the trees. My Mum doesn't even know the names of trees. If I want to know them, I have to look them up in a book.

Maggie: You feel you've had to do everything for yourself?

Tracey: Absolutely. Now if there's a form to fill in, I'm the one that has to do it. And my Dad bought a camera but I was the only one who could understand the instructions. My Dad's not stupid though. No, not at all.

My supervisor and I reflect on the poignancy of these words, especially those relating to Kew and the names of the trees, which are spoken in a dreamy and nostalgic tone of voice.

On many occasions, Tracey refers to a strong attachment to her father and a difficult relationship with her mother. She talks about her mother in a disparaging way. For example, she tells me on one occasion, 'She nags and nags my Dad. She'll be the death of him.' In response to my enquiry as to the state of 'Dad's' health, Tracey tells me he had a heart attack during the previous year.

Tracey: If he had died… Well that cow… Honestly, Maggie, I don't know what I'd have done.

Although the words themselves are angry, I see that Tracey's eyes are full of tears. When I say that the thought of losing her father makes her feel very sad, Tracey gives me an angry look but continues to cry.

For the most part, Tracey's physical self-presentation and speech has a stereotypically 'masculine' quality, echoed in her leisure activities. The liberally applied bright red lipstick that so jars with the rest of her seems to be added as an afterthought, a disconnected gesture paying 'lip service' to her female gender. As a woman with feminist sympathies, who loves the outdoor life, is happiest in T-shirts and jeans and shuns make-up, I am well aware of the dangers of 'masculine' and 'feminine' stereotyping! But I believe that the case material undeniably points to confusion and difficulty with regard to gender identification and Oedipal issues.

Tracey makes it clear that she wants a close relationship with her father and that she resents her mother. Her relationship with Pete, a married man for whom Tracey is not the first priority, recreates the dynamics of the original Oedipal triangle. Tracey herself underlines the parallels, commenting frequently on the striking physical similarities between Pete and her father. She has not met Pete's wife but sees her as another version of her mother, coming between Tracey and the object of her desire by being too demanding and 'wanting Pete to be around all the time'. Eventually it emerges that I am also perceived as wanting to come between Tracey and her sexual gratification. In the following passage, Tracey is again talking about her colleagues at work:

Tracey: Why do they get all the good cards and I get this rubbish hand? I mean, all right, I know you think I at least have a choice about carrying on with Pete. But Maggie, have you ever been without sex for a long time? I don't think I could stand it. I need my nookie! *(Tracey looks at me accusingly, as if this is something I might be trying to take away from her.)*

Freud originally saw Oedipal issues as coming into play in the third and fourth years of life but Klein dated them much earlier, from the first year of life onwards. For Klein, Oedipal issues and questions of envy and gratitude were closely connected. The infant's envy of the mother can spoil the mother's love and obstruct the establishment of a good internal object (1957). Without a sense of this 'primary source of goodness' (Klein 1952) negotiation of Oedipal rivalries and desires is especially difficult. Klein believed that envy was primarily a constitutional matter – that some infants are simply more envious than others. Winnicott took a more 'environmental' position, later incorporated into post-Kleinian thinking, arguing that infantile envy is in part a consequence of excessive frustration in the relationship with the mother.

Klein emphasised the importance of unconscious fantasies, which she referred to as 'phantasies'. In infancy, thoughts, fantasies and phantasies are all felt to have real power. The line that divides internal and external worlds is blurred and the workings of the internal world are equated in the child's mind with externally directed actions. Tracey's rage, distress and feelings of persecution in the present may arise, at least in part, from poor management of her normal incestuous desires towards her father and unconscious murderous intent towards her mother in infancy and childhood. The resolution of Oedipal conflict entails identification with the same-sex parent or a substitute figure. Tracey has resisted identifying with her mother, for reasons that are as yet unclear. Her anger, envy and sense of deprivation have continued unabated, leaving her in the grip of fantasies of forbidden action and adult retaliation.

Earlier, I mentioned my first infant observation, which involved 'Emma' and her family. Towards the end of that observation, when the situation in the family was much improved, I had the opportunity of observing good maternal management of Oedipal desire. I include an observation extract here that helped me to gain some insight into the kind of help that might have been lacking in Tracey's early experience.

Observation of 'Emma', age 17 months

Emma returns to the room. On the stairs she has picked up a silky cloth, multi-coloured in purple and yellow. 'Doo-doo-doo. Da-da,' she sings, fingering the shorts and draping and swishing them over her bare arms. 'Your favourite thing, Daddy's boxer shorts!' says Mother in an enthusiastic tone of voice.

We hear the front door open, and Father comes in. He puts some cardboard boxes down on the floor, opens them and briefly checks the contents, which are door handles and hinges. Emma goes over and peers in. 'No no. Those are mine,' says Father, then he picks Emma up and jiggles her. 'Ooh-ah-ooh-ah-ooh-ah,' says Emma in a rhythmic pattern. 'We're going to give you a bath a bit later, aren't we?' says Father. 'Yes,' says Emma enthusiastically. Father puts her down and she cries immediately. 'You were all right before I came, weren't you?' he says. 'No,' says Emma. 'Yes. You were,' objects Father and looks at her. Emma cries really bitterly and stretches up her arms. Father says, 'I'm sorry, I've just got to make some phone calls', and goes upstairs.

Mother comforts and distracts Emma, building towers out of bricks and encouraging her to knock them down. Emma throws the bricks around, seeming angry. 'Don't throw them please,' says Mother. Emma lies on her back on the floor, kicks her legs and screams loudly. 'What happened to you?' says Mother. 'I think I might get you a bottle.' She goes out to the kitchen.

Emma sidles over to the forbidden boxes and, making a huge effort, removes a heavy iron door handle. Then, with great difficulty, she climbs on to a high upholstered chair and sits up very straight, head against the back of the chair, legs straight out in front, arms evenly along the chair arms, in an upright, regal posture.

Mother returns. 'Yes, you're sitting in Daddy's chair!' she says. Emma looks extremely pleased with herself and shouts exuberantly, 'Yer-wa-wa-wa.' She finds Father's pad of paper on the chair seat, picks it up and leafs through it, then pulls the top sheet off and crumples it up. She looks at it hard and comments, 'A-a-a-tah.' Then she bumps her head back several times against the upholstered chair back and takes on a cheeky expression, shouting, 'Nayah! Nayah!'

Emma's experience of Oedipal desire and envy is mitigated by what Stern (1985, 1999) refers to as 'maternal attunement' and by her mother's capacity to acknowledge and contain Emma's intense feelings towards her father. Although we cannot be sure, it seems likely that Tracey's mother was not available to help her in this way. There is a striking sense of distance and coolness in all of Tracey's relationships with women, including with me. Tracey has two brothers but, as far as I am aware, no close female relative, such as an aunt or a grandmother, played a part in her upbringing. She mentions no female friends and spends many weekends in the predominantly male world of 'paint-balling'.

By this stage, Tracey is more willing and able to respond to my efforts to understand her childhood experiences, although I am invariably the one to raise the subject:

Maggie:	You know, although you've mentioned your mother in passing and I have gathered that you have very little time for her, I have no real idea of what it's like to be with her – of what it was like for you as a child.
Tracey:	*(thinks for a while)* I don't really know Maggie. I suppose – it was as if I wasn't really there.
Maggie:	As if you were invisible?
Tracey:	Something like that. You know, she never came to a parents' evening. And I was really good at the piano but she never said anything. I might as well not have bothered, for all she cared.
Maggie:	Are you saying she didn't really care for you – not in a way you recognised as caring?
Tracey:	I felt, what's the word, wiped out by her. She carried on in her own sweet way. Dad and me, I'd say that neither of us made the slightest difference.

This is an illuminating exchange, for the feeling of being 'wiped out' and of not making the slightest difference strikes an immediate chord. I have at times felt that nothing I say or do touches Tracey in any way. Tracey's comments again suggest the operation of projective identification, with Tracey communicating to me the way she herself has felt as a child, through unconsciously stirring up similar feelings within me. In connection with this material, I reflect on Winnicott's question 'What does the infant see when it looks into the mother's eyes?' and his answer: 'I am suggesting that, ordinarily, what the baby sees is himself or herself. In other words the mother is looking at the baby and *what she looks like is related to what she sees there*' (Winnicott 1971, pp.112–113). In the place of this maternal seeing, identified by Winnicott as a kind of mirroring, it seems that Tracey saw a mother who was self-absorbed, who could not or did not wish to see her.

Mollon (1985) writes about a client, a night-club singer in her twenties, who, like Tracey, is very dissatisfied with the quality of her sexual relationships. Reflecting on his client's difficulties, Mollon draws on the framework of self psychology, developed by Kohut (1971) and others in the USA. In self psychology, narcissistic disturbance is attributed to the absence of responsive mirroring by primary caretakers and the role of Oedipal conflict is de-emphasised. Mollon finds Kohut's account relevant but insufficient. In order to reach a fuller understanding, he has to take account of Oedipal difficulties and early failures of containment, as described by Bion (1962).

This same combination of understandings proves useful in my work with Tracey and I feel that I am finally grasping the meaning of Tracey's self-hitting and other difficulties. Tracey feels enraged, shamed and aggrieved by the narcissistic wound inflicted upon her by her mother's self-absorption, by her mother's failure to see and respond to her as a unique human being. These suppressed emotions interact with unresolved Oedipal issues. Repressed feelings emerge in the form of self-hitting and shaking, which may represent a fear of the violence Tracey experiences as locked up inside her. Her symptoms give expression, albeit indirect expression, to her difficulties. By making the invisible visible, they carry the hope of recognition and change and in this sense they serve a useful function.

I try to make sure that Tracey knows that I see her and acknowledge her, that I am interested in her as a whole person. She does not need to have symptoms in order to hold my gaze and my attention. She seems surprised to find that this is the case, particularly when I remember and bring into the session something that she has told me at a previous meeting. As the atmosphere improves, I decide to risk interpreting Tracey's self-sabotaging behaviour, rooted in her resentment of her mother.

Maggie: Because your mother didn't recognise that you were bright and clever, you haven't done anything much with those qualities yourself, have you? I mean, as far as I know, you've not even thought about a career change, about what you might need to do...

Tracey: *(hotly)* That's not true! I have thought about it.

Maggie: I wonder why you haven't mentioned it? Perhaps you thought I would be like your mother, that I wouldn't be interested.

Tracey: Are you interested then?

Maggie: You spend a lot of your life at work, many hours every week. And you tell them that your job is dull and doesn't challenge you. So I'm curious about what it means to you to stay there and, now you've told me you have other ideas, to hear what they might be. Perhaps this could be the place to think about some changes.

This conversation leads to a period of reflection and discussion that culminates in Tracey enrolling at university and beginning a part-time degree in philosophy. Given her background, her poor academic qualifications and her psychological difficulties, I find this a quite extraordinary achievement. Tracey makes good use of her sessions, talking through her fears about her interview, about managing the work and about driving her car to college, something that she is at last able to do. Our progress is also marked by an incident when, for the first time ever, we are able to laugh together.

Tracey: I bought a washing machine and I was going to pay to have it plumbed in, but Dad said, 'Oh, never mind that. I can do that for you.' He's always round at my flat you know. *(Smiles at me sheepishly.)* I told him, 'It's all right, you don't have to', but he said, 'Don't you worry, I can do that for my best girl!'

(I laugh. Tracey looks down, a little embarrassed, then looks up at me and laughs as well.)

Tracey: I'm afraid Pete does the same kinds of things for me.
                 He's coming over at the weekend to have a look at my
                 central heating.

The last six months of therapy bring changes that suggest Tracey is
beginning to be more in touch with her internal world. For the first time,
she begins to remember her dreams and to describe them to me in the
sessions. There is a marked change of atmosphere. Where the sessions were
dominated by accounts of concrete events, accompanied by much
complaining, we are now able to work fruitfully with symbolic material.
The dreams described seem to allude to some of the issues discussed above,
the Oedipal wishes, the destructive feelings towards the wounding
mother, the envious attacks on the parental couple and their relationship,
and the attendant paranoia. They testify to a bleak and devastated internal
world and, not surprisingly, Tracey finds them very disturbing.

Tracey: I had such a weird dream, Maggie. I was in a graveyard.
                 It was misty, then I saw loads of headstones and I could
                 hear this noise – like the wind howling. Then this kind
                 of ghoul appeared in a black cloak. I could only see it
                 from behind at first. *(Tracey stops and gulps.)* The worst
                 thing was, she turned around and her face was just a
                 skull, with empty sockets where her eyes should be.

Maggie: You seem to know it was a 'she'?

Tracey: Yes, it was me, wasn't it? It was me. *(Now Tracey is staring
                 fixedly at me and her face has gone very pale.)*

On another occasion, Tracey describes a dream of being in hospital and
finding she is a 'vegetable' kept alive on a life support system, fully aware
but unable to act. A few weeks after this, she comes with a dream that we
jointly identify as a horror-film version of her paint-balling weekends. In
the dream, the battlefield is a real one, strewn with real corpses. She
cautiously approaches a body in a khaki uniform and it leaps up and
pursues her. Running in terror, not looking back, Tracey hears a bayonet
blade swishing past her ears. She wakes up screaming. She is not sure
whether the figure pursuing her is a man or a woman.

Soon afterwards, Tracey tells me she has dreamt of being in a small room. The walls are covered in blood. She is in there on her own and has a small rag and bucket. Her job is to clear up the mess.

Maggie: This is quite a small room, isn't it?

Tracey: It could have been this room. It was just about this size.

Maggie: A lot has happened here. You are worried about how much mess is left to clear up. In the dream you are doing all this on your own. Do you still feel that you can't rely on me?

At this point, I recommend to Tracey – not for the first time – that she should come to see me twice a week, even if she can only manage this for a limited period. Initially Tracey seems open to this suggestion, although she is concerned about her finances, having recently taken on a mortgage. I offer her a reduced fee for a limited period of three months and say again that this is an important time and that I do feel concerned for her. She says she will think about it.

The following week, Tracey comes along and tells me she will have to stop her sessions as she has lost her job. She announces this in a very matter-of-fact way and does not seem at all upset. (In contrast, I feel shocked and upset.) My concern and my attempts to persuade her not to precipitate such a sudden and abrupt ending are in vain. Tracey just keeps telling me that she can no longer afford to come. Eventually, she agrees to come for one final session. At this session, she remains distant and pragmatic. Towards the end of the session, I ask about the possibility of my referring to our work together in a future publication. Tracey readily agrees to this and brushes aside my suggestion that she should think it over for a while and then let me know. She says in a dismissive tone more reminiscent of early sessions, 'To be quite honest, it doesn't bother me one way or the other.'

Interpretations of this kind of ending suffer from the fact that they cannot be explored with the client. At the point when she left, Tracey perhaps felt the practical gains she had made were under threat and so decided to call a halt to the proceedings. Her loss of her job played into this, of course, but I am convinced that it was not the only reason for her departure. There was, by this time, quite a lot to lose. Tracey was pursuing her studies and managing her assignments. She had bought her own flat and moved out of the family home. She had stopped harming herself. Her symptom of 'shaking' had improved and she was able to drink tea with her fellow students. For all of this, Tracey continued to find life enormously difficult. At college, she studied but did not socialise. She found seminar presentations a particular torture, imagining that the other students were waiting for her to make mistakes. (This was such an insuperable problem that Tracey eventually changed her course to one where she did not have to give verbal presentations.) She was able to drive but still found it almost unbearably stressful. She was still in a relationship with Pete, which continued to be a source of frustration and bitter complaint.

The content of Tracey's dreams suggests that the gradual softening of her defences in therapy led to her being overwhelmed by primitive and terrifying material. Some of this material had previously been absorbed and expressed in her psychosomatic symptoms and, in this sense, she was perhaps the victim of her own success, her symptoms no longer being 'available' to her as an outlet. Looking back, I am left to wonder whether I interpreted too little, leaving Tracey feeling that she had to bear her intense feelings alone, or whether I interpreted too much, moving at a pace that Tracey was unable to match. In a sense, by ending therapy in the way she did, Tracey had her final triumph over me as the quasi-maternal figure, leaving me feeling bemused and insecure.

Tracey's self-harming behaviour, disclosed several weeks into the work, was the main reason for my choosing to include an account of this particular piece of work. Readers will have gathered that very little time in the sessions was devoted to the discussion of self-harm. This is a true reflection of the work, which is not to say that the subject of self-harm was avoided. Because self-harm stirs up difficult feelings, it is possible to express a felt sense of urgency by focusing on it heavily, perhaps believing that the main aim of the therapy is to eliminate the self-harming behaviour. In my view, this approach is counter-productive. It is more important by far to recognise that self-harm is meaningful, that it is serving a purpose. Self-harm is a symptom of something else and it is that 'something else' that needs to be given the space to emerge. Analogies exist in the realm of purely physical illnesses. For example, there is no point in treating the symptom of coughing if the underlying disease of tuberculosis is not also identified and addressed.

In our work together, we came closer to understanding the 'something else' that lay beneath Tracey's self-harming tendencies. I was only sorry that at this particular point in her life, she did not feel able to continue the journey she had started.

9

A Body in Pieces: Working with Peter

A person is confronted with *overwhelming* affects; in other words, his affective responses produce an unbearable psychic state that threatens to disorganise, perhaps even destroy, all psychic functions. (Krystal 1988, p.137)

In this chapter I describe work with a client, 'Peter', whose self-harming behaviour is almost entirely hidden. People like Peter represent a silent majority among people who harm themselves – 'silent' because so few people know about their self-harm, 'silent' because their experiences so seldom feature in the professional literature. Peter is in therapy with me for two and a half years. On several occasions, when he is clearly in a fragile state, I discuss with him the possibility of coming twice a week. Peter never feels that this is right and pressure of work in any case makes it more or less impossible. He continues to see me once a week throughout the therapy.

My first impression on meeting Peter is of a man of around thirty who emanates charm and civilised living. He has a self-confident manner and a pleasing appearance, well-dressed, with just the right measure of casual elegance. I ask him where he would like to begin and he describes his current work situation. I learn that Peter has been 'fast-tracked' in his career in health services management and that this is putting him under considerable pressure. He tells me laughingly that he is 'always being over-promoted'. Peter also tells me he co-owns a house in Clapham in South London, where he lives with two friends, and that he has been in a relationship for just over a year with a woman called Anna.

I ask Peter what brings him to therapy. In response, he describes two 'symptoms' to me. First, he sometimes finds himself kicking a bush, a lamp-post or a bollard, without knowing why, as he walks along the street. Second, he finds himself, in the middle of washing up or some other domestic chore, saying out loud, 'Fuck you, Anna!' This exclamation is accompanied by an explosive action such as banging a plate down on the draining board. Peter's face takes on an expression of bafflement as he tells me about these incidents. He assures me that he could not think more highly of Anna and that he is deeply committed to her. I comment that different parts of him seem to be behaving in different, even contradictory ways, and that he is finding this very puzzling.

Peter is an articulate man. He speaks fluently and at times makes humorous, slightly self-deprecating comments. Over the next few sessions, he tells me a little about his life and his family. He has one brother, eight years older than himself, who lives in America. His parents, now retired, were previously school teachers in a small town in Surrey. The family was very respectable. As Peter puts it, 'My parents were pillars of the community.' I notice the ironic tone and say, 'Are you telling me that the family as seen from the outside was rather different from the family you experienced, living inside it?' Peter nods and there is a long pause. Then he heads off on a different tack.

Peter is so pleasant to be with, so personable, so successful, so engaging, that the sessions seem almost too easy. I am aware of how much I like him and of a rather seductive side to his personality. All of this is very much at odds with the aggression hinted at in his 'symptoms'. I begin to think in terms of a well-developed 'False Self' scenario (Winnicott 1960a). Peter's description of being repeatedly 'over-promoted' rather confirms this line of thinking. What he describes is persuading his superiors that he can do a job that he cannot, in fact, do except by means of staying at the office for upwards of seventy hours a week. This slightly removed 'as if' quality is a pervasive feature, both of Peter's way of being with me and of many of the situations he describes.

The term 'False Self' is sometimes understood as having only negative connotations, a reading that has been criticised, for example by Richards (1996). In fact, Winnicott emphasises that a certain level of False Self functioning is essential to health. Each of us has a private core of our being. The False Self protects this private area of experiencing, functioning in normal circumstances as a screen and a useful 'social self'. There is the potential, however, for the False Self to become a costly defence, taking over to the extent that spontaneity and authenticity are almost entirely lost.

The elusive counterpart of the 'False Self' is the 'True Self', described by Winnicott as emanating from 'the aliveness of the body tissues and the working of the body functions, including the heart's action and breathing' (Winnicott 1960a, p.148). If True Self functioning involves being in touch with and at one with physical functioning, then False Self functioning involves the opposite, namely a split between physical functioning on the one hand and emotion and thought on the other. Psychosomatic splitting of this kind can often be traced back to traumatic experiences. In the face of overwhelming distress, the individual has effectively said, 'Something is happening to me physically, but at the same time not to me. My body is not me. I am not really here.' Repeated experiences of trauma can lead to chronic and habitual splitting of this nature. Over time, the individual concerned loses access to what we refer to in everyday language as 'gut feelings'. Difficulties in mentalising come into play and are part of the same overall picture.

At his next session, Peter reveals that he has a whole range of ways of staying out of touch with feelings. At the weekends, he goes out drinking, takes 'recreational' drugs in clubs and gets very little sleep. Peter boasts a little about his double life:

Peter: People at work haven't got a clue what I get up to at the weekend. *(Laughs.)* You wouldn't believe how hard it is sometimes to get up and go in on Monday morning. *(Pause.)* I don't want you thinking that the drugs are a problem – I've got it all under control.

Maggie: You are not concerned about your drinking or drug-taking?

Peter: No, that's not a problem. *(At this point, however, he looks down at his hands and my sense is that he is embarrassed.)*

Peter describes a life that is programmed wall-to-wall with hectic activity.

Maggie: I find it very striking that you leave no space at all in
               your life – almost as if you were afraid of having a
               moment unoccupied.

Peter: I don't know why, but I do need to be occupied. I dread
               the prospect of a Saturday night when nothing is
               booked in. If I haven't got something arranged by
               Wednesday, I start to panic. I phone around one person
               after another until I've got something sorted out.

The relationship between action, thinking and feeling is an issue here, as in
the previous chapter. There is a great deal of action in Peter's life, along
with a great deal of intellectual thinking. In contrast, there is very little
access to feelings and very little thinking in relation to feelings. One
version of this situation emerges in Peter's identification with and support
for the feminist cause. He lectures me in an abstract and highly intellectual
way about the special difficulties experienced by women at work.
Eventually, I intercede:

Maggie: Well, it's clear that I am a woman, and I'm wondering if
               you feel that I am somehow being downtrodden in this
               work with you?

Peter: *(Taken aback, laughs.)* I was talking about women in
               general, not about you. *(Pause.)* But I suppose I might be
               a bit of a tricky customer.

Maggie: Perhaps you are. Can you say any more about that?

Peter: *(slightly sheepishly)* Well, you know…the drugs and
               everything.

Over the next two sessions, Anna's qualities are extolled even more than
usual. I feel that she has been raised almost to goddess status. After
listening once again to an account of her many virtues, I comment on this:

Maggie: How odd it must be for you to find yourself breaking out in fits of cursing her, where she is so worthy and above reproach and especially when you are so much on the side of women.

Peter: I just can't understand it. It seems to come out of the blue.

I described in the previous chapter, using the example of the 'Michelin Man', the way in which I am sometimes 'visited' by somatic sensations or images (or both) that have no obvious connection with the therapy material. A number of psychoanalysts have written about such phenomena. I will refer here to the work of the American psychoanalyst Thomas Ogden (1997), which I have found particularly helpful. Ogden develops his ideas from Winnicott's conception (1971) of a transitional space, a 'place where we live', a third area of experiencing between reality and fantasy. Into this third area of experiencing come images and feelings originating in situations outside the therapy setting. Ogden recommends close reflection on these experiences, which bring in the analyst's personal experience:

> A great deal has been written in recent years about the importance of the analyst's 'realness', i.e. his capacity for spontaneity and freedom to respond to the analysand from his own experience…in a way that is not strangulated by stilted caricatures of analytic neutrality.
>
> …My own technique rarely includes discussing the countertransference with the patient directly. Instead the countertransference is implicitly presented in the way I conduct myself as an analyst, for example, in the management of the analytic frame, the tone, wording and content of interpretations and other interventions. (Ogden 1997, p.25).

While working with Peter, I happen to visit a friend, 'Kay', who has a young son, 'Johnny'. While I am there, Johnny wakes up suddenly and becomes very distressed, kicking out and hurting himself before I can intervene. I am including a short observation of this incident, recorded after my visit, because images from the scene I witnessed often drifted into my mind during this phase of my work with Peter.

Observation of 'Johnny' at 9 months

When I arrive, Johnny is sleeping peacefully on a mat on the floor. Kay says, 'He fell asleep in the middle of playing with his Babygym. He is so tired.' She tells me that she is very tired as well, having spent hours in the night walking Johnny up and down while he cried with the misery of teething pains. I respond sympathetically, remembering only too well what it was like when my own children were teething. We chat for a few minutes, then Kay offers me a cup of coffee and goes down to the kitchen to make it.

Almost as soon as Kay leaves, Johnny wakes up, very suddenly and in a very agitated state. He lets out a series of loud cries. His face is bright red. He rubs his fists into his nose and into his eyes and his face is quickly covered with mucus. He kicks wildly and flings his arms out, screaming. He is quite beside himself. He inadvertently kicks a chair leg, intensifies his howls and then I see him, apparently deliberately, kick the chair leg again.

All of this happens in just a few moments. I automatically jump up to go to the rescue but Kay is ahead of me. She comes in, rushing upstairs from the kitchen, bends down and gathers Johnny up in her arms. 'Oh dear, oh dear! You poor little thing!' she says, sounding distressed herself. 'This is terrible!' She holds Johnny firmly against her chest and rubs his back, making soothing sounds, 'Shush, shush. There, there… It's OK. It's going to be OK. You just keep waking up, don't you? You don't want to wake up and it makes you so angry.' She moves her weight from one foot to the other, so that they both rock gently back and forth.

It takes ten minutes for Johnny to calm down. At times he snuggles into Kay's shoulder and seems OK, but then he lifts his head and tenses his body and starts to roar all over again in an angry and dismayed tone. Twice Kay offers him a bottle of milk.

On both occasions he takes it from her and flings it forcibly to the ground. The intensity of the outbursts gradually diminishes, until Kay is able to sit down and Johnny sits quietly on her lap, leaning his body floppily against her breast and looking very sleepy.

As part of her ministrations, Kay receives and names Johnny's feelings, identifying anger and frustration (rather than feelings, for example, of deep sadness). She puts into words what is happening for him – he is in this state because he is exhausted and keeps waking up. This is a classic example of what Bion refers to as 'containment'. Kay 'detoxifies' the situation further, soothing Johnny with the words, 'It's OK… It's going to be OK.' These words create a narrative skin around Johnny and help to calm him, even though he does not understand the meaning of the words as such. Physical holding and rocking and the weaving of a web of words both play a part in Kay's response.

In the course of a normal childhood, experiences like this are repeated over and over again. On each occasion, the child has the opportunity to identify with the mother's ability to remain thoughtful in the face of difficult feelings and situations. Gradually, this ability becomes part of his internal repertoire and he becomes more able to manage difficult experiences on his own. The intrusion of these images into my work with Peter seem to be drawing my attention to the fact that, as with many clients who self-harm, Peter has an inadequate or damaged capacity for self-containment and self-care. Because he seems in many ways to manage so well, this is not at all obvious from the surface material.

I do not speak about my images of Johnny with Peter. However, I am soon to find them helpful in what Ogden describes as the 'management of the analytic frame'. Peter arrives at his sixth session with his hand and wrist heavily bandaged. He tells me he has decided to stop therapy. I experience a start of alarm and have a fleeting image of Johnny lashing out on the floor. I express my surprise, which is entirely genuine, and wonder aloud what can have led to such a change of heart.

Peter:	I've decided that it's all to do with stress at work. I'm working too much. If I get the work under control, my symptoms will disappear.
Maggie:	Talking of symptoms, what happened to your hand?

Peter describes one of his drink and drug sessions at the weekend. It ended with Peter throwing a wild punch at another man, missing the man, and crashing his fist into a door. He had to get a taxi to Accident and Emergency, where he was told that his hand was just bruised but that he had sprained his wrist. At the end of this account, he adds a comment:

Peter:	You're probably right. I should stop going on these benders and lead a more sensible life.
Maggie:	I don't recall having given you that advice. But perhaps you feel that's what I should have said?

A stiff silence follows. Thinking again about Johnny, I feel that I must grip on to Peter harder, not let him go crashing off into pieces of furniture and other dangers. I want to offer an interpretation, linking his current wish to flee to repressed feelings of anger and fear, but my mind doesn't seem to be functioning well and such thoughts refuse to form themselves into sentences. Determined not to allow Peter's rage to make me drop him, and unable to come up with anything more erudite, I find myself appealing, in a very non-analytic manner, to Peter's rational and reasonable side.

Maggie:	Even if your symptoms are to do with work stress, and I'm not entirely sure about that, we still don't know why they take the particular form that they do. Why should work stress come out specifically in these physical actions of kicking concrete objects and banging dishes down? It is as if your body is in separate pieces, each going about things in its own way. If you leave now, you will not be any closer to understanding that. You will not have accomplished what you came to do.

By appealing to his intellect, I succeed in re-engaging Peter. He acknowledges that the symptoms still don't make any sense and that he is still curious about them. Perhaps because I have brought the psychosomatic nature of the presenting problems back into the picture, Peter feels able to tell me about another physical symptom:

Peter:	I suppose I should tell you… I can only have an orgasm when I'm not inside a woman. I mean, it's perfectly easy for me to ejaculate when I masturbate but I can't ejaculate inside a woman. I don't think this is really a problem for Anna. She doesn't seem to mind.
Maggie:	You're telling me this now and I think it's perhaps linked to your wish to leave. There is a question of how much control you can let go of with Anna and also how much control you can let go of with me in the consulting room.

My words are followed by a long but apparently thoughtful silence. As Peter doesn't speak and the matter of his continuing in therapy is still not resolved, I speak again:

Maggie:	You have had the idea of leaving, of sorting things out by yourself and maybe you are a bit surprised to discover that I really do mind, that I really do think it matters and that I want you to follow through what you have started here.
Peter:	*(Laughs, slightly embarrassed.)* Well, I'm not sure about that. But I will keep coming along, at least for the time being.

The next phase of the therapy is particularly taxing and I rely heavily on supervision. Almost every week, Peter arrives for his session with some kind of new injury. Kicking a bollard, he breaks a toe. Frying chips, he spills the fat and burns himself. Climbing railings under the influence of alcohol, he trips and breaks his ankle. He drives his car into a wall, fortunately escaping serious injury. He is full of bravado and scorn and seemingly unreachable. My supervisor and I discuss these incidents in terms of communication in the transference. What is Peter's unconscious message to me and how am I to interpret it? The following exchange ensues.

Maggie: With all of these injuries, I think you are trying to tell me how badly I am failing you.

Peter: *(a little bit irritated)* No, really. It's nothing to do with you. There's no need to make things more complicated.

Maggie: But these injuries are a communication to me. I feel there is a kind of reproach in them. When you show me your new plasters and bandages, you are telling me I'm really not doing such a great job.

Peter: *(angrily)* Sometimes you therapists do get on my nerves. Everything has to be to do with you! You think you're so clever. Well, actually, you're not that important. It's got nothing at all to do with you.

Suddenly, Peter gets up and storms out of the room. He slams the door behind him. I feel shaken by what has happened and sit berating myself, feeling that my words were clumsy and ill chosen. At the same time, I experience a sense of relief, related to the fact that some of Peter's rage is finally coming into the open.

Peter arrives for the next session, sits down looking contrite, and stares at his hands.

Peter: I'm sorry about last week.

(I nod, but say nothing.)

Peter: I want to say something, but it's really difficult.

(I nod again and wait.)

Peter: I cheat on Anna all the time. She doesn't know. I go to women I've known in the past in other parts of London and just shag them. I still do it. I don't know why. I despise them and I despise myself. *(Pause.)*

Peter: *(looking up at me)* You're going to say that I hate all
                    women, aren't you? *(Pause.)* I couldn't bear it last week
                    when you said I treated you with contempt.

(I reflect that this was not quite what I had said, but do not speak.)

Peter: Really, you're not very like my mother.

Maggie: You haven't really told me yet how you feel towards
                    your mother, but I do think you feel angry towards me.
                    In fact, I think there are times you feel enraged with me,
                    without understanding at all what that rage might be
                    about.

Peter: Well, if I do, it probably does have to do with my
                    mother. I really do hate her. I feel nothing but
                    contempt. My father was a violent man, but I get on OK
                    with him now. I quite like him in a way.

Maggie: It is the woman in the story that you hate?

Peter: She always covered things up. She kept up this pretence
                    that everything was normal and kind of bought me off.
                    Once when my father had given me an awful beating –
                    the full works with getting out the belt and making me
                    stand still and wait until he started it – she gave me a
                    bunch of grapes.

(Peter looks down and tears begin to roll down his face.)

Peter: *(looking up)* What use is a bunch of grapes to a child?
                    (Pause.) It was the same with my brother. She always
                    gave us money or bought us records and we all played
                    the game and said nothing.

*(Peter picks at his jacket, as if removing something sticky from it, his face bearing an
expression of profound contempt and disgust.)*

Maggie: You feel contaminated by your part in this deal? You
                    hate the fact that you were bribed into playing your part
                    and letting your father off the hook.

Peter: It was really so sick. I just can't stand her. When I go to
              visit, which isn't very often, I can hardly bear to be in
              the same room. *(Pause.)* I'm a big supporter of women's
              rights. But my behaviour towards women is horrible. I
              can't stand to be this way. *(He buries his face in his hands
              and sobs for a long time.)*

Maggie: *(after a while)* You're afraid you may be like your mother,
              that she may not be the only one with double standards.
              You often complained to me about how unfairly Anna
              was treated at work, but now you're admitting that you
              are treating her unfairly yourself.

Peter: Are you saying that I'm like my mother? If I'm like her,
              I may as well top myself.

*(Peter bangs his fist forcefully down on the wooden arm of the chair and breaks into
renewed sobbing. The session is close to the end and I am concerned about how upset
Peter is. I wait a while and his crying begins to abate.)*

Maggie: I understand now that you have been raging against
              yourself because you fear you are like your mother. Your
              accidents, which are really too numerous to be
              accidents, are beginning to make more sense to me. But
              your mother never embarked on the journey that you
              are undertaking. Her way was to turn her back on
              problems but you have decided to look them in the face.

Peter: *(sighs)* I really need to think about this some more. I'll
              see you next week.

When Peter returns, he says no more about his violent father and
appeasing mother. Instead, he talks a great deal about Anna and his
relationship with her. Among other things, he tells me that he sees very
little of her because he is working such long hours but that, fortunately, she
understands, because she is in a very similar position. I get a sense that this
relationship with Anna is in trouble, although I notice that Peter does not
see it this way and wonder if I am misreading the situation. One day,
however, Peter arrives, sits down heavily and leans forward in his chair, his

hands extended towards me on his knees, palms upwards, in a beseeching gesture.

Peter: Anna has finished with me. It's over. She's finished it.

Peter begins to sob heavily, looking down at his hands. He continues to cry through most of the session, with only occasional pauses to look up at me or to speak. I find that I am feeling relieved rather than disturbed by his crying. I keep my gaze upon him and listen calmly when he chooses to speak. Peter blurts out a number of denigrating comments about Anna's new lover but is not apparently angry with Anna herself. After a while, he looks up at me and says the following:

Peter: So it's over. What now, I wonder?

I find myself leaning towards Peter and mirroring his hand position with my own hands. A talk comes to mind, given by the child psychotherapist Dilys Daws for the Squiggle Foundation (a London-based organisation, which disseminates and supports the development of the work of D. W. Winnicott.) Referring to her psychotherapeutic work in a baby clinic, Daws described positioning herself for part of the time near the baby weighing scales. Here, she was able to observe how a mother might 'wrap the baby around with her gaze and her voice', while the baby was being weighed, and how this helped the baby to hold himself together through this weighing procedure. These associations convey something of the quality of my presence with Peter in this session. I feel that I am 'wrapping him around', though without physical contact. I feel also that Peter is allowing himself to return to a time and state of being long forgotten, before he was hardened by experience or weighed down with pain or complication.

In this first year of therapy, much of Peter's communication takes the form of projective identifications. Rather than telling me about his feelings, Peter stirs up what he feels, or refuses to feel, within me. The recurrent image of Johnny in distraught mode alerts me to the process in play. For a while, Peter's most 'telling' communications are, in fact, 'showings' (Schafer 1992). They take the form of plasters and bandages, of storming out of the room, of the dark shadows beneath his eyes and the strain in his face when he has been working and drinking until all hours. This channel of communication is supplemented by 'tellings' (Schafer 1992), narratives of 'benders' and 'shagging'. Catching a sense of what Peter has himself been through, without yet knowing the story, I am able to help him put words to some of his experiences. When I can keep my head above water, I manage to offer interpretations of the desperate feelings expressed in his 'invited' injuries and his undisclosed but palpable rage. Peter can be very contemptuous and I know I run the risk of being humiliated, but take comfort in the fact that, by offering interpretations, I continue to insist upon the idea that understanding might be possible.

During this time, I sometimes experience my own thinking as paralysed and notice that my breathing becomes shallow, that I virtually stop breathing. At times, I have a sensation of blankness and emptiness just as I am about to say something. I have found that somatic experiences in the countertransference, such as these, are inherently meaningful. Where the therapist has a good level of somatic awareness and is willing to reflect on physical sensations and symptoms, his or her body can serve as a sensitive instrument, tuned in to the client's unconscious and picking up communications that are not being put into words.

I have described the body elsewhere as 'a barometer of psychological change' (Turp 2001). At the time of writing, a television commercial is frequently shown, with the caption, 'Only 7% of communication is verbal.' What I am describing, then, is not something unusual but the refinement of something perfectly ordinary, namely our receptivity to non-verbal cues in our interactions with others. I have found the experience of psychoanalytic infant observation particularly helpful in the refinement of these sensitivities. Being with the undercurrents within a family in the role of observer, being actively present but not directly involved, has made me much more aware of the fine detail and nuance of non-verbal communication. The meaning of my 'symptoms' when I am with Peter is at first a mystery. Later, Peter's descriptions of childhood scenes help me to make sense of the alteration in my breathing patterns and my sense of 'going blank'. And eventually Peter will also refer to episodes where he 'stopped breathing' and 'stopped thinking' during his father's unpredictable and apparently senseless outbursts of rage.

I have suggested that one way of looking at self-harm is as a particular form of psychosomatic disturbance, in the sense that psychological distress is being expressed in a bodily way. Winnicott's work draws our attention to the positive value of psychosomatic difficulties. In his view, they express a tendency 'not altogether to lose the psychosomatic linkage' (Winnicott 1966). Peter's various 'symptoms' stand in the way of his living on an entirely 'False Self' basis. In this sense, they perhaps represent the survival of the 'True Self' aspects, confirming the reality of emotional life, attesting to the existence of 'gut feelings' that have been split off and denied other avenues of expression. Even more than in the case of other psychosomatic symptoms, self-harm has a nuisance value – in this case both for Peter himself and for his local Accident and Emergency department! According to Winnicott's understanding, antisocial behaviour, such as delinquent behaviour in young people, contains the hope of finding the environment that is needed. It represents a refusal to 'go quietly', to simply give in and give up. Paradoxically, the things that baffle Peter and that he complains about may be the same things that keep alive the possibility of more authentic living.

When Peter loses his relationship with Anna, he is able for the first time to drop his mask of self-sufficiency and turn to me for help. This brings into play the kind of symbolic touching and holding described above. Such unconscious communications, involving no physical contact, play a very important part in the psychoanalytic process, one that is not always fully acknowledged. I have suggested (Turp 2000a, 2001) that symbolic equivalents of physical touching become increasingly important as we grow older. When my daughter was a toddler and wanted to climb, I held her hand. When she was involved with gymnastics during her primary school years, I went along to watch her. Sometimes she turned towards me, seeking confidence, seeking my 'touch', which was experienced as our eyes met.

It seems that Peter does feel held and touched in the sessions where he breaks down and weeps. From this point on, he becomes more open and reveals many experiences that he has not mentioned up until this point.

These revelations, and his attempts to begin to try to come to terms with them, occupy most of the second year of the work. Gradually, a clearer picture emerges of Peter's childhood. I learn that his father was prone to unpredictable outbursts of violence against both of his sons. He would beat them with a belt for any or for no reason. The abuse carried on for many years until Peter was, as he put it, 'as tall and strong as my father and prepared to hit back'.

Peter:	There's a scene in my mind from when I was quite young, maybe six or seven. I'm sitting at the top of the stairs and my father is arguing with my brother, who has come home later than he should have. They start to fight and somehow the glass in the front door gets smashed. I think Martin must have done it. I thought he's had it then. I was absolutely terrified.
Maggie:	Do you remember what you did?
Peter:	I sat there, knowing it would be the end of me if they saw me. I was supposed to be in bed. In fact, I think I had been in bed but when I heard the shouting, I kind of felt compelled to creep onto the landing and watch. I know it happened more than once. Anyway, I couldn't tear myself away and go back to my bedroom. I couldn't think. It was as if I was transfixed. I remember kind of freezing, stopping breathing, praying that nobody would look up. My mother brought it to an end. She said something to Martin – 'Get up to your room', or something like that. Then I remember her saying to my father that we didn't want the whole street knowing our business.

This is painful material to listen to and I feel very moved by Peter's story. We sit for a while in a sad and thoughtful silence. In a subsequent session, Peter tells me this:

Peter:	I remember one time. I was about twelve and I had · homework to do. The light bulb in my room had gone but I didn't dare to ask for a new one. I just sat there in

the dark and worried about my work and about the trouble I would be in when my father found out. One night, he came up to my room. He found me sitting in the dark and started shouting about how stupid I was, screaming at me and hitting me. I tripped and fell down –it was still dark, you see. I remember hitting my head on something, then crawling across the room to get away from my father.

Maggie: I find it hard to imagine how terrible those times must have been for you. It seems there was no way at all for you to get things right.

Peter: My mother didn't say a word. She just carried on as if everything was hunky dory. That's what I find the hardest to stomach. The double standard of it all. *(Pause.)* After that, I bought my own light bulbs out of my pocket money and put them in myself. I didn't want to have to care. I didn't want to have to worry. I just wanted to look after myself.

Winnicott argues that, in health, the psyche–soma functions in an integrated way and the individual experiences a sense of 'unit status'. Excessive trauma and 'impingement' (Winnicott 1956) is associated with the extreme defensive splitting that results in a 'duality psyche–soma'. The soma, where emotions reside, is split off, is no longer 'indwelt' in the sense of being at one with and properly inhabited by the psyche. In this situation, mental functioning can become overdeveloped, with an intellectual 'caretaker self' standing in for the mother who is not there to take care or who cannot be trusted. With reference to this situation, Winnicott writes: 'I want to make clear my point that *this type of mental functioning is an encumbrance to the psyche–soma,* or to the individual human being's continuity of being which constitutes the self' (Winnicott 1949, p.248). These comments are relevant to Peter's precocious yet necessary attempts at self-caretaking.

According to Winnicott, the encumbered and exiled soma desperately calls attention back to itself by means of psychosomatic symptoms, taking the unconscious route of psychosomatic illness or the conscious route of self-harm. Symptoms and behaviours of this kind express an unconscious wish for a return to full and integrated functioning:

> Psychosomatic illness, like the antisocial tendency, has this hopeful aspect, that the patient is in touch with the possibility of psycho-somatic unity (or personalization) and dependence, even though his or her clinical condition actively illustrates the opposite of this through splitting, through various dissociations, through a persistent attempt to split the medical provision and through omnipotent self-caretaking. (Winnicott 1966, p.515)

Having been repeatedly obliged to 'freeze' his physiological functioning – to stop breathing and quieten the beating of his heart – Peter has lost contact with his emotional self, particularly with feelings of rage, which were too dangerous to allow to surface within the family. At this point, I feel sure that this frozen part of him is being mirrored in disturbances of my own breathing in his presence. Thus, split off feelings are making themselves known via the process of projective identification and also via hidden self-harming behaviour and other expressions of psychosomatic disturbance, such as the sexual difficulties described above.

Over the course of my career, I have worked with many clients who injure themselves or who 'invite' apparently accidental injury. Many of them, like Peter, have had very limited experience of containment during their childhood years. In psychotherapy, they at last encounter 'the human capacity for bearing pain through thinking' (Shuttleworth in Miller *et al.* 1989, p.36). Now that Peter is able to speak, cry and rage about his bleak and frightening childhood, the fights, accidents and injuries that have been such a regular feature of our time together fade away. In their place come feelings of depression and hopelessness.

Peter: I feel very low. I don't know where all this has got me. I still go out to clubs at the weekend but I don't enjoy it any more. It seems kind of meaningless.

Maggie: Your old ways of coping and keeping yourself buoyant aren't working any more.

Peter: The worst thing is, I still visit those women I talked to you about. I'm still shagging them and I despise myself. I don't even enjoy it!

Maggie: You have laid all the blame for your childhood misery at your mother's door. Your contempt is reserved for her and it spills out on other women too.

Peter: But I've always been very sympathetic to women and women always like me and say that they feel I understand them.

Maggie: You idealise women and see yourself as on their side. But isn't that rather at odds with the way you sometimes treat them?

Peter: *(slowly)* I can't deny that. And I feel kind of torn into pieces. *(Pause.)* It wasn't all my mother's fault, was it? Well, I suppose you're not going to answer that. What I mean is, why don't I blame my father more?

(There is a long pause, during which I remain silent, reflecting that I have indeed wondered at times why Peter's father is let off so lightly.)

Peter: No, that old bastard has got to take his share of the blame as well. He was a headmaster, you know. Nobody who sent their child to his school had the slightest idea how he was at home. *(Pause.)* I got out of that house the moment I could. As soon as I was seventeen, I was off. I stayed at a friend's house to do my A-levels and they couldn't do a thing about it. They were too worried I'd blow the gaffe. And look how far away Martin has gone.

The session continues in this vein as Peter expresses increasingly angry feelings towards his father. In the next session, Peter begins by talking for quite a while about his brother, Martin, who has recently been in touch to say that he is getting married.

Maggie:	This is the first time you've really talked to me about Martin. Do you ever talk to him about what all this was like for him?
Peter:	It's funny you should say that. I'm going to go over for the wedding and I think I might talk to him. We've never mentioned what happened. We were eight years apart, you see. Not close companions. And he left when he was eighteen and went to university. I would only have been ten then. But he went through a lot of similar things at home. I know that.
Maggie:	I'm pleased that you're going to see him and perhaps to bring into the open the experiences you shared. I've felt at times that he's rather lost to you.
Peter:	*(crying)* I feel rather lost to myself just at the moment. *(Pause.)* I've never thanked you, have I, for persuading me to keep coming along. There was so much shit, all swept under the carpet. The carpet was almost up to the ceiling. But I'm beginning to feel that it's clearing now.

Peter has travelled a long road. His manic defence against emotional pain and his physical self-abuse are being replaced with full, often painful contact with a whole range of emotions. His relationship with me has changed a great deal. I am neither idealised nor denigrated now. Instead, Peter is able both to disagree with me at times and, as in the passage above, to express genuine gratitude towards me. These gains are consolidated in a very fruitful period of work. At the start of the third year of therapy, Peter says this to me:

Peter:	You haven't asked, but I expect you've guessed. I don't go to visit those women any more.
Maggie:	What does it mean to you, to give that up?
Peter:	I've lived a double life, just like my parents. There was the person on view and the other person operating in a dark world, a private hell really. It made me hate myself and take all kinds of risks. I didn't want to see that. But now it's different. Stopping the shagging is like

stopping doing the drugs. It's just not what I want any more. I have to move on.

Shortly after this session, Peter begins a new relationship with a woman he meets at work, whom I will call 'Suzanne'. Suzanne knows nothing of Peter's history of drinking, drug-taking and promiscuous sex. Peter goes through a period of feeling excruciatingly ashamed of his former way of life. This coincides with him taking an AIDS test and waiting for the result. When he finds that the test result is negative, he begins to feel less haunted by the past. For the first time in many months, he feels optimistic. His relationship with Suzanne puts him in touch with new feelings.

Peter:	Suzanne has a big scar on her abdomen. She had to have a major operation as a child. I've been avoiding looking at it properly. I was a bit afraid.
Maggie:	Afraid that Suzanne is not perfect, that she is not a goddess?
Peter:	Well, perhaps that's it. Anyway, I looked carefully at the scar last night and, well, it's not very nice. It's really rather ugly. But I felt this great wave of tenderness.
Maggie:	We all carry scars. Your own are not so visible, but they are still there.
Peter:	*(nodding and crying)* I used to loathe my scars, loathe myself because of what had happened to me and what I had become. I couldn't even spend an evening in my own company…

There is something very moving about the dissolving of Peter's false sense of assurance and its replacement with remorse and tenderness, accompanied by a fresh look at previous attitudes and assumptions.

Peter:	She wore a very nice cardigan last night. It had flowers embroidered on it. Anna would never have worn something like that. It wasn't really trendy. But she looked lovely in it. *(Pause.)* You know, I've been thinking about where I live. I think I'd like to get a place with Suzanne. She wants to give things a bit more

time, but I can see she's excited about the idea. *(Pause.)* Clapham is supposed to be very up and coming but I think I might rather like to live in Crouch End. That would be a much better place for children and, well, it's nice.

I never felt like this about Anna. It was much more of a working partnership, supporting each other, being very politically correct. I thought my world had come to an end when she finished with me, but she was right. There was no real depth of feeling there. And in lots of ways we were just competing with each other.

Maggie: I know that you don't kick lamp-posts any more, but you've never told me what has happened about your sexual difficulties?

Peter: At first I was worried I wouldn't be able to ejaculate with Suzanne and so I warned her about the problem. But then it just happened. I guess it was all just a part of the mess I was in.

Maggie: So there's really not a lot that you hold back with Suzanne?

Peter: No, and it does make me feel kind of exposed. *(Laughs.)* But you never said that getting my feelings back would make life easy. I don't like feeling so vulnerable and our relationship hasn't been going on for long enough for me to feel really secure. But I have to say as well that I'm happier than I've ever been before.

Two months later, Peter raises the subject of ending therapy:

Peter: I've been thinking that I'm ready to stop coming to therapy. But I'm not sure. When I wanted to leave before, it would have been such a terrible decision. Thank goodness you stopped me!

Maggie: But I think that things are different this time around.

Over the next few weeks, Peter comes to feel secure in his wish to end therapy and I also feel happy with his decision. We discuss what it means to end and spend some sessions reflecting on the work that has been done. When Peter finally leaves, we are both sad and at the same time happy that he has achieved so much. Peter willingly gives me permission to publish details of our work, saying that he knows that he has paid for the sessions, but even so, he is really pleased to be able to give me something more than this.

In psychoanalytic psychotherapy with an individual who self-harms, the practitioner's aim is to discover the nature and personal meaning of acts of self-harm through assisting the client in his or her telling and re-telling of a personal story. As part of this process, I have offered myself as a recipient of and container for Peter's projections and have myself been contained by my supervisor. I have been able to provide a safe environment, where events that are difficult to speak about can begin to be put into words. Gradually, 'showings' of disturbance have been replaced by 'tellings' of a difficult story. Now the experiences in question can be properly thought about and it becomes possible to make sense of physical symptoms, including mysterious actions and eruptions such as those described by Peter.

Psychoanalytic psychotherapy has put these concerns at the very centre of its thinking. Many of the clients who come to us have experienced high levels of childhood trauma. For one reason or another, they have not been well contained. Through receiving projections, thinking about them and searching for a suitable form of words, the therapist enables the client to enter more fully into the original experience, to feel again and subsequently to reflect on the emotions evoked at that time. In doing this, he or she repeatedly models the capacity to think in the face of distress. For the therapist, it is very rewarding to work with a client like Peter, who is able to take full advantage of the opportunity to identify with this capacity and take it into his own repertoire, establishing it as a permanent internal resource.

10

Self-Harm by Omission: Working with Kate

> Trauma means the breaking of the continuity of the line of the individ-
> ual's existence. It is only on a continuity of existing that a sense of self, of
> feeling real, and of being, can eventually be established as a feature of the
> individual personality. (Winnicott 1986, p.22)

In this chapter I describe work with a client whose action, or rather
inaction, is at the limit of what many practitioners would count as
self-harm. Of all the scenarios described in the book, this is the one where
self-harming behaviour comes closest to being completely hidden. As with
Peter, it is only in the course of the therapeutic encounter that self-harming
tendencies are recognised and acknowledged. In the course of the research
described in Chapter 2, a vignette of this case was presented to a gathering
of practitioners. Seventy per cent of them gave a 'Yes' response to the
question: Is this an example of self-harm? Seventy per cent was the cut-off
for inclusion, so this case study just made it into the book. In the discussion
of the vignette, a number of practitioners said that they liked the term
'self-harm by omission' and that it helped clarify their understanding.

The client 'Kate' telephones me, having found my name and details in
the BACP directory. When we meet for the first time, I find myself in the
presence of an attractive, well-dressed woman in her late twenties, with an
Irish accent. I notice that her posture is poor – she is slightly stooped – and
that she moves quite stiffly. I warm very much to Kate in our first meeting.
She seems relieved to have an opportunity to begin to tell her story and
says at the end of the session that she would definitely like to work with
me. Because her husband's company is due to be relocated and a house

move is planned, the end date for therapy is known in advance, one year from the time we begin. We agree to begin meeting once a week and this arrangement continues up until the time Kate leaves.

When Kate tells me about her line of work, I am really quite surprised and am brought face to face with one of my own stereotypes! She is a 'high-flyer' with a firm of stockbrokers in the City. Currently, however, she is on extended sick leave and in the middle of a legal claim against her firm, seeking compensation for work-related injury. Describing her work, which involves spending most of the day operating a keyboard, Kate begins to talk about the issue that has brought her to therapy. She is suffering from repetitive strain injury (RSI), which has 'turned her life upside down'.

I ask Kate to give me a history of her symptoms. She tells me she began to be aware of pain in her hands and wrists three years ago. At first, she 'thought nothing of it'. After a year, when the pain showed no sign of going away, she visited her GP, who suggested that it might signal the beginning of arthritis.

Maggie: That must have come as a bit of a shock…

Kate: Well, yes, I suppose so. I was only 26 after all… I carried on as I was, though. I didn't think much could be done for arthritis.

Maggie: You didn't think at that time of taking further advice?

Kate: Well, I've never been one to fuss about being ill. The doctor was a very busy man and, well, I felt I shouldn't bother him again.

I am immediately aware of feeling concerned, even slightly alarmed. I wonder about the meaning of this response, which seems disproportionate to the events described. In contrast, Kate's tone of voice suggests resignation and something close to indifference. Kate goes on to tell me that her problems have become worse and worse. Eventually, using a keyboard became excruciatingly painful. She noticed that the muscles in her arms were feeling weak and she was plagued with pains in her neck and shoulders. As I clarify the details with her, I learn that it was more than a year before she consulted a doctor again, in this case her company's doctor. He immediately suspected repetitive strain injury (RSI) and this diagnosis was confirmed by a specialist. It was only then that Kate ceased to use her keyboard. By this time, she was having difficulty not only with using a keyboard but also with many household tasks.

Maggie:	Looking back, do you think you realised that working on the keyboard was aggravating your condition, or did that come as a surprise to you?
Kate:	I always knew it was to do with using the keyboard, because it would be at its worst on Friday night and at its best again by Monday morning. I know what you must be thinking…
Maggie:	What I 'must be thinking'… What do you imagine that would be?
Kate:	Well, that I'm making an awful fuss about this thing… That if I really put my mind to it, I could find a way through it and get back to work.

It is clear from this exchange that Kate has no hope or expectation of a helpful emotional response from me. Her fantasy of my response is quite different from my actual felt response. I feel dismayed as I hear about her continuing to work on the keyboard, literally for years, knowing that she is doing herself harm. My mind keeps returning to the words 'I always knew it was the keyboard…'. Thinking about this countertransference response, I wonder where Kate has learned to expect so little, has come to believe that 'making a fuss' is a pointless course of action. Although it is only the first session, it feels important to find a way to speak about these matters:

Maggie:	You think I must be forming a very bad opinion of you…
Kate:	Well, I wouldn't blame you. Not many people know anything about RSI. I'm sure a lot of people think, you know, not that I'm making it up exactly but that I could turn it round if I really put my mind to it.

Maggie: I wonder what gives you this idea – that you will be seen as 'making a fuss'? Tell me, is that what you think about yourself?

Kate: *(shaking her head and looking down)* No. For a long time I thought that, but I've had to face up to the fact that it's not true.

When Kate looks up, I see that her eyes are full of tears and I myself feel tearful. I wait to see if she will say more but on this occasion she switches to a different topic.

Fonagy (1991) describes how a client is continually engaged in developing a 'theory of mind' of the therapist. Whether child or adult, she (or he) is engaged in a process, sometimes conscious and sometimes unconscious, of imagining what the therapist may be thinking about her. Her reading of the situation is reflected in the way in which she positions herself vis-à-vis the practitioner. This is a quite normal, indeed indispensable, aspect of one-to-one relating. Most of us, on reflection, can identify examples of engaging in such 'reading of the other' and 'positioning of self' in everyday life. Attending to this process in the client and to one's own responses to the fantasies, thoughts and feelings that are projected is a central aspect of psychoanalytic work, generally referred to as 'working in the transference and countertransference'.

As many readers will know, the term 'transference' refers to the elements that are 'transferred' from previous relationships, usually relationships with parents and siblings, into the relationship with the therapist. Transference elements colour all personal relationships but play an especially important part in the therapeutic relationship. Because the therapist is a relatively unknown figure, in the sense that her personal history, her family situation, her political opinions and so on remain undisclosed, the client has considerably less information to go on than in other situations. The client's 'theory of mind' is therefore more than usually affected by the assumptions and expectations she brings with her into the consulting room. These are founded partly on prevailing cultural norms and partly on the client's past experience and personal interpretation of that experience. What emerges in what Ogden (1997) refers to as the 'matrix of unconscious communication' is a picture of the client's inner world, of the emotions and dynamics that dominate and of the personal lens through which events are perceived.

The term 'countertransference' has a long and complex history. It was first used to refer exclusively to the therapist's response to the client's transference and was considered by Freud an unwelcome phenomenon, an obstruction to the therapist's clear-sightedness and objectivity. Over time, it has been recognised that the therapist's response to the client's transference cannot be separated from her response to the client as a whole and the term has come to be used to refer to all aspects of the therapist's response to the client. At the same time, we have come to understand that our personal responses – in thought, feeling, imagery and physical sensation – are our most valuable clinical resource, provided that we have the capacity to recognise and reflect upon them. As described by Heimann:

> The analyst's emotional response to his patient within the analytic situation represents one of the most important tools for his work. The analyst's countertransference is an instrument of research into the patient's unconscious. (Heimann 1950, p.81)

In a variation on this theme, Winnicott developed the idea of a 'transitional space', particularly in relation to the 'as if' experience of playing in childhood and the enjoyment of cultural activities such as music and theatre in adult life. The transitional space is seen as an area of shared experience that is contributed to and drawn upon by both therapist and client. Ogden refers to this as a third element in the consulting room. What is being referred to in each of these accounts is the intersubjectivity, the 'here and now' of the relationship between client and practitioner. As this relationship carries echoes of the client's earlier significant relationships, a window is opened up on the client's inner world. Thinking about these matters as they unfold in the present is a central concern of psychoanalytic psychotherapy.

Much has been made in some quarters of the distinction between therapeutic approaches that 'work with the body' (body psychotherapy and a number of humanistic psychotherapy approaches) and those that, allegedly, do not. My own view is that it is impossible *not* to work with the body. We are all embodied – practitioners and clients alike. We meet body to body in a consulting room and are physically affected by each other's presence, words and actions. Our concern, whatever our therapeutic approach, is with emotion and emotional conflict. Keleman, a body psychotherapist, wrote in 1985 that 'the body is the somatic architecture of feelings'. This statement is as relevant to the 'talking cure' therapies as to those where the body is directly moved or touched, for speech is, of course, a physical as well as a mental phenomenon:

> In the beginning, the word is just one aspect of bodily experience. To the new-born infant, it is all cadence, rhythm, volume and tone. Words soothe, tease, excite or shock; sustain or cut across the infant's own sense of its being. At this stage, the meaning of words resides in their physical impact alone. Later, words are understood to have a representational value also. If I say to a friend, 'Look! The cat has come in', the words themselves have a meaning. But the physicality of the words remains crucial to a more complete understanding. It is the manner of my delivery, and that alone, which will reveal whether the cat is an accursed nuisance or a loved and welcomed family member. (Turp 2001, p.3)

A therapeutic encounter is a physical experience and the therapist's use of his or her body as a sensing device and a barometer of change has probably always been a part of psychotherapeutic practice. I say this because I believe it to be impossible to avoid being physically affected by the close presence of another human being for fifty minutes at a time, week upon week. Since it is part of our work to reflect on what transpires between two people in the consulting room, it is also impossible to imagine that we would not reflect on physical aspects of our experience. I first came across the idea of somatic countertransference in an excellent paper entitled 'Listening with the Body' (Field 1989). As I read it, I recognised a great deal that I had experienced and reflected on over the years, without ever thinking to give it a special name. What has happened in recent years is that somatic aspects of countertransference experience have been made more explicit and discussed in depth in both body psychotherapy and psychoanalytic circles.

The verbal exchange cited above offers an example of these processes in play. The feeling tone of my response involves a sense of 'shock' and 'dismay' that is missing from Kate's own account. Physically, I experience a hollow feeling in my chest, a sense of lack, of emptiness, of something missing and, a few minutes later, of tearfulness.

During the first three months of our time together, Kate spends much of each session describing the details of her condition and its effects upon her, usually without emotion and in a methodical way. One week, she concentrates on her arms and shoulders and her physiotherapy. The next week, she renders a full account of the apparently torturous experimental treatments to her hands that she has undergone in accordance with the wishes of her consultant. At the story unfolds, I have an impression of somebody who is being used as a guinea-pig for various RSI treatments. Her specialist has tried out a number of approaches, all relatively new and untested. Some of these treatments have been extremely painful and, as I hear about them, horror-film images drift into my mind. I hear about prolonged immersion of hands in hot wax, about injections into joints and tourniquets applied to reduce the flow of blood to the hands. Kate tells me that none of these interventions has been of any benefit at all.

I talk about this in supervision, expressing my anger and disgust with these 'experts'. My supervisor says: 'It's as if she is being bullied and you are the knight in shining armour. You want to ride in and rescue her.'

Kate has not mentioned being bullied and I let my supervisor's comment pass. I go on to reflect on a sense of something cut off and deadened in Kate, of her body as a 'not me' object to be pushed and pulled around. This calls to mind other clients in therapy who harm themselves. Many of them speak sooner or later of feelings of numbness and deadness, states of mind that fit with psychoanalytic descriptions of 'dissociation' and 'depersonalisation'. For some of them, self-harm brings relief, enabling them to return from a limbo-like and unreal place into the normal world of feeling, thinking and action.

The Bristol Survey refers to a number of examples where self-harm is enacted in order to appease feelings of numbness, deadness and isolation:

> I used to feel like the world was going on around me but I was not part of it. I interacted with it like a robot. The real me was locked up inside but I couldn't reach it. I was sealed off and I would get really desperate to break out. (Arnold 1995, p.14)

It is perhaps this sense of a body not properly inhabited, of a disturbance of 'the indwelling of the psyche in the soma' (Winnicott 1970), that provides the clearest link between actively perpetrated self-harm and self-harm that arises from lapses in self-care. Winnicott has argued that psychosomatic symptoms – and here I would include both self-harm by commission and self-harm by omission – serve the dual purpose of expressing and attempting to remedy experiences of depersonalisation:

> In psycho-somatic illness of one kind there is in the symptomatology an insistence on the interaction of psyche and soma, this being maintained as a defence against threat of a loss of psycho-somatic union, or against a depersonalisation. (Winnicott 1962a, p.62)

In actively perpetrated self-harm, this 'insistence' is more graphic, easier to read. It may be that such self-harm is in a sense 'healthier', in that it signifies that the individual in question is holding on to an unconscious hope of psychosomatic union being restored. Self-harm by omission is often an aspect of a more depressed presentation and a more profound dissociation. The underlying split between psyche and soma is expressed in a deeply hidden way, through failures of self-care. This scenario can also be thought about in terms of psychic skin, as discussed earlier. I have in mind particularly Briggs' extension of Bick's original contribution, where the idea of a 'porous skin' is used in relation to certain infants with feeding difficulties. Briggs describes two infants, Hester ('impervious'), who refuses to allow food into her mouth and becomes embroiled in a battle of wills, and Michael ('porous'), who allows the food in but then dribbles it out or regurgitates it:

> Alongside the idea of different infantile responses to problems in the relationship with mother, is the question as to which kind of infant has the greater capacity for resilience; is it the more impervious or the more porous infant who is more able to develop and maintain internal resources which enable, despite difficult and adverse circumstances, the capacity to maintain relationships and relatedness to others? (Briggs 1998, p.48)

My reading of Briggs' work coincided with the observation of the infant 'Emma', also referred to in earlier chapters, who received very little responsive handling in the early months of her life, a situation that appeared to derive from her mother's (undiagnosed) post-natal depression. Over time, it becomes clear that this situation is affecting Emma's whole physical way of being:

Observations of Emma at 14 weeks

When Mother leaves the room to make her telephone calls, I have to bear the full impact of Emma's unmet psychological needs, her distress and her disturbance. These are only too evident in her lack of liveliness, her slumped posture, her pallid and tired appearance and her constantly running nose. When Mother is out of the room, Emma sags down, chin on chest, and cries half-heartedly in a way that seems quiet and despairing rather than demanding. Her eyes are open but vacant and unfocused. Like Mother, she seems emotionally depleted and lacking in physical energy. It is said that some babies become quite manic and try to cheer up and 'entertain' their depressed mothers, but Emma seems rather to pick up on her mother's feelings of weariness and inadequacy and becomes somewhat depressed herself. This mood is extremely infectious and I again depart from the observation feeling tired and low in spirits.

In the wake of my early sessions with Kate, I experience again this feeling of weariness and low mood and wonder about its meaning. The word 'psychosomatic' has many connotations and is sometimes (incorrectly) used to suggest that an illness is not real. Kate's illness is absolutely real. The damage is measurable and may be irreversible. Although this is not yet exactly known, there may be a biological predisposition, something about her joints that has made her particularly susceptible to RSI. Undoubtedly, though, her overriding of early symptoms has played a major role in the situation. Bearing in mind my sense of shock and dismay in the countertransference, I am inclined to think that her determination to 'carry on regardless' is a kind of self-harm. In Winnicott's terms, it is a psychoso-

176 / matic disturbance that

matic disturbance that both expresses and defends against, albeit in a more subtle way than in the case of active self-harm, an absolute 'loss of psycho-somatic union'. In Briggs' terms, Kate expresses a disturbance of psychic skin in the form of 'porous skin'. She is passive in the face of her specialists' intrusions, cannot stand up for herself and, like Emma, is pallid and weary.

Over time, details emerge about the impact of RSI on Kate's life. Her condition has brought her career to an end and is affecting her day-to-day life in many ways. She is embroiled in a bitter legal battle with her company, involving financial uncertainty and a series of humiliating medical encounters, where she is called upon to 'prove' the extent of her disabilities. This is especially stressful for her, as in all other contexts she does her utmost to play down her limitations. She finds herself in a dilemma when, for example, she is presented with a saucepan full of water and told to pick it up – something that she has already said she cannot manage. Should she comply and strain herself to manage the task, even though she knows it will cause her additional pain for the rest of the day? The manner in which these events are described perplexes me. Kate's tone of voice is wooden and distant, while I am fuming at the humiliation being inflicted upon her! It seems that she preserves her equanimity by her dissociating herself from parts of her body. She tells me:

Kate: They told me to pick up a saucepan but my arm would
                   not do it.

I have a sense, as with Peter, of a 'body in pieces' rather than an experienced whole. I wonder whether, by breaking down the impact of RSI into its constituent parts, Kate is keeping at bay intense feelings associated with the impact of the overall experience. I offer an interpretation along these lines but it is not taken up. Either I am missing the point or my intervention is premature. Until meeting Kate, I have not had contact with a client, or indeed a friend or relative, with RSI and I am not well informed. Now, I find myself inclined towards doing some reading outside the sessions to discover the 'facts' of the condition. This is not a thought that would usually occur to me. I resist the inclination and wonder to myself whether there is a way in which I want to set myself up as an expert and to 'pull rank' on Kate. At this point, my supervisor's comment about bullying comes briefly to mind.

For the next month, the focus continues to be on practical details of Kate's disabilities. Kate describes not being able to drive and not being able to shop. On one occasion, she becomes very upset, telling me how long it takes her to cook dinner for her husband (Jim) and how, the previous evening, she found herself unable to complete the task. Most days, Kate tells me, she can lift the empty saucepan onto the stove using both hands, then add water with a jug and, finally, add the vegetables she wants to cook. The previous night, however, she had been unable to manage this. Jim came home to find her lying on the sofa in tears. I find myself feeling very stirred up, silently asking the question, 'How could it have come to this?' I find myself wanting to turn back the clock and intervene. Talking about this in supervision, I am asked what it is I would want to say or do. I reply that I would say, 'Stop and think. Can't you see the harm you're doing to yourself? You shouldn't hurt yourself in this way.' By now, both my supervisor and I are seriously considering Kate's narrative as, in part, one of self-harm. As yet, however, it does not feel possible to explore this possibility with Kate herself.

As the therapeutic alliance develops, Kate shows that she is ready to move on from her factual and emotionally inhibited account and into the work of mourning. Kate knows that her prognosis, in terms of recovering full use of her hands and arms, is very poor. On one occasion, I say this to Kate:

Maggie: I think you probably came to therapy partly so that you could begin to address some of the terrible losses you have suffered. But now you are here, you are finding it difficult to do that. I wonder whether this idea that you will be making a fuss comes into your mind and gets in your way.

Kate allows herself to cry at this point. She is able to acknowledge that she needs to grieve her many losses but that she finds it hard to allow herself to 'give in to the sad feelings'. Over the next few weeks, we name and think about some of these losses together. The first issue is Kate's self-image as a person who is hard-working and who can be relied upon 'to get the job done whatever the odds against it'. I suggest that, for the time being, it is more appropriate for Kate to think of herself as somebody in need of rest and care and that she finds this very difficult.

She tells me that Jim holds a senior management position and, fortunately, their difficulties are not complicated by financial strain. Nevertheless, her loss of earning power does affect her. For many years, she was a high earner in her own right with a successful career. Now she is dependent on her husband's income and this is a major blow to her self-esteem. In the home, domestic tasks – the only way to make a contribution that she feels is left to her – are particularly difficult since they involve physical work. She cries as she tells me about her painful and inadequate efforts to vacuum the hall or clean the bath.

Maggie:	As you know, I'm no expert on RSI, but I feel rather shocked when I hear about you trying to do these things.
Kate:	I shouldn't really, I suppose, but I just don't know what to do.
Maggie:	As you said to me the first time we met, your world has been turned upside-down.

The most serious loss to be addressed is the apparent loss of the possibility of Kate having children of her own.

Kate:	The worst thing of all is – I haven't wanted to get around to this – but we always assumed we would have a family and now is about when we'd be thinking of it. But my specialist has absolutely forbidden me to get pregnant.
Maggie:	He has absolutely forbidden you?
Kate:	Yes. He says I'll never manage it. I shouldn't even consider it. *(She sits and weeps.)* He says I won't be able to lift a child in my arms. I won't be able to push a pram up a hill.

The feeling of intense sadness is cut off after a minute or two when Kate pulls herself together and says with an apologetic smile:

Kate: I'm sorry. You must think I'm a real complainer.

Maggie: You think I will feel critical because you are so sad?

Kate: Well, maybe not. But what's the point of me wallowing in self-pity? I know how they think about me at work. They would much prefer that I just disappeared. And I hate that. I used to be really well regarded and now I'm just a pain. It's not Jim, really, or you. There's my mother too...

Maggie: How does your mother see things?

Kate: Well, it's not that she says I'm making it up. But she never asks. I don't think she wants to think about it.

Kate has been reluctant to speak about her childhood and I only know the outline details. These are that she was one of seven children, and the only girl, and that she grew up in Ireland where her father was a shoemaker. My sense has been that the work of mourning needed to take precedence and that only when this had been addressed might we be able to turn to other issues. Now, with seven months still to go and a good therapeutic alliance established, I seize the opportunity to delve further.

Maggie: You've not been keen so far to talk about your family and it may not be relevant but I just have this feeling that there are important things about your childhood that you've not said.

Kate: I was doing fine until the RSI, though. I don't really think it's my childhood.

Again taking this work to supervision, I find that I remain unconvinced. My supervisor and I both feel there is something important that has yet to come to light. When I next meet Kate, she tells me about another new treatment that she is being pressured to try.

Kate: I don't suppose it will do any good. Nothing else has
                 done any good and I think they're just using me to try
                 things out. I suppose I'll go ahead, though.

Maggie: As you describe it, the medical experts are treating you
                 as a bit of a guinea-pig. You seem to find it very difficult
                 to stand up for yourself, though.

Unconscious communication is a mysterious process. Sometimes
something is not consciously experienced by the therapist but is
nevertheless communicated on to the supervisor, who is able to identify
and name it. Joseph (1989) gives an excellent example of this
phenomenon in her chapter 'The Total Transference'. This proves to be the
situation with regard to my supervisor's earlier reference to bullying. Her
words come back to mind, along with my recognition of my own wish to
'bully' Kate by becoming an expert and talking down to her. Eventually,
when Kate is again discussing her treatments, I say to her:

Maggie: I suppose that if I'm honest, I feel that you are being
                 bullied.

Kate sits in silence for a long time. Then she embarks, rather haltingly at
first, on a long and sad story. She tells me that she had older twin brothers,
who bullied and threatened her and who made family life unbearably
miserable. Her mother's response to their violent and disruptive behaviour
was to try to appease them, to plead with them and to offer them sweets for
being 'good boys'. Kate's father kept a low profile and refused to get
involved. Once she starts to speak about these matters, Kate returns to
them many times. She relives her feelings of betrayal and abandonment by
both her mother and father, feelings that have coloured her relationships,
including her relationship with me, into the present.

Kate: Christmas was so terrible, I think it was the worst time.

Maggie: The time when everything should be nice – but not for
                 you by the sound of it?

Kate: Every year it was the same thing. Mum got up early and
                 cooked a turkey, all the trimmings and so on. We would

sit down to eat but in a few minutes everything would be ruined. The twins would argue about the food and start pulling the turkey apart. Then they started throwing bones and potatoes and things across the table. Mum got upset and, well, a total shambles and that was Christmas dinner – the same every year. I used to dread it. I was in such a state that I couldn't have eaten anyway, knowing what was coming...

Then after lunch there would be presents for unwrapping and Mum would try to make it nice again. But the twins snatched our toys and everything got broken. By the middle of the afternoon, everything was ruined.

Maggie: It sounds just awful.

Kate: *(crying)* I should have done something for my little brother. I should have protected him. The bigger ones were OK really. If the twins hit them, they just hit back. But my little brother had a really hard time. And mostly I was hiding in a cupboard or under the table.

Maggie: It was all you could do to save yourself.

Kate talks more about her younger brother, whom she was unable to protect from the twins' bullying, and I come to understand that this is a particular source of shame and misery to her. This brother now leads an isolated life with no sexual relationship. Kate feels that his life has been ruined and that she is responsible. These are sad sessions. We talk about 'survivor guilt' and I suggest to Kate that the situation was not in fact her responsibility and that as a child in the family she would not have been able to make things right.

By this time, things are considerably clearer. Kate is recalling and reliving a childhood that was in many respects, truly terrible. She spent a great deal of time in dread and in hiding from the twins. When they found her they would tease and torment her in many different ways. Sometimes, one twin would hold her down while the other pulled her hair or her ears. Once, they pulled off her shoes, put her socks in the toilet and defecated on them. And watching her younger brother being frightened and hurt was every bit as terrible for Kate as the things she went through herself.

In the light of these revelations, Kate's difficulties in taking care of herself start to make a lot better sense. It is with both relief and sadness that Kate begins to recognise and acknowledge her own failures of self-care and the way in which they have contributed to her RSI. All at once, many things fall into place for her. She tells me about a severe bout of flu when she took only one day off from her work at the stockbrokers, even though she felt, in her own words, 'half dead'. She speaks of regularly working very long hours. I ask whether it is common in the City stock market environment for people to work excessively and Kate tells me that people work 'all hours'.

Kate: You have to draw the line yourself but it's very hard.

At this point I share with Kate the anecdote about the death of the Japanese worker and the coining of the term 'karoshi'. She is very moved and tells me, 'I was headed that way. Something had to happen to make me stop.'

Kate's 'self-harm by omission' includes failure to insist on proper investigation of her symptoms early on, failure to take a reasonable amount of time off work when ill, failure to insist on her legitimate rights and needs, a willingness to be experimented upon and an overall tendency to compromise her health through overworking. As far as the latter is concerned, it must be said that much that might be considered 'self-harm' in a less work-oriented culture counts as a 'casha' in our particular society. Rather than being frowned upon, overwork is widely applauded.

Later in the year, I find myself referring back to earlier sessions and reminding Kate of her perception of me as somebody who would see her as 'making a fuss'. Kate adds to what I have to say, telling me that the pattern with Jim is more or less the same. She knows, she says, that he is a kind man who loves her; she is at least sure of that. He has no desire for her to engage in hours of struggle in order to cook him a meal. He would prefer to go out to eat but she finds it difficult to give up struggling and to let him take the strain. We look again at Kate's childhood experiences and link them to her current difficulties in taking care of herself and accepting care from others. In failing to control the behaviour of the twins, Kate's parents communicated to her that she was not deserving of care, protection and respectful treatment. In the wake of this phase of the work, Kate makes a number of positive changes, which come as a complete surprise to me, in the world outside the consulting room.

Two months before we are due to finish, Kate rings to say that she will have to miss a session because she is going to visit her family in Ireland. On her return, she tells me that she raised the matter of the twins and the misery they had caused in her childhood with her mother. They had a good talk, during which her mother acknowledged tearfully how bad things had been. Kate learned that as infants, before she was born, the twins showed a lot of strange behaviour, such as head-banging. Her mother did not know how to deal with this and had no-one to help her. She felt 'at the end of her tether'. Because thwarting the twins led to more outbursts of aggression and self-injury, she settled for a policy of appeasement. Kate's mother admitted that she knew, looking back, how hopeless and wrong this had been. It was clear from Kate's emotional account that this was a healing conversation and that it set the scene for further reparation.

Later on in the same visit, Kate's mother expressed profound regret that she had not been able to spend more time with Kate as a baby. She had felt absolutely thrilled to have a girl but the twins (two years older than Kate) took up the lion's share of her time and energy because they were so difficult. Kate remembers her mother's words as follows: 'I always wished I'd had more time to sit and hold you. I had to put you on the bottle before I wanted to. You were too little really and I've always felt bad about it.'

After this, more changes come in quick succession, with the fast-approaching end date of therapy playing its part. No longer in the role of the 'helpless younger sister', Kate stands up to her consultant and refuses further experimental treatments, telling him that only her physio-therapy has ever helped her. She also tells him that a decision about having children rests with her and Jim, although they will take full account of the special difficulties caused by the RSI. I have an image of a football crowd, of a goal being scored and of a huge cheer going up! I ask Kate if she is feeling pleased with what she has done and she looks proud and happy.

This is a very nice moment, when we sit and share a feeling of real achievement.

Kate's growing capacity for self-care is expressed in many different ways. She decides to have an afternoon sleep and to go swimming every day, even if she cannot swim very far, rather than staying home and struggling to cook and clean. I am particularly interested in Kate's decision to go swimming. In earlier work I describe an anorexic client (identified as 'W' in 1997 and as 'Sheila' in 2001) for whom swimming became very important as a source of sensual pleasure and a symbol of overall recovery and better self-care. As with this anorexic client, though for different reasons, Kate seems to have lacked appropriate and responsive maternal handling in infancy and childhood. The idea of swimming as a kind of benign 'self-handling' seems to apply in both cases, contributing to a recovery of a good quality of psychosomatic indwelling:

> The experience of moving in a large pool of water is in many ways a touch experience, involving a feeling of being carried or supported, sensations of cold or warmth, the flow of moving water over bare skin, and afterwards the towelling dry. (Turp 2001, p.172)

My feelings about swimming echo something expressed in a passage by Winnicott many years ago. He also seemed to recognise the special quality of this particular physical activity:

> When we provide a swimming pool and all that goes with it, this provides links with the care with which the mother bathes her infant, and with which she generally caters for the infant's need for bodily movement and expression, and for muscle and skin experiences that give satisfaction. (Winnicott 1962a, p.69)

Along with other changes, Kate is changing her body storyline, taking it in a new direction. Changes in her physical appearance are mirrored in changes in her spoken narrative, with passivity and inertia being replaced by purposeful activity. Some of the changes are difficult to pin down in words. I notice that Kate is less stiff and stooped. I have a sense of her 'bodily integrity', as described in relation to 'Esther' in Chapter 4, and sometimes of the beginnings of 'sensual muscularity', as described by Richards (1994). Kate now looks at home in her skin and is a quietly energetic presence in the room.

Kate spends her last month in therapy looking towards the future. We talk about what she wants to do and what she might be able to do. She has a great love of literature and her enforced inactivity has allowed her to return to a path of serious reading. (As a passionate reader myself, I feel an immediate sense of recognition and a mild stab of envy.) Kate decides she would like to formally study English literature and maybe later to teach. She enrols at a college near her new home to begin to study for a degree in English, set to begin the following autumn.

I am very impressed by the way that she pursues her rights, as a student with disabilities, to tape-record the text of her essays and have it transcribed. In the face of considerable difficulty and bureaucratic obstruction, she also manages to negotiate special examination arrangements. Kate tells me that she had realised through our work that it is okay to ask for her special needs to be taken into account. She now recognises that she deserves to be adapted to, to be responded to in a way that acknowledges and respects her special needs.

By this time, Kate is on the verge of moving out of London and our work together is in any case reaching a natural conclusion. In one of our last sessions, she tells me that she no longer regards RSI as an unmitigated disaster. She and Jim both had such high-powered jobs that they rarely saw each other. Their relationship is now much improved and they 'talk as we have never talked before'. In another late session, Kate tells me that she has never really known herself and has lived in a superficial way. Now she knows what is really important to her. Moving out of London is part of moving to a less frenetic life. She grew up in the country and feels again her attachment to it, no longer marred by the painful episodes of her childhood. She and Jim have found a house close to shops and with flat walks around, with the idea of children and Kate's probable difficulties with prams and pushchairs in mind.

It is part of the work of the psychotherapist to agree not to know, not to see the client's dreams realised. Nevertheless, in my mind's eye, I see Kate in a small town or village somewhere in England or Ireland, with the family she and Jim so wanted and with a flourishing career as a sensitive and successful teacher of English literature.

11

Reflections on Case Study Themes

> It is generally agreed that traumatic events such as neglect, and physical
> and sexual abuse, are linked with the later need to harm oneself, and can
> lead to basic alterations in the experience of the body. (Gardner
> 2001, 21)

Why self-harm?

Some understandings of self-harming behaviour reflect the belief that the
individual who self-harms is fundamentally flawed, that he or she is either
'mad' or 'bad'. These ideas may be expressed in the formal language of
'personality disorder' or the informal language of 'provocation' and 'attention-seeking'. Other accounts emphasise the long-term emotional damage
that accrues when an individual is subject to physical assaults and/or psychological insults, including inattention and neglect, particularly (but not
exclusively) where such experiences are sustained during the formative
years of childhood. It is into this general area of discourse that my own
contribution falls.

Certain psychoanalysts, for example Welldon (1988), view self-harm
as essentially sexualised behaviour. This perspective is at odds with my
personal experience and that of other community-based practitioners with
whom I have spoken, perhaps because we are working with a different
client group:

> I would like to reflect on this notion of sadomasochism in relation to
> self-harm. Few people who self-harm talk of enjoyment of the physical
> pain they inflict on themselves. They talk more in terms of the tension it
> relieves or the pride they feel in being able to withstand the pain. (Collins
> 1996, pp.465–466)

Collins goes on to suggest that the person who self-harms 'becomes sadistic in relation to parts of herself and acts towards those parts of her body as if they were not her'. This statement is in line with Welldon's understanding that the person may treat parts of her body as 'part objects', perhaps because she herself was treated as a 'part object' in childhood, that is to say as an extension of the mother rather than an individual in her own right. This description seems apt, for example, in relation to Lorraine's entangled relationship with her mother, to Kate's disregard of the pain in her hands and her 'offering up' of those hands for experimental treatments, and to Peter's experience of 'a body in pieces'.

These phenomena do not necessarily require us to think of self-harm as sexualised behaviour. The client's state of dissociation, of psychosomatic fragmentation, is sufficient explanation for the behaviour described. Dissociation makes the act of self-injury *possible*, because the person is in a kind of trance. (Lorraine, for example, said she felt no pain when she cut herself but knew that the pain would come.) Dissociation also makes the act of self-injury *necessary*. The experience of physical pain, whether suddenly inflicted or gradually worsening, creates an alternative focus and helps to restore a normal sense of embodiment.

In the case studies presented, self-harm emerges as a mode of self-handling and self-soothing, as a coping strategy that curtails unbearable states of mind by translating invisible internal damage into visible external damage, and as an unconscious communication from client to practitioner. In discussion of the clinical material, I have relied primarily on post-Kleinian concepts of projective identification, containment and second skin formations and on Winnicott's concept of the psyche indwelling in the soma.

In Chapter 5, I identified theory as a 'tool for thinking' rather than a statement of facts or underlying realities. This point of view allows for the co-existence of various theories. It follows that the situations described in the case study chapters can be thought about in many different ways. To say this is to subscribe to a postmodern perspective, involving the acceptance of alternative and even competing 'truths', the adoption of 'a critical stance towards taken-for-granted knowledge' (Burr 1995, p.3) and the abandonment of any attempt to arrive at one final 'true' version of events:

> There is no reason why psychoanalysts should agree with one another...nor is there any reason to believe that if the perfect synthesis of competing theories is achieved it will speak inside the analyst like a God telling him what to do in the ordinary disarray of a psychoanalytic session. A repertoire might be more useful than a conviction, especially if one wants to keep in mind that there are many kinds of good life. (Adam Phillips 1993, p.xvi)

Fonagy (1999b) argues that psychodynamic practice is not directly governed by the logic of theory. In the session itself, our full attention is turned towards the client. Inevitably, theoretical frameworks are there in the background, unconsciously colouring our perceptions and understandings, but they only come explicitly into the picture after the session is over, particularly during the process of reflection that takes place in supervision. Theories are in any case not absolute truths but narratives that help us make sense of our experiences, in this case experiences that involve us in a close encounter with another human being. The same material lends itself to many different narrative possibilities, many different kinds of understanding. It follows that the manner in which psychotherapeutic encounters are framed theoretically is to some extent a matter of personal preference.

My own preferences are influenced by a number of different factors. I have long felt drawn to the subtlety and eloquence of object relations accounts. I have a desire to communicate these ideas in a manner that is accessible to a wide range of practitioners and to clients and service users whose interests lie in this direction. Because psychoanalytic accounts are not simplistic, do not reduce complex human dilemmas to a few broad brushstrokes, I realise that there is hard work involved for the lay reader. I try to meet him or her halfway, to avoid obscurity and complexity for the sake of complexity. It is also relevant that the theoretical frameworks I use are 'old friends' of mine, familiar landmarks that have long served as a secure base for my thinking, teaching and writing.

'Looked-after' children

In the past as a social worker, I sometimes worked with young adults leaving care who were not engaged in obvious self-harm, such as self-cutting or self-burning, but who seemed unable to take proper care of themselves. They 'forgot' to make a necessary appointment with a GP or a dentist or to buy food for a meal later in the day. They relied heavily on 'cashas' such as drinking, smoking and recreational drug-taking. Up to a point, this is normal adolescent behaviour, but these teenagers tended to go beyond that point and to put themselves at risk.

Only one of the clients described, Lorraine, has spent periods of time in local authority care. Perhaps more people who have been 'looked-after' children would find their way to me if they had ready funds or supportive adults to help them gain access to counselling. I say this because research confirms a high incidence of self-harm, both 'active' and 'by omission', among looked-after children and young adults leaving care.

Evidence about the health needs of looked-after children reveals:

- undiagnosed chronic health conditions, including poor and uncorrected eyesight, significant weight problems, glue ear, asthma and eczema

- uncompleted immunisation programmes and courses of treatment

- serious and widespread mental ill-health, including self-harming, attempted suicides – most between the ages of 15-18 (when the majority were leaving care) – and stress, loneliness and risk-taking behaviours, particularly amongst young people leaving care

- poor physical health and high levels of substance abuse.

(Stein *et al.* 2001, p.125)

Other studies, for example Saunders and Broad (1997), have produced similar findings. In discussing the infant observation studies, I considered some of the ways in which good parental care might support the individual's self-caring tendencies and allow them to emerge and evolve.

With this in mind, it is perhaps not surprising that poor and disrupted care or institutional care regularly results in an impoverished capacity for self-care, leaving the individual unusually vulnerable to self-harming tendencies.

Looked-after children are sometimes doubly disadvantaged, with early failures of care being compounded by inadequate preparation for the responsibilities of adult life. The transition from 'care' to independence is relatively rapid and abrupt. It comes at a time when most children who have grown up in families are still enjoying considerable practical and emotional support:

> In comparison to their peers in the general population young people leaving care have to cope with the challenges and responsibilities of major changes in their lives – in leaving foster and residential care and setting up home, in leaving school and entering the world of work, or more likely, being unemployed and surviving on benefits, and in being parents – at a far younger age than other young people. (Stein *et al.* 2001 p.90)

Deprived of the opportunity of a gradual and well-supported transition into adult life, looked-after children are left terribly vulnerable to depression, failures of self-care and active self-harm.

To seek help is in itself an act of self-care. Because of the stigma associated with self-harm, it is not an easy step to take. Many people seek help only when their problems have become severe and entrenched. They suffer in silence and secrecy for years, because they are ashamed to admit – sometimes even to themselves – that they are engaging in self-harming behaviour. I hope that the understanding that compromised self-care and self-harm are not 'crazy', are not in fact so very uncommon, may give people the confidence to approach a counsellor and begin to work on their difficulties sooner rather than later. This would be a welcome development, one that would substantially improve the likelihood of full recovery from the difficulties being experienced.

Failures of containment

Each of the clinical examples points to the importance of early failures of containment. In Lorraine's case, her mother (in each of the cases the mother has been the primary carer) behaves in a way almost guaranteed to stir up states of 'nameless dread' (Bion 1967a) in her young daughter. In other cases, maternal failures have taken the form of significant omissions. Tracey and Ellen May describe mothers who were not really interested in them, who were self-absorbed. Narcissistically preoccupied mothers are, by definition, not well attuned to their children and are not in a position to exercise containing functions. For Peter and Kate, interactions with other family members have been traumatic. Peter has been terrorised by a violent father and Kate by bullying twin brothers. Failures of maternal containment in these cases have taken the form of failures of protection. The child has been left to face terrifying situations alone and unsupported.

Comparing the different cases, it seems fair to say that, of all the clients described, Lorraine is the one who has suffered the most obvious and sustained abuse. Nevertheless, she has doggedly pursued her quest for counselling, remaining resolute in the face of repeated setbacks. She seems to have an implicit sense of what care and self-care might be, something that sustains her efforts and enables her to appreciate and make use of the containing environment when those efforts finally pay off.

We might say, as Rustin and Rustin say of Harry Potter, that 'These are the preconceptions of the hopeful child whose adverse early years have not crushed an expectation that the world contains beauty and good feelings' (Rustin and Rustin 2001, p.277).

Individuals do vary in their ability to make the most of such care as is offered. As far as we can tell, Lorraine's capacity for self-care is based on the year's care and containment offered by her partner's parents when she was a teenager and by the continuing and mutually supportive relationship she enjoys with this same man. It may be that caring for her brothers and sisters as a child and her nephews as an adult has also helped her, bestowing a vicarious sense of being cared for and keeping alive the idea of the possibility of love and care.

Physical and psychic skin

Like Bion's work, Bick's work on 'psychic skin' and 'second skin' is a post-Kleinian development and the two areas of theory have much in common. The concept of psychic skin has offered an eloquent metaphor for considering the interaction between traumatic experiences and the client's capacity for self-care. A trauma, as described earlier, is literally a 'piercing'. In the case of physical skin, good functioning involves strength, flexibility, resilience and a certain degree of permeability. Where all is in order, the skin has an elastic quality. It cannot be easily pierced and, if it is pierced, then the damage will heal. The time required for healing will vary, depending on the severity of the wound, the care given and the individual's capacity for recovery.

The same is true symbolically of psychic skin, the point of negotiation of connectedness and separation between self and others. I have referred to distortions of psychic skin functioning involving both 'porosity' and 'toughening'. The case studies suggest that these two possibilities are not mutually exclusive. In some individuals one or the other is emphasised, while in others porosity and toughening are equally apparent. In the case of toughening, Bick refers to the skin being 'impermeable'. The individual lacks sensitivity and compassion for others. At the same time, he or she finds it difficult to allow others to make meaningful contact. When working with Tracey, I saw myself 'moving towards her and bouncing off again'. Tracey's sense of grievance sustains an impoverished mode of relating. Early on in the therapy, she is a 'hard nut' impervious to the sufferings and difficulties of others and, in a way, to her own sufferings. Her tough shell makes it difficult for her to take advantage of the possibilities offered by psychotherapy. Both Tracey and Ellen May keep me at a distance through the exercise of 'verbal muscularity', expressed in a harsh and dismissive style of speech.

Peter has also to some extent 'toughened' himself, relying on his intellectual prowess – another kind of verbal muscularity – and an over-developed 'False Self' (Winnicott 1960a) or 'Social Self' (Modell 1990) to push himself through a punishing work and leisure-time schedule. Incessant activity and excessive use of alcohol and drugs contribute to a state of dissociation that keeps disturbing memories and feelings at bay. Nonetheless, the underlying difficulties emerge in a series of apparently incomprehensible actions and symptoms. When he comes into therapy, Peter is also 'toughened' in the sense of being out of touch with his more tender feelings. He has settled for an intellectualised relationship on the one hand and casual 'shagging' of women for whom he feels no affection on the other.

A 'toughened' second skin formation – Bick's 'hippopotamus hide' – confers a measure of protection against further trauma. 'Piercing' this skin is difficult. Where self-harm is inflicted through self-cutting, self-burning or self-scalding, areas of 'hippopotamus hide' can become a physical reality as well. The scar tissue that forms is literally thickened and toughened. There is a reduction in flexibility, permeability and sensitivity in the area affected. In all cases of toughening, meaningful interaction with others, where feelings are communicated and shared, is impeded. Accordingly, the individual tends to find himself or herself in a state of painful emotional isolation. There is a pervasive sense of lack or deficit, an absence of a sense of connectedness to others. Feeling numb and walled off, the individual becomes desperate to break out, to 'feel real'. Self-harm offers some kind of respite, with physical pain or illness serving to restore a feeling of normality, of connection to self and others.

When porosity comes to the fore, the individual seems almost entirely unprotected. Piercing is easy, as the skin offers no resistance. All the clients whose stories have been included express this kind of difficulty at one time or another. Ellen May, for example, seems almost 'skinless' at times. Things seem to spill out of her in an unsorted jumble. A state of almost constant agitation and internal chaos emerges in last-minute cancellations, failures to turn up for appointments, narratives of missed college deadlines and of sleeping all day and being up all night. Ellen May's experience is of a fragmented existence. She cannot keep in mind any overall picture or plan but instead becomes obsessed with small and immediate details, such as how many turkey burgers to eat for supper. Porosity is indicated too by the way in which any small difficulty – her jeans feeling tight or her father expressing relief that she has not lost more weight – can tip her over into a self-destructive state of mind. A horror of seeing herself naked, of having to look at her own skin is one of the difficulties Ellen May brings to therapy, as if she is unconsciously aware of something terribly wrong in the arena of skin functioning. Kate seems to exemplify difficulties associated with porosity in a different way. She comes over as lacking in strength and vitality. She has allowed herself to be driven by work pressures, even after her physical symptoms became serious, and now she is being bullied into acting as a 'guinea-pig' for experimental treatments.

Self-harm as a psychosomatic issue

In previous work (Turp 1999a), I have suggested a sub-division of psycho-somatic disturbances into those that remain deeply unconscious, emerging in physical illnesses and symptoms without any apparent organic base, and those that take a more conscious route, emerging in self-harming behaviour of all kinds. In many cases, the two routes are in simultaneous use. Ellen May and Kate are bothered by a whole raft of minor symptoms – sinus problems, back problems, digestive upsets and the like – unusual not in their nature but in the frequency of their occurrence. Peter describes sexual dysfunction, in the form of an inability to ejaculate during intercourse.

Much of my work has drawn on Winnicott's writing on the themes of psychosomatic indwelling and psychosomatic splitting. For Winnicott, these were matters of central importance. The source of authenticity, the possibility of becoming 'the person who is me', resides in our awareness of physical functioning. Indeed, Winnicott describes the 'True Self' (1960a) as 'little more than the summation of sensory-motor aliveness'. This sensory-motor aliveness finds expression in the infant's 'spontaneous gestures'. The 'good enough' mother does not replace these gestures with her own, causing the infant to comply with her way of being. Instead, she recognises and implements the gestures, investing them with symbolic meaning. In this way, the infant is supported in his or her personal mode of self-expression and hence in 'feeling real' (Winnicott 1949). This is the basis for authentic relating which, in Winnicott's account, is the key to the overall health of the individual: 'Let us say that in health a man or woman is able to reach towards an identification with society without too great a loss of individual or personal impulse' (Winnicott 1967, p.27).

Winnicott's ideas have been extended in work by Bollas (1993) on 'idiom' and 'idiomatic investments'. In this work, as in my own, physical experience and physical self-expression are taken to be both meaningful and communicative. Winnicott refers to 'feeling real' (1949), 'the psyche indwelling in the soma' (1960b, p.45) and 'a psyche–soma that lives and works in harmony with itself' (1967, p.29). The appearance of the 'duality psyche–soma', an experienced sense of 'mind' on the one hand and 'body' on the other, is not a normal phenomenon. It is the consequence of defensive splitting in the face of 'impingements' from the environment that are too severe or too often repeated. At the time when he was writing, Winnicott's rejection of the philosophy of mind–body dualism was startlingly radical. Since then, we have seen the idea of separate 'mind' and 'body' functioning gradually yielding to the idea of ongoing and meaningful embodiment and integrated functioning.

In some psychoanalytic accounts of psychosomatic disturbance (McDougall 1974, 1989; Wilson and Mintz 1989) the focus is on the nature of 'mysterious leaps' from mind to body. Examples of such 'leaps' can be found in the clinical material presented in this book. They include actions such as kicking a bollard, cutting skin, uncontrollable shaking when picking up a drink, and self-induced vomiting. In each case, the action or symptom is physical, whereas the underlying difficulty is evidently psychological. In a dualistic version of events, the gap or chasm that is 'leapt' is not, in itself, noteworthy, for it is taken for granted that mind– *res cogitans* – and body – *res extensa* – are separate phenomena:

> Rene Descartes was responsible for the pronouncement that mind and body were separate entities, composed of different substances and subject to different laws. He advocated different research methods for the two phenomena he had distinguished. The body, being a material object, could be explored via scientific investigation but the mind was of a 'higher' order and could only be investigated via introspection. (Turp 2001, pp.46–47)

For those of us who subscribe to a holistic point of view, the situation looks rather different. Naturally, we attend to symptoms when this is a priority, as

I attended to Ellen May's need for immediate strategies to ward off the urge to vomit. But the existence of a gap or a chasm to be 'leapt' is of more fundamental interest than the symptom itself. The 'mysterious leap' is a symptom of underlying damage, of psychosomatic splitting, and it is this damage that needs to be addressed. Our endeavour is to try and understand, in collaboration with the client, the circumstances that have led to the development of this 'chasm', this unnatural divide between physical and psychological aspects of functioning.

Winnicott suggests that symptoms and behavioural eruptions are essentially health-seeking, representing unconscious attempts to *remedy* the underlying damage. With psychosomatic splitting, bodily experience is damped down through the reduction in somatic awareness. Through symptoms, bodily self-experience is restored, although in a way that is convoluted, distorted and the source of further difficulties. As we have seen in some of the examples, physical symptoms and behaviour that results in pain have the potential to relieve experiences of dissociation and deper-sonalisation and to restore a feeling of normality. In this sense, they express a tendency 'not to altogether lose the psychosomatic linkage' (Winnicott 1966, p.113).

Symptoms also make explicit the plight of the individual concerned, representing a silent but powerful plea for help. Now something visible, something on the outside, draws attention to the pain and damage on the inside. Self-harm, in common with other psychosomatic manifestations of distress, brings the body decisively and visibly back into the picture. It opposes the loss of psychosomatic union, which at an experiential level is a loss of feeling real, feeling normal or feeling 'sane'. Cutting a gash in the skin may, in desperate circumstances, usher in a sense of being held together: 'It's a solution that means I'm not going to flip out completely and kill myself. It's something I do for myself, it's mine, a way of feeling I am in control of what I am doing' (Arnold 1995, p.14).

Psychoanalysis and neuroscience

A dualistic perspective on 'mind' and 'body' continues to dominate at the 'coal-face' of medical practice. It is illustrated, for example, in the marked separation between 'physical' and 'mental' health services. This separation persists, untouched by the understanding that psychological factors are involved in many physical illnesses, for example in cardiac disease. In philosophy, sociology and psychoanalysis, and at the cutting edge of science, the situation is very different. The last decade has seen a marked shift away from dualistic perspectives on 'mind' and 'body'. There is something approaching a consensus on the idea of one single entity, the ever-embodied self, to be researched and described (Bermudez *et al.* 1995; Damasio 1994; Schore 2001; Turp 2001).

This shift has been fuelled by, and is reflected in, the rapid development of the discipline of neuroscience. The embodied self can now be described, at least in part, in terms of neurological structure and function and the fine detail of chemical and electrical activity within the brain. Overwhelming evidence has emerged of the dynamic and integrated nature of brain functioning (Edelman 1989; Pally 1997). Development and maturation of neuronal circuits has been shown to be heavily dependent on the individual's experience of the environment, in both its physical and emotional aspects, and the early years of life have been confirmed as a crucially sensitive period. We now know that much of the brain is 'soft-wired' at birth. It seems likely that certain neural connections, particularly those involved in intimate relating, cannot be made at a later time if – as a result of extreme deprivation – the building blocks are not laid down at an early stage (Schore 1997, 2001).

Damasio (1999) explores the subject of the neuro-anatomy of con-sciousness. One of his conclusions is that our sense of individuality, our 'singularity of self', has its roots in the fact that we are embodied beings, that each of us inhabits one body that is not shared with any other human being. Pally (2001) describes how non-verbal cues not only express emotion but also regulate body physiology and the ways in which individuals behave towards each other. At the neurophysiological level, the impact of non-verbal communication is mediated in many different ways, by circuits involving the limbic structures in the brain, by changes in hormone levels and by neurotransmitters, all of which influence the functioning of the autonomic nervous system. These same systems are involved in the development of primary attachments and in the ongoing interactions between an individual and his or her social and emotional environment.

Of particular interest in relation to self-harm are new understandings of the physiological mechanisms implicated in experiences of trauma, and the inscription and activation of memories of trauma (Diamond 2001; Schore 2001). The trauma 'pierces' the individual. It creates a state of neurological disturbance, a heightened level of arousal. What has happened cannot be processed, cannot be thought about in the normal way, and remains lodged, a situation that is reflected in a chronically raised level of arousal, a 'hyper-alert' physiological state. In the absence of processing, of a narrative of thoughts and words, physical activity and physical symptoms are obliged to carry the whole burden of the distress. I have found it interesting to be aware of neurophysiological versions of behaviour such as Lorraine's constant fidgeting and compulsive cleaning, Peter's sexual dysfunction, Tracey's self-hitting and 'paint-balling' and Ellen May's enactment of chaos.

The similarities between the narrative suggested by neuroscience findings and the narrative offered by object relations and attachment theory are striking. There is a buzz of excitement and a growing literature testifying the interest that has been generated. Sulloway (1975) and, more recently, Schore (1997) link these recent developments back to Freud's original project:

> In his 1895 'Project for a Scientific Psychology', Freud attempted to construct a model of the human mind in terms of its underlying neurobiological mechanisms. In this endeavor 'to furnish a psychology which shall be a natural science', Freud introduced the concepts that to this day serve as the theoretical foundation and scaffolding of psychoanalysis. (Schore 1997, p.807)

It cannot be said that this particular ambition of Freud's has shown much sign of being realised. Up until recently, the relationship between natural science and psychoanalysis has been characterised by hostility and scepticism. The scientific method – reductionistic and mechanistic, focusing on small subdivisions of behaviour and ignoring the context of larger whole – has had little to offer in a psychoanalytic context. The argument of behavioural psychology, that only that which can be directly observed should be researched, stood in direct opposition to the psycho-analytic interest in what lies beneath the surface, in currents that *cannot* be directly observed. Until recently scientific research focused on the search for linear cause–effect relationships, in marked contrast to the psychoana-lytic interest in complex and multi-causal interactions of different influences on the individual and of the individual on his or her environment.

Different tendencies were always present within natural science but it is only in the last decade that they have come decisively to the fore. In the place of linear cause–effect relationships, scientists are now inclined to think in terms of feedback loops, field theories and chaos theory, where nothing can ever be exactly predicted (Marshall and Zohar 1997; Turp 2001). In the light of recent developments, Schore asks: 'A century after Freud's project: Is a rapprochement between psychoanalysis and neurobiology at hand?' (Schore 1997, p.807).

Perhaps we can venture a cautious 'Yes'. For, broadly speaking, neuroscience findings corroborate psychoanalytic understandings concerning the development of the human individual and the complexity of his or her interaction with the environment. Beyond such corrobora-tion, there is the potential for understandings to be enhanced and refined. For the first time in many decades, a meaningful dialogue has opened up between psychoanalysis and biological science. Referring to 'possibilities for mutual gain' Olds and Cooper write:

> Where once we were concerned about the reductionism of some forms of biology, today's biological forefront is based on hierarchical systems theory, recognising emergent properties, and is unconcerned with trying to reduce poetic understanding to neuronal activity. (Olds and Cooper 1997, p.221)

One consequence of these developments is the need to reconsider the term 'psychosomatic'. If the 'mind', the 'brain' and the 'body' are all one, are merely different expressions, different versions of one ever-mindful, ever-embodied organism, then is it meaningful to continue to use the terms 'mental', 'physical' and 'psychosomatic'? Many years ago, having defined 'mind' as 'no more than a special case of the functioning of the psyche–soma', Winnicott (1949, p.244) suggested that we should continue to use the words 'mental' and 'physical' in daily conversation but not 'in scientific discussion'. He referred to the 'muddle' and 'precarious position' of psychosomatic disorders and, by way of clarification, offered the following suggestion:

> Let us attempt, therefore, to think of the developing individual, starting at the beginning. Here is a body, and the psyche and the soma are not to be distinguished except according to the direction from which one is looking. One can look at the developing body or at the developing psyche. I suppose the word psyche here means the *imaginative elaboration of somatic parts, feelings and functions*, that is, of physical aliveness. (Winnicott 1949, p.244)

These words were written many years ago. In 2002, they succinctly summarise the perspective on embodiment subscribed to in this book. We can perhaps identify some experiences and actions, for example jogging, self-cutting or asthma attack, as *essentially physical*, in the sense that their physical aspects are defining. They make these phenomena what they are. Other experiences and actions, for example dreaming or writing a book, can perhaps be thought of as *essentially mindful*. They are also physical, in the sense that the body is involved, in the case of the dream, at the level of neurophysiology and, in the case of the book, in the movement of fingers over a keyboard. However, their physical aspects are not defining. To know about REM sleep does not bring us closer to the feeling of the dream and the book would, in all major respects, remain the same if it were dictated rather than typed.

We sometimes need to refer to physical actions and physical symptoms that are first and foremost expressions of psychological distress. 'Psychosomatic disturbance' perhaps remains the phrase best suited to this purpose. A holistic point of view includes the understanding that psychological distress is always physiologically represented as well as subjectively experienced. Instead of envisaging a world of physiological events and a world of subjectively experienced mental events, we increasingly think in terms of one world, a world that can be described in different terms, at different levels of detail and from different points of view. Thus, my use of the term 'psychosomatic' does not imply, as has sometimes been implied in the past, that psychological distress 'causes' physical symptoms or self-harming behaviour. As neuroscience findings have confirmed, the causative agent is *trauma* and cause–effect relationships, which are in any case complex and non-linear, are between the environment and the organism as a whole.

As described above, the fine detail of the physiological version of events is beginning to emerge as neuroscience research proceeds. Broadly speaking, neuroscience findings corroborate an object-relations account of the individual in interaction with the environment. As well as providing a welcome 'triangulation' of findings (Denzin 1970), arriving at similar conclusions through the application of different methodologies, neuroscience offers psychoanalysis an opportunity to identify shortcomings and errors and to refine its understandings.

Body storylines

In linking the clinical material in this book to previous work on 'body storylines', I find myself referring to a 'lack', to an absence of something that can usually be taken for granted, namely a state of 'good enough' embodiment or indwelling. Satisfactory 'indwelling' is a normal consequence of good enough maternal care. Winnicott describes how the handling we receive as babies gives us a sense of a personal shape and physical boundaries.

> The infant becomes a person, an individual in his own right. Associated with this attainment is the infant's psychosomatic existence, which begins to take on a personal pattern; I have referred to this as the psyche indwelling in the soma. (Winnicott 1960b, p.45)

He describes one of the primary maternal tasks as 'joining up' emotional and physical aspects of experience:

> The beginning of that part of the baby's development which I am calling personalization, or which can be described as an indwelling of the psyche in the soma, is to be found in the mother's ability to join up her emotional involvement, which is originally physical and physiological. (Winnicott 1970, p.264)

Winnicott identifies 'handling', the physical aspect of maternal 'holding', as having a special function in this 'joining up' and hence in the establishment of 'indwelling'. Clients who suffer from psychosomatic symptoms or harm themselves are, almost by definition, suffering from disturbances of indwelling. We might also see their symptoms, whatever other meanings are involved, as unconscious requests for help with the task of 'joining up' emotional and physical experiences.

The question arises: How might such joining up best be supported? As psychoanalytic practitioners, we do not, for various reasons, physically handle our clients (Kertay and Riviere 1993; Turp 2000a, 2001). On the other hand, we do *symbolically* handle our clients, in our quality of gaze, tone of voice, movements towards or away from them and in the general tenor of our presence with them, expressed in posture, breathing, facial expression and so on. In the consulting room, free from the distraction of other activities, we are in an excellent position to attend to the client's somatic self-expression and to help him or her clothe non-verbal communications in words. In cases of psychosomatic disturbance, I have found it useful to focus particularly on these matters, paying close attention to somatic countertransference experiences, to the client's physical appearance, posture and stance and to narratives or fragments of narratives referring to physical experience and physical activity.

As has been emphasised in postmodern writing, cultural embeddedness is ongoing, as is individual embodiment. I have written about body storylines in terms of a person's posture, liveliness or inertia, physical quality of presence, sense of calm vitality or chaotic energy, viewing all of these as a non-verbal record of personal experiences in the physical domain (Turp 1999c, 2001). I am aware, however, that this is not a full account. Cultural influences on self-experience and self-presentation are equally important and cultural and individual influences are inextricably intertwined. Contemporary sociology, expressing a postmodern ethos, explores embodiment in terms of 'habitas'. The way in which the body is 'worn' attests to the taste, distinction and social standing of the 'owner' of the body in question (Bourdieu 1987). Fox (1999) also offers an interesting exploration of embodiment written from a postmodern perspecttive.

These matters are brought into sharp relief in the plays of Oscar Wilde: 'With a profound comic realism he plays at the dangerous edge of social convention, both as a member of the glittering classes of his day and simultaneously undercutting all they depend on' (Rustin and Rustin 2002, p.180). Wilde's principal characters articulate the Victorian preoccupation with wealth, respectability and 'breeding'. In this context 'Relationships are viewed as steps on the social ladder, and the natural dependence of the child has no place in the scheme of things' (*ibid.* p.177).

Posture is a mark of class and social standing and, as such, a form of 'symbolic capital' (Bourdieu 1977, 1987). In this passage from *The Importance of Being Ernest* Lady Bracknell is assessing the suitability of Cecily, whose 'breeding' is uncertain, for marriage to her nephew Algernon:

> LADY BRACKNELL: *(then bends, with a practised style to Cecily)* Kindly turn round, sweet child. *(Cecily turns completely round.)* No, the side view is what I want. *(Cecily presents her profile.)* Yes, quite as I expected. There are distinct social possibilities in your profile. The two weak points in our age are its want of principle and its want of profile. The chin a little higher, dear. Style largely depends on the way the chin is worn. They are worn very high, just at present. (Wilde 1899, Act 3)

Matters of 'habitas' on the one hand and the bodily inscription of individual experience, particularly traumatic events, on the other are not to be entirely disentangled. There is a complex interaction between the two. A psychoanalytic approach with a 'body storylines' flavour, the approach illustrated in the case studies, is marked by an emphasis on unconscious somatic communication and on client narratives of physicality, for example descriptions of past and present experiences of touch and physical activity. Cultural shaping of experience and perceived meaning, in the area of bodily self-presentation as in other areas, is recognised but it is the individual colouring that is of central clinical interest:

> Different people tend to construct experiences of the same event differently, each for reasons of his or her own. Many of these reasons originate early in life and therefore give rise to primitive forms of emotional and cognitive experience that persist unconsciously and influentially into adult life.

These individual variations add individual coloring to otherwise standardized responses to the conventions of one's culture. (Schafer 1992, p.xiv, my italics)

A long history of personal involvement in sport and recreational exercise has undoubtedly influenced my interest in the client's history of physical 'handling' and physical activity, and encouraged me to make space for reflection on the client's physical activities or the absence of such activities. Scenarios considered in previous work have included difficulties in getting out of bed, regular 'gentle bumps', sought out by one client on his daily underground journeys, and engagement with essentially physical activities such as walking, swimming or running (Turp 2001). The situations considered in this book involve physical action of a different kind, namely self-inflicted harm, whether occurring by commission or by omission.

Three clients – Lorraine, Ellen May and Kate – also make reference to psychologically helpful physical activities. Lorraine refers to walking, glass painting and, later, to planning a holiday. Ellen May remembers her love of volleyball and Kate starts to swim regularly. I will argue here, as I have argued elsewhere, for recognition of the potential value of somatic self-expression, and again voice my objection to any automatic pathologising of physical activity. On some occasions physical activity is inimical to, and may stand in the way of, thinking and reflection. (In my view, this was the case with Tracey's 'paint-balling' weekends.) At other times, physical activity is complementary to thoughtfulness and, in its tendency to enhance somatic awareness, helps to reconnect the client to his or her internal world of memory and emotion. Rhythmic and vigorous physical activity in particular can serve as a strong unconscious link to 'memories in feeling' (Klein 1957) of maternal handling and early physical achievements. When used rather than abused, the activities in question help to restore and conserve the individual's continuity of being and to sustain his or her quality of indwelling.

In summary, physical activity has both a negative and a positive psychological potential. The body can serve as an arena where pathology is expressed, where pain, tension and anxiety are played out in the form of psychosomatic symptoms or self-harm. It can also serve as an arena for the expression of healthy tendencies, where healing, recovery and enjoyment of living can take root and grow. Building on and enhancing positive potential is not a matter of offering activity or exercise recommendations but of helping the client to identify activities that feel 'right', that feel meaningful, to him or to her. This process involves being receptive, responding to and amplifying the client's 'spontaneous gesture' towards meaningful physical self-expression. This gesture may make itself felt unconsciously in the countertransference or emerge from the client's self-narrative (or both).

These matters are especially important when self-harm is the issue in question. It is perhaps too much to expect that the creation of a verbal narrative will immediately release the client from the compulsion to express his or her difficulties in a physical way. In many cases, the client has been using physical sensation to ward off and manage potentially overwhelming emotions and intolerable states of mind for a very long time. It is surely legitimate to help the client find his or her way towards alternative physical activities, activities that are psychologically sustaining rather than damaging re-enactments of trauma and emotional pain. Over time, dependence on physical self-expression tends to lessen, as a 'capacity to mentalise' – to create a narrative and find a form of words – improves. The body will, of course, continue to play a vital and complementary role in self-expression and communication, as is the case for all of us throughout our lives.

I will conclude this chapter by emphasising that working with body storylines falls naturally within the remit of psychoanalytic psychotherapy. The aim of psychosomatic integration is unlikely to be well served by any compartmentalised consideration of physicality. Instead, opportunities are taken to encourage the client to reflect on the changing experiences of physicality over the years of living and months of psychotherapy. These matters are considered as they emerge, alongside the consideration of other issues – self-harming behaviour, relationship difficulties, issues of personal creativity, difficulties in making decisions or whatever else the client brings to the sessions.

The principle of 'being with' rather than 'doing to' holds firm. In special cases (for example, when working with children), physical as well as verbal contact may form part of the interaction. In most cases of adult psychotherapy, symbolic experiences of touch, physical contact in the form of gaze, gesture and tone of voice, are sufficient and allow the transference–countertransference dynamic to evolve without undue disturbance. The primary therapeutic factor is understood to be the gradual internalisation by the client of the therapist, as a figure who holds in mind the client's physical and emotional needs, and who feels concerned that these needs should be met in a non-destructive way.

12

The Self-Harming Individual
and 'The System'

> Professionals are often terrified by self-injury. Their normal empathy
> with others' distress and their confidence in their ability to help often
> desert them when faced with someone who persistently hurts herself.
> This problem reflects a serious and widespread lack of understanding of
> self-injury, which results in great inconsistency and inadequacies in
> services. (Arnold 1995, p.1)

Up to this point, the book has focused on the relationship between a client
and a counsellor or psychotherapist. In this chapter, the discussion is
broadened to include encounters between individuals who harm
themselves and other practitioners working in a health or social care
context. Self-harm, once disclosed, is likely to bring an individual into
contact with a number of different agencies (Keene *et al.* 2000). Practitioners in these agencies, for example nurses working in accident and
emergency departments, mental health nurses, psychiatrists and general
practitioners, do not usually enjoy the level of support available to
counsellors and psychotherapists. Where incidents of self-harm impinge
upon a practitioner who is inadequately supported and supervised, we
have the makings of a situation where treatment standards may fall well
short of best practice.

It has saddened me, in the course of clinical practice and, more
recently, of writing this book, to hear about incidents that suggest a serious
breakdown in a practitioner's capacity to remain thoughtful and compassionate when confronted by self-harming behaviour. In the worst cases,
the response to the individual who has harmed herself has been neither

ethical nor professional. Dawn Collins, a counsellor who has worked extensively with young people who self-harm at the Hackney Off Centre in London, offers the following comment:

> The self-harmer often becomes re-abused in a system that fails to see the injury as a communication of the trauma, but views it instead as manipulative. For a young person crying out for help to be regarded as attention seeking carries maladaptive connotations, and this just provokes more of the same (silence, ignoring the injury, punitive responses). (Collins 1996, p.464)

The psychoanalytic approach set out in this book leans on the understanding that self-harming behaviour is the client's way of managing very difficult internal states. Through the process of projective identification, the state of mind being warded off by the client is stirred up in the practitioner. A practitioner may become 'terrified', as described by Arnold, in the presence of a client who is threatened by feelings of terror, or enraged in the presence of a client who has been harmed by the rage and violence of others in the past. Understanding this helps, I think, but is not in itself a guarantee of good practice.

> Attitudes bordering on contempt for psychiatric patients are not confined to ancillary staff and some biological psychiatrists; they are also common enough in the thinking of psychoanalysts and psychoanalytically oriented therapists. Although this attitude may be paradoxical inasmuch as psychoanalysis is based on respect for the intrapsychic focus and the unconscious, it nevertheless exists, especially in the context of the treatment interaction. (Giovacchini 1993, p.ix)

Self-harm as transgression

Where a person has intentionally cut, bruised, burned or poisoned herself, or interfered with wound healing or incurred injury through reckless behaviour or self-neglect, there is always a danger of a judgmental and punitive reaction. As discussed in Chapter 2, 'cashas', for example heavy smoking, often result in more serious damage to body organs and systems than acts of self-harm. Nevertheless, smoking-related lung cancer or heart disease do not provoke the same level of shock and outrage as self-cutting, even when the injury is relatively mild

What we call self-harm is distinguished first and foremost by the fact that it is not culturally accepted, is not permissible. Most of us remain within the limits of acceptable ways of injuring ourselves, or courting injury, or undermining our health. If we step outside these limits, our actions will start to be described as 'self-harm', and we may find ourselves perceived as seriously disturbed on the one hand, or angry and attention-seeking on the other.

The perception of self-harming behaviour as 'mad' or provocative is tied in with the emotional response of alarm, dismay, anger or fear provoked by this transgression of limits. At a physiological level, such emotional responses are associated with increased levels of adrenaline and cortisol circulating in the brain and the autonomic nervous system. The practitioner is in a state of hyper-arousal, in the grip of a primitive 'fight or flight' response, and we should not underestimate the challenge represented by this level of disturbance and distress. Even when good support and supervision are in place, he or she may become temporarily disabled and unable to think, as I myself became disabled and unable to think at various points during my work with my own clients.

The individual who self-harms feels, often quite reasonably, that he or she has been transgressed against in the past. The original transgression is re-enacted in his or her behaviour, which transgresses the cultural rules setting the limits for physical expression of self-destructive tendencies. A client's re-enactment of the original transgression, whatever it may have been, has an impact on the practitioner, who now becomes the one who feels transgressed against. The nurse feels personally insulted and assaulted by the patient's picking apart of the carefully stitched cut. I myself feel demeaned by Ellen May's lofty and superior claims to be the one who really knows about eating disorders, who can help her 'girls' back in the hospital.

The sequence continues when the practitioner himself or herself re-enacts the transgression. Clients who self-harm regularly speak of being treated dismissively and sometimes report that their wounds have been roughly treated or sutured without anaesthetic. Reports of such incidents are too widespread and numerous to be dismissed as inventions or exaggerations. I applaud efforts by the National Self-Harm Network and others to highlight these matters and demand that they be taken seriously. Nurses are not, of course, supposed to stitch cuts without anaesthetic or to swab them with methylated spirits. Such behaviour is a transgression of the ethics of nursing practice. Similarly, the 'attitudes bordering on contempt' referred to by Giovacchini are not a part of ethical counselling and psychotherapy practice. Similar problems arise in encounters between clients who self-harm and psychiatrists:

> I saw a psychiatrist. I waited months for the appointment and then he was so cold, clinical, impersonal, firing intrusive questions which left me reeling from the pain of disclosure and lack of support. The next psychiatrist I saw was much better but I didn't dare tell her about my self-harm. After six months I did and she was so shocked, ignorant, punitive, saying, 'if you don't stop cutting we can't do any work'. (Arnold 1995, p.18)

In a further twist, practitioner countertransference may translate into emotionally abusive behaviour that is justified in terms of behavioural psychology. Theory associated with the 'Behaviourist' school of psychology offers a rationale for withholding caring attention to injuries, on the grounds that such attention will offer 'positive reinforcement' and make a repeat episode more likely.

> I used to see a clinical psychologist but she was very unsympathetic. She thought cutting myself was an attempt to manipulate her and that it was disgusting. (Arnold 1995, p.18)

> I wanted to go to the day hospital, but they said they wouldn't take me until I'd sorted out my eating and my cutting. I thought, 'If I could do that then I wouldn't need to come here.' (Arnold 1995, p.19)

Behaviourist ideas have been influential in the field of mental health nursing and practitioners are widely encouraged to show a muted reaction to self-harming behaviour. Sometimes this is done in a sympathetic and ethical way. One nurse told me that he shows patients how to attend to and dress their own wounds but stays with them while they do so. He encourages them to come and talk to him at any time, emphasising that they do not need to harm themselves in order to have his care and attention. Others interpret this ethos of 'non-dramatisation' and 'non-reinforcement' in a very different way. At a conference workshop, I heard a mental health nurse present a case study involving self-cutting where he repeatedly referred to the behaviour as 'not serious' and as 'just attention-seeking'. This prompted another nurse in the group to say: 'If they do that on my ward I just give them the mop and the bucket and they can bloody well clear up the mess themselves.'

Supporting self-care

As Fonagy (1998) has noted, our increased understanding of the developmental pathways involved in psychological disturbance opens the door to prevention initiatives. The infant observation studies presented early on in the book indicate that a resilient capacity for self-care emerges naturally in the context of 'good enough' mothering: *the best way to support adult self-care is to support maternal capacities in parents, by ensuring that children are not brought up in poverty, that parents have time to be with their children and that emotional support is available as and when it is needed.* Under the current Labour administration in the UK, some steps have been taken in this direction, including the reform of child benefit and tax regimes and the introduction of the 'Sure Start' programme, aimed at children up to 6 years old. Much remains to be done, particularly in relation to the needs of 'looked-after' children.

Child psychotherapists work increasingly with severely damaged children, doing invaluable work that can transform the individual's prospects of enjoying a good quality of mental health in adult life. Nevertheless, as practitioners working with adults, we will continue to come face to face with self-harming behaviour. In this situation, some practitioners, particularly in Accident and Emergency nursing, have told me that they feel utterly helpless. They have not been educated to understand the possible meanings and functions of self-harming behaviour. They are overwhelmed by emotion and have no context for thinking about what might be going on. In a sense, it is no surprise to learn that the feelings stirred up sometimes spill over in reactive and punitive behaviour. When this happens, we can say that both the element of transgression and the failure of containment expressed in the act of self-harm have been echoed in and compounded by the practitioner's reaction. Having experienced yet another failure of containment, the client may feel propelled towards further acts of self-harm, as described by 'Lorraine' in Chapter 6.

It is useful for the practitioner to be aware of courses of action that are likely to be helpful. While not every practitioner will feel able to explore functions and meanings of the self-harming behaviour, the possibility of supporting self-care is open to all. A good starting-point involves the identification of occasions when a person has felt like harming herself but has not done. Family therapists White and Epston refer to this as the identification of 'unique outcomes' (1990). The case study of Ellen May offers an example of this approach. Effectively, I ask her: 'When you manage to resist the urge to vomit, what do you do instead? What helps?' Over time, we are able to identify a set of 'survival strategies', ways in which Ellen May can soothe and calm herself without resorting to bulimic behaviour. This fairly straightforward way of working has positive consequences for the client–practitioner relationship. It puts the two parties on the same side, engaged in a joint endeavour, and at the same time encourages the recovery of the client's damaged capacity for self-care.

By encouraging the client to speak freely and by listening sympathetically, the practitioner is already offering a form of 'treatment', acting as a source of containment for the distress and difficult feelings that lie behind the act of self-harm. It is important to acknowledge the impossibility of consistently providing such containment without supportive supervision. Mollon (1997) describes the thinking involved in a psychoanalytic style of supervision as a free-associative 'right-brain' mulling over, rather than a linear, logical 'left-brain' activity. Many factors have the potential to interfere with the creativity of this space. Ideally, supervision should be provided by a person who is not the practitioner's line manager, so that the practitioner need not feel inhibited in describing, digesting and detoxifying the difficult feelings stirred up by self-harming behaviour. In some NHS settings, where cost is a major consideration, I have suggested regular peer group supervision with a paid external facilitator, as an alternative to individual supervision.

The organisation where treatment is offered – whether a GP surgery, a social services office, a voluntary organisation, a youth detention centre or a psychiatric out-patients department – is also a potential source of containment. Because of the possibility of multidisciplinary working, the on-site support of colleagues and ready access to other services if needed, it is possible to work with more severe manifestations of self-harming behaviour in these settings than in private practice.

As well as supportive supervision and a supportive environment, an understanding of the dynamics that fuel self-harming behaviour is, in itself, a source of containment. The practitioner who is equipped to think about what might lie behind self-harm, to consider how the actions themselves might function as a coping strategy for the individual concerned, is less likely to behave in a retaliatory way than a practitioner who does not have these tools for thinking:

> As Bion has described, developing an understanding is in itself contain-ing of anxiety. It offers terms in which one can think about and think through what has happened, rather than feeling that one must *act,* whether in a rescuing or punitive manner. (Turp 1999a, p.311).

The question of containment brings the discussion around to the practitio-ner's capacity for reflection and insight, which links to his or her work on self. Counselling and psychotherapy training requires students to undergo a substantial period of personal psychotherapy, and I have identified infant observation as a second valuable sensitising experience. It is not so much a matter of learning techniques as of sensitising and strengthening oneself and thus becoming a more effective instrument of healing.

'Sally' and 'Janet'

Psychoanalytic practitioners believe that their work can only be effective if they are able to recognise within themselves something of the state of mind expressed in a client's behaviour. In a paper addressing the way in which individuals are affected by counselling training when they return to their core profession, Richards cites an account given by a probation officer. The speaker speaks about the issue of containment, then draws attention to the fact that those who offend are, in a sense, offending for all of us:

> I actually gained some understanding of what I'd been doing in the past as well, about the importance of the relationship; of providing a con-

tainer; of providing a clear space of time and confidentiality and trust in which people could use me, to a certain extent… There is very much a growing culture which says, 'There are offenders, and there are the rest of us.' There is this great separation, rather than the recognition that crime is something that is in all of us. It is out there being expressed for us by these other people, but of course, it is part of ourselves that is being acted out. But there is this increasing notion that there are two populations, those who do and those who do not break the law. But, of course, the distinction is much more blurred than that. (Richards 2002 forthcoming)

Similarly, clients who harm themselves, whether their behaviour is 'high visibility', as in the case of self-cutting and self-burning, or 'low visibility', as in the case of picking scabs or pulling out individual hairs, express self-destructive tendencies for us all. All of us, at times, hate ourselves and would like to hurt ourselves. Clients who harm themselves by omission also express self-destructive tendencies that we all share. They give expression to the parts of us that 'don't care', 'don't give a damn' and 'can't be bothered'. If we wish to work compassionately and effectively with clients who self-harm, we need to reach towards an understanding of our own self-destructive tendencies and of the ways in which they find expression in injurious and health-impairing behaviour. The following clinical vignette underlines some of the therapeutic possibilities inherent in recognising similarities between our own behaviour and that of our clients:

> A counsellor in supervision with me, whom I shall call Janet, discusses a new client, 'Sally'. At her second session, Sally reveals that she has intentionally cut herself. In response to Janet's enquiry, she says that she has done the same thing before, but not for over a year. She describes how this time she felt compelled towards self-cutting and yet tried to resist the compulsion. Her eyes kept being drawn to the kitchen drawer. Eventually she took out a sharp vegetable knife that she knew was there. She replaced it, then took it out again. She 'hid' it, went out and bought a pint of milk. But when she returned, she retrieved the knife and cut herself on her arm. (At this point, Janet describes to me a 'clenching feeling' in her stomach.)

Sally says that she had 'kind of gained control over the situation' but had then allowed herself the self-injury. She tells Janet, 'I knew I was on the edge. It was the only way to be sure that I wouldn't start hitting the kids and screaming at them five minutes after they got in from school. I wanted us to have a nice evening.' Janet keeps her outward response neutral and plays for time, saying that this is clearly a subject that will need careful consideration.

In supervision, Janet wonders whether Sally is a suitable client for the kind of counselling she offers – psychodynamic counselling on a once weekly basis. She feels she might find it too difficult to work with Sally, that Sally is perhaps too 'disturbed'. I bring into the supervision session the Kleinian concept of projective identification (1946), reminding Janet that the feelings being unconsciously stirred up within her by the client are there to be thought about and are likely to emerge as meaningful in the longer term. Janet identifies her primary emotional response as fear and begins to wonder whether Sally herself has felt very afraid in the past and, if so, what has been so frightening for her.

We note that Sally has made an early reference to difficulties in managing anger, speaking of a fear of 'hitting' and 'screaming at' her children. We identify a need both to keep the underlying anger in mind and, at the same time, for Janet to work in a sensitive way. Inevitably, the meanings of Janet's communications will be coloured by Sally's past experiences and we are aware that many individuals who harm themselves have at some point been 'accused' of being angry, manipulative or provocative. In this supervision session, I take the Bristol Survey off my shelf and quote to Janet an experience described by one of the respondents: 'I saw a psychiatrist who just said: "You're too angry to treat, psychiatry can't help you"' ('Woman E', Arnold 1995, p.19).

As we talk further, Janet brings into the conversation her current endeavour to give up smoking. Apparently, this sometimes involves taking out a cigarette and replacing it several times, 'hiding' the packet and distracting herself by going for a walk or to buy some shopping. Janet is making progress but still 'gives in' to a cigarette from time to time, particularly when she is feeling angry or upset.

These two developments – reflecting on the potential meaning of her emotional response and recognising parallels with her own behaviour – are directly helpful to Janet, and indirectly helpful to Sally. Janet now feels fairly confident about working with this troubled client and hopeful about the possibility of establishing a good therapeutic alliance. In her next session with Sally, she comments on the high priority Sally places on being a good parent. Referring back to the self-cutting incident, Janet reflects that, at that time, cutting herself had felt like the only way for Sally to calm herself down and be the kind of mother she wanted to be. Sally is clearly moved by Janet's comment and becomes quite tearful.

Subsequently, Sally seems more trusting of Janet. Her responses are less guarded and Sally's feeling of wariness ebbs away. These changes find physical expression at the end of the session when Sally says that her cut is healing well and pulls up her sleeve to show Janet the dressing. The counselling continues for a further year (this being the time limit at the voluntary organisation where Janet works). Sally cuts her arm once more during this time. In her sessions, she is able to talk about being seriously physically abused by her father, who tied her up and beat her. Janet helps her to name and describe her terrible feelings of rage and humiliation. Sally uses the time well and makes a number of significant changes in her life.

The case for early intervention

'Sally's' self-harming behaviour has not become altogether entrenched. It is not yet a regular part of her way of getting by. In many ways, Sally is still functioning well. We could say that the self-harm has not yet 'taken over'. In the absence of the counselling she undertakes with Janet, might Sally's self-harm become more severe? The words spoken by 'Woman B' suggest that the answer may be 'yes': 'I have been self-harming since I was very young, starting from a slight scratch to bruises, burns and serious wounds to various parts of my body' (Arnold 1995, p.7).

Although self-harm is not to be confused with suicidal behaviour, statistics suggest that 10 per cent of people who harm themselves eventually go on to commit suicide. Without intervention, which of my clients might have featured in this 10 per cent? Would it have been Sarah or Kate in a prolonged episode of depression and dissociation? Or Tracey or Peter in a violent outburst, disguised as an accident of one kind or another? Or Lorraine, by means of a final, fatal overdose? Or Ellen May, finally succeeding in starving herself to death?

In a recent submission (July 2002) to the National Institute for Clinical Excellence (NICE), I pointed out that, at present, services for individuals who self-harm are oriented towards and used almost exclusively by individuals engaging in 'high visibility' self-harm. In many cases, individuals reach counselling or psychiatric services at a point where their self-harm has already become entrenched. The behaviour in question is a well-established mechanism for coping with the stresses and strains of everyday living, a task that, as we have seen, is often exacerbated by a history of early trauma.

Self-harm that is heavily relied upon and continues over a long period develops a momentum of its own and becomes addictive, so that change becomes ever more difficult. This situation (described, for example, by Gardner 2001) finds support in recent neuroscience research, which has identified a possible physiological underpinning for such entrenchment. The feedback loops involved in pain and response to pain can become overloaded, setting up the electrical equivalent of the screeching noise, similar to that heard when a feedback loop develops in an auditory system. The individual resorts to more and more extreme acts of self-harm in an effort to rid herself of this painful and intense 'noise' (Carroll 2002).

On the other hand, people whose self-harm has not yet 'taken over' often respond well to counselling interventions. Such evidence as is available suggests that clients find 'unstructured' psychodynamic and narrative approaches more helpful than 'structured' cognitive-behavioural interventions. As well as preventing a great deal of human suffering and contributing significantly to best practice, an early intervention initiative would be likely to be highly cost-effective, since early intervention is likely to be associated with a shorter period of treatment and a much improved success rate. The establishment of such a service is one of the few options available with the potential to stem the rising tide of 'high visibility' incidents of self-harm. A first practical step might be the setting up of a single early intervention unit, to provide a flagship clinical service and to serve as a centre for multi-professional education, supervision and support of practitioners in all relevant fields and further research.

A number of obstacles stand in the way of the establishment of a successful early intervention programme. The first stems from the 'qualitative leap' model of self-harm itself. Because they are not conceptualised within this model, compromised self-care and mild self-harming behaviour are not recognised as self-harm. Thus, there is no mechanism for responding to them as early warning signs. Officially speaking, there is no self-harm in evidence until the individual progresses to more severe 'high visibility' self-harm.

Moving on to services for clients whose self-harm falls into the 'high visibility' category, an enormous obstacle to the improvement of services is the widespread stigmatisation of clients who harm themselves. 'Personality disorder' diagnoses, although not usually intended as stigmatising, are particularly problematic. They have an insidious effect on how *all* individuals who self-harm are perceived. For many people, the immediate association to the phrase 'personality disorder' is 'psychopathic personality disorder', which obviously has very negative connotations. Among the psychiatrists who have also expressed concern are Tantam and Whittaker (1992) and Ryle, who notes that: 'At the present time many of these patients receive little in the way of effective treatment' (1997, p.xi).

A linked problem is the understanding, enshrined in British law, that personality disorders are untreatable. Classifying self-harming behaviour as a symptom of borderline or multi-impulsive personality disorder encourages a culture of indifference and neglect. Those who make policy decisions and control budgets are invited to conclude that people who harm themselves cannot be helped, so there is little sense in investing resources in them, for example by ensuring access to counselling services. This is a callous conclusion, one that pays no regard to the very real distress that drives people to harm themselves.

Most individuals who harm themselves say that they want to try a counselling approach. They want a space where they feel listened to and understood and are given an opportunity to try to understand themselves:

I was lucky that when I went to College there was a counselling service and I finally got the help I needed. That was after several years in the psychiatric system, during which no-one ever tried to help me get to the reasons I was in such a state. There should be places where you can just walk in and get some real help without having to be seen as 'ill'. (Arnold 1995, p.27)

Like the client cited above, many people are not in a position to pay for private treatment. Some, like 'Lorraine', struggle for years to find their way to a counsellor or therapist, becoming involved with many different agencies along the way but not finding the help they are seeking. In Lorraine's case, good work could still be done although precious time had been lost. Inevitably, though, there are some cases where the delay leads to the behaviour becoming seriously entrenched and, as a consequence, only limited improvements are possible.

The expansion of counselling in primary care currently being pursued by the UK government presents an opportunity to radically improve the situation. The case examples suggest that what is needed is ready access to a normal counselling service, as well as the provision of a specialist service for especially difficult cases. They suggest also that 'low visibility' self-harm can be effectively treated in once- or twice-weekly counselling or therapy. A better option than a psychiatric referral when a patient who self-harms comes to the attention of a general practitioner or a nurse in Accident and Emergency is a period of counselling.

The table below, reproduced from the Bristol Survey report, gives an overview of what individuals who harm themselves experience as helpful.

Table 12.1

Service used	Total no. attending	% satisfied	% dissatisfied	% partially satisfied
Psychiatrist	34	15	82	3
Counsellor/ therapist	30	63	30	7
GP	24	37	46	17
Psychiatric hospital	23	4	96	0
Accident and Emergency	16	6	69	25
Social worker	10	20	70	10
Psychologist	9	22	77	0

This evidence highlights the need for individuals who are struggling with self-harming tendencies to have easy access to counselling services. The 'satisfaction' figures for counselling and psychotherapy, 63% satisfied and a further 7% partially satisfied, while no cause for complacency, are much higher than for any other kind of intervention. Counselling and psychotherapy are, by a very long way, the services that individuals who self-harm find most helpful. As has been emphasised, the practitioners undertaking the work need to be well supervised and to feel emotionally supported in their work. With a change of attitude and an increase in this kind of provision, we might at last begin to see a decrease in the incidence of severe and dramatic acts of self-harming behaviour.

Concluding thoughts

Self-harm is a 'multi-professional' issue. Social workers, general practitioners, teachers, accident and emergency nurses, mental health nurses, police officers, probation officers, prison wardens and youth workers may all, at times, be called upon to respond to self-harming behaviour. Through the presentation of individual case examples, I have argued for a 'talking cure' approach, with the aim of getting the sense of and putting into words the distress behind the symptom. To recognise that self-harm is an expression of emotional distress is to open oneself to the possibility of compassion. This is in itself helpful, for, where people who self-harm are concerned, compassion is sometimes in short supply.

I have concentrated on examples of low visibility and hidden self-harm. My work does not bring me into contact with more acute disturbance, such as might be encountered in inpatient psychiatric settings or in working with autistic or brain-damaged individuals, hence I am not in a position to comment on the potential value of the approach described in such cases. If the account I have given were to prove helpful to those working with higher levels of disturbance, this would be an added bonus. There has been a trend within psychoanalysis from working with less serious to working with more serious disturbance. At the beginning of the twentieth century, Freud saw the efficacy of the 'talking cure' as limited to the treatment of neurotic disorders. A hundred years later, psychotherapists, particularly child psychotherapists, work effectively with 'looked-after' children who have been very damaged and with individuals suffering from autistic and psychotic disturbances (Alvarez 1992; Margaret Rustin 2001; Margaret Rustin *et al.* 1997; Tustin 1972,). Similarly, accounts are beginning to emerge of effective psychoanalytic interventions in cases of entrenched and severe self-harm, as described, for example, in Gardner (2001).

A recurrent theme in this book has been the need to listen to what service users have to say. In the case study chapters, I have tried to ensure that the client's voice is heard. In this chapter, I have again included the voices of those who took part in the Bristol Survey, speaking in detail about their self-harming behaviour and their experience of practitioner responses. I will conclude by adding my voice to the voices of clients and other practitioners, calling for the provision of an adequate, affordable and non-stigmatising counselling service, available to all who find themselves concerned about either active self-harm or serious failures of self-care.

Bibliography

Abram, J. (1996) *The Language of Winnicott*. London: Karnac.

Addley, E. and Barton, L. (2001) 'Who Said Hard Work Never Hurt Anybody?' *The Guardian*, 13/03/01.

Alvarez, Anne (1992) *Live Company*. London: Routledge.

American Psychiatric Association (1994) *Diagnostic and Statistical Manual of Mental Disorders, Fourth Edition*. Washington DC: APA.

Amez, S. and Botero, H. (2000) 'The Mother, the Baby, the Pouch and the Observer: Feeding Difficulties of an Infant on the Kangaroo Mother Programme.' *The International Journal of Infant Observation 3*, 2, 46–54.

Anzieu, D. (1989) trans. C. Turner. *The Skin Ego*. London and New Haven: Yale University Press.

Arnold, L. (1995) *Women and Self-Injury – A Survey of 76 Women*. Bristol Crisis Service for Women, P.O. Box 654, Bristol BS99 1XH.

Bell, D. (2001) 'This is How It is for Me, I Think.' *Times Literary Supplement*, 8/06/01.

Bermudez, J. L. *et al.* (eds) (1995) *The Body and the Self*, Cambridge, Massachusetts: MIT Press.

Bick, E. (1968) 'The Experience of the Skin in Early Object Relations.' *International Journal of Psychoanalysis 49*, 484–486.

Bion, W. R. (1962) *Learning from Experience*. London: Heinemann.

Bion, W. R. (1967a) *Second Thoughts*. London: Heinemann.

Bion, W. R. (1967b) 'Notes on Memory and Desire.' In E. Bott Spillius (ed) *Melanie Klein Today. Vol. 2 Mainly Practice*. London: Routledge (1988).

Bollas, C. (1987) *The Shadow of the Object*. London: Free Association Books.

Bollas, C. (1993) *Being a Character*. London: Routledge.

Bourdieu, P. (1977) *Outline of a Theory of Practice* (trans. R. Nice). Cambridge: Cambridge University Press.

Bourdieu, P. (1987) *Distinction: A Social Critique of the Judgement of Taste* (trans. R. Nice). Cambridge Mass: Cambridge University Press.

Briggs, S. (1997) *Growth and Risk in Infancy*. London: Jessica Kingsley Publishers.

Briggs, S. (1998) 'The Contribution of Infant Observation to an Understanding of Feeding Difficulties in Infancy.' *Infant Observation 1*, 3, 44–59.

Buckroyd, J. (1994) 'Eating Disorders as Psychosomatic Illness: The Implications for Treatment' *Psychodynamic Counselling 1*, 1, 106–118.

Burr, V. (1995) *An Introduction to Social Constructionism*. London: Routledge.

Carroll, R. (2002) 'Why Psychosomatisation is Complex: Going beyond "cause–effect".' Address to 'Confer' lecture series *Working with Psychosomatic Symptoms*, London, 06/02/2002.

Casement, P. (1985) *On Learning from the Patient*. London: Tavistock.

Chasseguet-Smirgel, J. (1990) 'On Acting Out' *International Journal of Psychoanalysis 71*, 77–86.

Collins, D. (1996) 'Attacks on the Body: How Can We Understand Self-Harm?' *Psychodynamic Counselling 2*, 4, 463–475.

Crossley, N. (1996) *Intersubjectivity: The Fabric of Social Becoming*. London: Sage.

Damasio, A. (1994) *Descartes' Error: Emotion, Reason and the Human Brain*. New York: Putman.

Damasio, A. (1999) *The Feeling of What Happens: Body and Emotion in the Making of Consciousness*. London: Heinemann.

Denzin, N. K. (1970) *The Research Act*. Chicago: Aldine.

Diamond, N. (2001) 'Towards an Interpersonal Understanding of Bodily Experience.' *Psychodynamic Counselling 7*, 1, 41–62.

Edelman, G. (1989) *The Remembered Present*. New York: Basic Books.

Elliott, A. and Frosh, S. (1995) *Psychoanalysis in Contexts: Paths between Theory and Modern Culture*. London: Routledge.

Favazza, A (1989a) 'Normal and Deviant Self-Mutilation: An Essay Review.' *Transcultural Psychiatric Research Review 26*, 2, 113–127.

Favazza, A. (1989b) 'Why Patients Mutilate Themselves.' *Hospital and Community Psychiatry 40*, 2, 137–145.

Feldman, M. (1988) 'The Challenge of Self-Mutilation: A Review.' *Comprehensive Psychiatry 29*, 3, 252–269.

Field, N. (1989) 'Listening with the Body: An Exploration in the Countertransference.' *British Journal of Psychotherapy 5*, 4, 512–522.

Field, T. M. (ed) (1995) *Touch in Early Development*. New Jersey: Lawrence Erlbaum Associates.

Fonagy, P. (1991) 'The Capacity for Understanding Mental States: The Reflective Self in Parent and Child and its Significance for Security of Attachment.' *Infant Mental Health Journal 12*, 3, 201–218.

Fonagy, P. (1998) 'Prevention, the Appropriate Target of Infant Psychotherapy.' *Infant Mental Health Journal 19*, 2, 124–150.

Fonagy, P. (1999a) 'Attachment, the Development of the Self, and its Pathology in Personality Disorders.' In J. Dersen, C. Maffei *et al.* (eds) *Treatment of Personality Disorders*. New York: Kluwer/Plenum.

Fonagy, P. (1999b) 'Relation of Theory and Practice in Psychodynamic Therapy.' *Journal of Clinical Child Psychology 28*, 4, 513–520.

Fonagy, P. (2001) 'The Human Genome and the Representational World: The Role of Early Mother-Infant Interaction in Creating an Interpersonal Interpretive Mechanism.' *Bulletin of the Menninger Clinic 65*, 3, 427–448.

Fonagy, P. and Target, M. (1995) 'Understanding the Violent Patient: The Use of the Body and the Role of the Father.' *International Journal of Psychoanalysis 76*, 487–501.

Foucault, M. (1970) *The Order of Things*. London: Tavistock.

Foucault, M. (1984) 'Space, Knowledge and Power.' In P. Rabinow (ed) *The Foucault Reader*. New York: Pantheon.

Fox, N. (1999) *Beyond Health: Postmodernism and Embodiment*. London: Free Association Books.

Freud, S. (1923) 'The Ego and the Id.' In *Standard Edition Vol. 18*. London: Hogarth, 1958.

Freud, S. and Breuer, J. (1893) 'Studies in Hysteria.' In *Standard Edition Vol. 2*. London: Hogarth, 1958.

Gardner, F. (2001) *Self-Harm: A Psychotherapeutic Approach*. London: Brunner–Routledge.

Giovacchini, P. L. (1993) *Borderline Patients. The Psychosomatic Focus and the Therapeutic Process*. New Jersey: Jason Aronson.

Glaser, B. G. and Strauss, A. (1967) *The Discovery of Grounded Theory*. Chicago: Aldine.

Greenspan, G. and Samuel, S. (1989) 'Self-cutting after Rape.' *American Journal of Psychiatry 146*, 789–790.

Harvey, D. (1989) *The Condition of Postmodernity*. Cambridge, MA, and Oxford, UK: Blackwell.

Heidegger, M. (1927) *Being and Time*. Trans. J. Macquarrie and E. S. Robinson (1962). New York: Harper and Row.

Heimann, P. (1950) 'On Counter-transference.' *International Journal of Psychoanalysis 31*, 81–85.

Hopkins, J. (1990) 'The Observed Infant of Attachment Theory.' *British Journal of Psychotherapy 6*, 457–469.

Joseph, B. (1989) *Psychic Equilibrium and Psychic Change*. London: Routledge.

Keene, J., Bailey, S., Swift, L. and Janacek, G. (2000) 'The Tracking Project: A Collaborative Multi-Agency Database for Shared Clients/Patients to Inform Policy Development.' *Journal of Interprofessional Care 14*, 4, 325–336.

Keleman, S. (1985) *Emotional Anatomy: The Structure of Experience*. Berkeley: Center Press.

Kertay, L. and Riviere, S. (1993) 'The Use of Touch in Psychotherapy: Theoretical and Ethical Considerations.' *Psychotherapy 30*, 1, 32–40.

Klein, M. (1946) 'Notes on Some Schizoid Mechanisms.' In *Envy and Gratitude and Other Works 1946–1963*. London: Hogarth, 1987.

Klein, M. (1952) 'On observing the behaviour of young infants.' *Envy and Gratitude and Other Works 1946–1963*. London: Hogarth 1987.

Klein, M. (1957) 'Envy and Gratitude.' In *Envy and Gratitude and Other Works 1946–1963*. London: Hogarth, 1987.

Kohut, H. (1971) *The Analysis of the Self*. London: Hogarth.

Krystal, H. (1978) 'Self Representation and the Capacity for Self Care. *Annual of Psychoanalysis 6*, 209–246.

Krystal, H. (1988) *Integration and Self-Healing: Affect, Trauma, Alexithymia*. New Jersey: Analytic Press.

Lacan, J. (1979) *The Four Fundamentals of Psychoanalysis*. London: Penguin.

Lacey, J. and Evans, C. (1986) 'The Impulsivist: A Multi-Impulsive Personality Disorder.' *British Journal of Addiction 81*, 641–649.

Lesser, R. C. (1996) '"All That's Solid Melts into Air": Deconstructing Some Psychoanalytic Facts.' *Contemporary Psychoanalysis 32*, 1, 5–23.

Levinas, E. (1961, trans. 1969) *Totality and Infinity*. Pittsburgh: Duquesne University.

Likierman, M. (2001) *Melanie Klein: Her Life and Work in Context*. London: Continuum.

Ludington-Hoe, S., Nguyen, N., Swinth, J., Satyshur, R. (2000) 'Kangaroo Care Compared to Incubators in Maintaining Body Warmth in Infants.' *Biological Research for Nursing 2*, 1, 60–73.

Marshall, I. and Zohar, D. (1997) *Who's Afraid of Schroedinger's Cat?* London: Bloomsbury.

McDougall, J. (1974) 'The Psychosomatic and Psychoanalytic Process.' *International Review of Psychoanalysis 1*, 437–454.

McDougall, J. (1989) *Theatres of the Body: A Psychoanalytical Approach to Psychosomatic Illness*. London: Free Association Books.

Merleau-Ponty, M. (1962) *Phenomenology of Perception*. Trans. Colin Smith. London: Routledge and Kegan Paul.

Miller, L., Rustin, Michael, Rustin, Margaret and Shuttleworth, J. (eds) (1989) *Closely Observed Infants*. London: Duckworth.

Modell, A. H. (1990) *Other Times, Other Realities. Towards a Theory of Psychoanalytic Treatment*. Cambridge, MA/London: Harvard University Press.

Mollon, P. (1985) 'The Non-Mirroring Mother and the Missing Paternal Dimenson in a Case of Narcissistic Disturbance.' *Psychoanalytic Psychotherapy 1*, 2, 35–47.

Mollon, P. (1997) 'Supervision as a Space for Thinking.' In G. Shipton (ed) *Supervision of Psychotherapy and Counselling: Making a Space to Think*. Bristol: Open University Press.

Moran, D. (2001) *Introduction to Phenomenology*. London: Routledge.

Ogden, T. (1997) *Reverie and Interpretation: Sensing Something Human*. New Jersey: Jason Aronson.

Olds, D. and Cooper, M. (1997) 'Dialogue with Other Sciences: Opportunities for Mutual Gain.' *International Journal of Psychoanalysis 78*, 219–225.

Orbach, S. (1995) 'Countertransference and the False Body.' *Winnicott Studies 10*, 3–13.

Orbach, S. (1999) *The Impossibility of Sex*. London: Allen Lane, The Penguin Press.

Pally, R. (1997) 'How Brain Development is Shaped by Genetic and Environmental Factors.' *International Journal of Psychoanalysis 78*, 587–593.

Pally, R. (2001) 'A Primary Role for Nonverbal Communication in Psychoanalysis.' *Psychoanalytic Inquiry 21*, 1, 71–93.

Parker, I. (1992) *Discourse Dynamics: Critical Analysis for Social and Individual Psychology*. London: Routledge.

Pattison, E. and Kahan, J. (1983) 'The Deliberate Self-Harm Syndrome.' *American Journal of Psychiatry 140*, 867–872.

Pembroke, L. (2000) *Cutting the Risk*. Rochdale: The National Self-Harm Network.

Pert, C. (1990) 'The Wisdom of the Receptors: Neuropeptides, The Emotions, and Body–Mind.' In R. Ornstein and C. Swencionis (eds) *The Healing Brain: A Scientific Reader*. New York: Guilford.

Phillips, Adam (1993) *On Kissing, Tickling and Being Bored*. London: Faber and Faber.

Phillips, Adam (1999) *Darwin's Worms*. London: Basic Books.

Phillips, Asha (1999) *Saying No: Why it's Important for You and Your Child*. London: Faber and Faber.

Pines, D. (1977) 'Skin Communication: Early Skin Disorders and their Effects on Transference and Counter-Transference.' *International Journal of Psychoanalysis 61*, 315–23.

Potter, J. (1997) 'Discourse Analysis as a Way of Analysing Naturally Occurring Talk.' In D. Silverman (ed) *Qualitative Research*. London: Sage.

Reid, S. (1997) *Developments in Infant Observation: The Tavistock Model*. London: Routledge.

Rhode, E. (1993) 'Book Review of *Cogitations* by W. R. Bion.' *British Journal of Psychotherapy 9*, 4, 503–504.

Richards, Barbara (2002 forthcoming) 'Ripples in the Pond: A Qualitative Study of Graduates' Perceptions of the Impact of Counselling Training upon their Work within the Core Professions.' *Psychodynamic Practice 8*, 3.

Richards, Barry (1994) 'The Glory of the Game.' In B. Richards (ed) *Disciplines of Delight*. London: Free Association Books.

Richards, V. (1996) 'Hunt the slipper.' In V. Richards (ed) *The Person Who is Me: Contemporary Perspectives on the True and False Self.* London: Karnac.

Rodman, F. (ed) (1987) *The Spontaneous Gesture: Selected Letters of D. W. Winnicott.* Cambridge, Massachusetts: Harvard.

Rowling, J. K. (1997) *Harry Potter and the Philosopher's Stone.* London: Bloomsbury.

Rowling, J. K. (1998) *Harry Potter and the Chamber of Secrets.* London: Bloomsbury.

Rowling, J. K. (1999) *Harry Potter and the Prisoner of Azbakan.* London: Bloomsbury.

Rowling, J. K. (2000) *Harry Potter and the Goblet of Fire.* London: Bloomsbury.

Rustin, Margaret (2001) 'The Therapist with her Back against the Wall.' *Journal of Child Psychotherapy 27*, 3, 273–284.

Rustin, Margaret, Rhode, M., Dubinsky, A. and Dubinsky, H. (eds) (1997) *Psychotic States in Children.* London: Routledge.

Rustin, Michael (1997) 'The Generation of Psychoanalytic Knowledge: Sociological and Clinical Perspectives. Part One: "Give Me a Consulting Room…".' *British Journal of Psychotherapy 13*, 4, 527–541.

Rustin, Michael and Rustin, Margaret (2001) *Narratives of Love and Loss: Studies in Modern Children's Fiction* (revised edition). London: Karnac.

Rustin, Michael and Rustin, Margaret (2002) *Mirror to Nature: Drama, Psychoanalysis and Society.* London: Karnac.

Ryle, A. (1997) *Cognitive Analytic Therapy and Borderline Personality Disorder.* Chichester: John Wiley & Sons Ltd.

Saunders, L. and Broad, B. (1997) *The Health Needs of Young People Leaving Care.* De Montfort University, Scraptoft, Leicester LE7 9SU.

Schafer, R. (1992) *Retelling a Life: Narration and Dialogue in Psychoanalysis.* New York: Basic Books.

Schore, A. (1994) *Affect Regulation and the Origin of the Self: The Neurobiology of Emotional Development.* New York: Lawrence Erlbaum Associates.

Schore, A. (1997) 'A Century after Freud's Project: Is a Rapprochement between Psychoanalysis and Neurobiology at Hand?' *Journal of the American Psychoanalytic Association 45*, 3, 807–840.

Schore, A. (2001) 'The Effects of Early Relational Trauma on Right Brain Development, Affect Regulation, and Infant Mental Health.' *Infant Mental Health Journal 22*, 1, 201–269.

Scott, A. (1998) 'Trauma, Skin: Memory, Speech.' In V. Sinason (ed) *Memory in Dispute.* London: Karnac.

Sifneos, P. E. (1965) *Ascent from Chaos: A Psychoanalytic Case Study.* London: Oxford University Press.

Sokolowski, R. (2001) *Introduction to Phenomenology.* Cambridge: Cambridge University Press.

Sorensen, P. (2000) 'Observations of Transition-Facilitating-Behaviour – Developmental and Theoretical Implications.' *The International Journal of Infant Observation 3*, 2, 46–54.

Spitz, R. (1945) 'Hospitalism: An Inquiry into the Genesis of Psychiatric Conditions in Early Childhood.' *The Psychoanalytic Study of the Child 1*, 53–74.

Stein, M., Sufian, J. and Hazlehurst, M. (2001) *Supporting Care Leavers: A Training and Resource Pack for Young People Leaving Care.* First Key, Oxford Chambers, Oxford Place, Leeds LS1 3AX.

Stern, D. N. (1977) *The First Relationship: Infant and Mother.* Cambridge: Harvard University Press.

Stern, D. N. (1985) *The Interpersonal World of the Infant: A View from Psychoanalysis and Developmental Psychology.* New York: Basic Books.

Stern, D. N. (1999) 'Vitality Contours: The Temporal Contour of Feelings as a Basic Unit for Constructing the Infant's Social Experience.' In P. Rochat (ed) *Early Social Cognition: Understanding Others in the First Six Months of Life.* New York: Lawrence Erlbaum Associates.

Strong, M. (2000) *A Bright Red Scream: Self Mutilation and the Language of Pain.* New York: Penguin.

Sulloway, F. J. (1975) *Freud, Biologist of the Mind: Beyond the Psychoanalytic Legend.* New York: Basic Books.

Tantam, D. and Whittaker, J. (1992) 'Personality Disorder and Self-Wounding.' *British Journal of Psychiatry 161*, 451–464.

Taylor, M. and Loewenthal, D. (2001) 'Researching a Client's Experience of Preconceptions of Therapy: A Discourse Analysis.' *Psychodynamic Counselling 7*, 1, 63–82.

Trevarthen, C. (1979) 'Communication and Cooperation in Early Infancy: A Description of Primary Intersubjectivity.' In M. Bullowa (ed) *Before Speech.* Cambridge: Cambridge University Press.

Trevarthen, C. (1998) 'Intersubjectivity.' In R. Wilson and F. Keil (eds) *The MIT Encyclopedia of Cognitive Science.* Cambridge, MA: MIT Press.

Turp, M. (1997) 'The Role of Physical Exercise in Emotional Well-Being.' *Journal of Psychodynamic Counselling 3*, 2, 165–177.

Turp, M. (1999a) 'Encountering Self-Harm in Psychotherapy and Counselling Practice.' *British Journal of Psychotherapy 15*, 3, 306–321.

Turp, M. (1999b) 'Touch, Enjoyment and Health: (1) In Infancy.' *European Journal of Psychotherapy, Counselling and Health 2*, 1, 23–39.

Turp, M. (1999c) 'Working with Body Storylines.' *Psychodynamic Counselling 5*, 3, 301–317.

Turp, M. (2000a) 'Touch, Enjoyment and Health: In Adult Life.' *European Journal of Psychotherapy, Counselling and Health 3*, 1, 61–76.

Turp, M. (2000b) 'Handling and Self-Handling: an Object Relations Perspective on Leisure Exercise.' *Psychodynamic Counselling 6,* 4, 469–488.

Turp, M. (2001) *Psychosomatic Health: The Body and the Word.* London: Palgrave.

Turp, M. (2002) 'The Many Faces of Self-Harm.' *Psychodynamic Practice 8,* 2, 197–217.

Tustin, F. (1972) *Autism and Childhood Psychosis.* London: Karnac.

Walsh, B. and Rosen, P. (1988) *Self-Mutilation: Theory, Research and Treatment.* New York: Guilford Press.

Welldon, E. V. (1988) *Mother, Madonna, Whore: The Idealisation and Denigration of Motherhood.* New York: Guilford.

White, M. and Epston, D. (1990) *Narrative Means to Therapeutic Ends.* New York: Norton & Company.

Wilde, D. (1899) *The Importance of Being Earnest.* London: Leanard Smithers and Co.

Wilson, C. and Mintz, I. (eds) (1989) *Psychosomatic Symptoms: Psychodynamic Treatment of the Underlying Personality Disorder.* New Jersey: Jason Aronson.

Winnicott, D. W. (1949) 'Mind and its Relation to the Psyche–Soma.' In *Collected Papers: Through Paediatrics to Psychoanalysis.* London: Tavistock, 1958.

Winnicott, D. W. (1953) 'Transitional Objects and Transitional Phenomena.' In *Collected Papers: Through Paediatrics to Psychoanalysis.* London: Tavistock 1958.

Winnicott, D. W. (1956) 'Primary Maternal Preoccupation.' In *Collected Papers: Through Paediatrics to Psychoanalysis.* London: Tavistock, 1958.

Winnicott, D. W. (1960a) 'Ego Distortion in terms of True and False Self.' In *The Maturational Processes and the Facilitating Environment.* London: Hogarth, 1965.

Winnicott, D. W. (1960b) 'The Theory of the Parent–Infant Relationship.' In *The Maturational Processes and the Facilitating Environment.* London: Hogarth, 1965.

Winnicott, D. W. (1962a) 'The Child in Health and Crisis.' In *The Maturational Processes and the Facilitating Environment.* London: Hogarth, 1965.

Winnicott, D. W. (1962b) 'Ego Integration in Child Development.' In *The Maturational Processes and the Facilitating Environment.* London: Hogarth, 1965.

Winnicott, D. W. (1966) 'Psycho-Somatic Illness in its Positive and Negative Aspects.' In C. Winnicott, R. Shepherd and M. Davis (eds) *Psycho-analytic Explorations.* London: Karnac, 1989.

Winnicott, D. W. (1967) 'The Concept of a Healthy Individual.' In C. Winnicott, R. Shepherd and M. Davis (eds) *Home Is Where We Start From.* London: Penguin, 1986.

Winnicott, D. W. (1970) 'On the Basis for Self in Body.' In C. Winnicott, R. Shepherd and M. Davis (eds) *Psycho-Analytic Explorations.* London: Karnac, 1989.

Winnicott, D. W. (1971) *Playing and Reality.* London: Tavistock.

Winnicott, D. W. (1986) 'The Concept of the Healthy Individual.' In C. Winnicott, R. Shepherd and M. Davis (eds) *Home Is Where We Start From.* London: Penguin, 1986.

Winnicott, D. W. (1988) *Human Nature.* London: Free Association Books.

Wise, M. (1989) 'Adult Self-Injury as a Survival Response in Victim-Survivors of Childhood Abuse.' *Journal of Chemical Dependency Treatment 3*, 1, 185–201.

Yin, R. (1993) *Case Study Research.* London: Sage.

Young, L. And Gibb, E. (1998) 'Trauma and Grievance'. In C. Garland (ed) *Understanding Trauma: A Psychoanalytic Approach.* London: Duckworth.

Zalidis, S. (2001) *A General Practitioner, his Patients and their Feelings.* London: Free Association Books.

Subject Index

abuse 32, 74, 82, 83, 88, 158–9, 162
accidents 32
acting, feeling and thinking 119–41
acts of self-harming, culturally accepted 20–1
'Anna' 144, 146, 152, 163–4
anorexia 32, 99–100

'Bernie' 25–6, 27, 32, 33
bodily integrity and psychic skin 53–66
body storylines 120, 202–7
borderline features 108–9
Bristol Survey 29, 35, 79, 85, 173, 221
British Association for Counselling and Psychotherapy (BACP) 81, 84, 119, 167
bulimia 32, 99–100
bullying 180–1

cashas 9, 20–1, 30, 31, 33, 36, 71, 210
CASSEL Centre 81, 89, 92
'Clare' 81–95
clinical examples
  from counselling and psychotherapy 74–7
  from group supervision 24–7
  selection of 32–3
concern for others, evolving 46–7
containment
  failures of 192
  holding and handling 61–2
continuity, narratives of 62–6
continuum model of self-harm 29–30
counselling and psychotherapy, examples from 74–7
countertransference 171

defining self-harm 36–7
description, value of 67–9
dramatic repetition and trauma 79–95
DSM IV 101

early intervention, case for 218–22
eating disorders 32, 37, 99–100
eczema 32
'Ellen May' 24, 32, 76, 97–117, 192, 193, 194, 195, 196, 199, 205, 211, 214, 219
'Emma' 60, 64–5, 133–4, 174–6
'entitlement' and self-care 49–51
'Esther', observations of 43–51, 53–8, 61, 62–5, 111, 185
exercise, inappropriate and excessive use of 32

'False Self' 144–5, 157, 193
feeling, acting and thinking 119–41

'going-on-being' and 'impingement' 56–8

Hackney Off Centre 210
'Harry' 26, 27, 32, 33, 60
Harry Potter 112–13, 192
health 39
'Helen' 43, 45, 53–5, 57, 65, 111
holding, handling and containment 61–2

ICD-10 101
'impingement' and 'going-on-being' 56–8
individual who is self-harming, and the system 209–23
infancy, physical dependency in 40–1
infant observation, psychoanalytic 41–3
intersubjectivity and postmodernism 69–70
intervention, case for early 218–22

'Janet' 216–18
'Jim' 177, 178
'Johnny' 147–9, 155

karoshi 10
'Kate' 24, 32, 60, 76, 167–70, 173, 175–86, 188, 192, 194, 195, 205, 219
'Kay' 147–9

'Lesley' 98–9
'looked-after' children 190–1
'Lorraine' 24, 76, 79–95, 97, 188, 190,
    192, 199, 205, 219, 221
'Louise' 64

maternal care, self-worth and self-care 47–9
meaning of self-harm 23–37
'Mike' 84, 90–1, 95

narratives of continuity 62–6
National Institute for Clinical Excellence
    (NICE) 10, 219
National Self-Harm Network 29, 211
neuroscience and psychoanalysis 197–202

object relations theory 40, 47
Oedipal issues 132–6
omission, self-harm by 167–86
overworking 32

parental sensitivity 43–5
'Peter' 24, 32, 60, 76, 143–7, 149–65,
    188, 192, 194, 199, 219
physical dependency in infancy 40–1
physical enjoyment and physical hazards
    55–6
postmodernism and intersubjectivity 69–70
psychic skin
    and bodily integrity 53–66
    and physical skin 58–61, 193–5
psychoanalysis
    in modern era 72–3
    and neuroscience 197–202
psychoanalytic infant observation 41–3
psychodynamic understandings 15–18
psychosomatic issues, self-harm as 195–7
psychotherapy and counselling, examples
    from 74–7

qualitative leap model of self-harm 27–8

'Rachel' 26–7, 32, 33
recognition of achievements 45–6

repetitive strain injury (RSI) 32, 168–9,
    173, 175–6, 178, 179, 182, 184,
    185
'Rob' 43, 45–6, 47, 54, 55, 57, 62, 65
'Ruth' 24–5, 27, 32, 33

'Sally' 214–18
'Sarah' 12–14, 24, 32, 33
'second skin' phenomena 113
self-care 18–20
    capacity for 39–51
    and 'entitlement' 49–51
    failure of 32
    maternal care and self-worth 47–9
    supporting 213–15
    vicissitudes of 33–6
self-cutting 11, 79–95, 97–117
self-injury, types of 79–80
self-worth, maternal care and self-care 47–9
services used by individuals who experience
    self-harm 221–2
skin
    infection 322
    see also psychic skin
'Social Self' 193
social transgression and self-harm 30–2
Squiggle Foundation 155
stereotypes of self-harm 70–2
supporting self-care 213–15
Sure Start 213
'Suzanne' 163, 164

themes and theoretical frameworks 67–77
theory and practice 13–14
thinking, feeling and acting 119–41
touching and being touched 53–4
'Tracey' 24, 76, 102, 119–41, 192, 193,
    199, 219
transference 170
transgression, self-harm as 210–13
transitional space 171
trauma 16–17
    and dramatic repetition 79–95
'True Self' 145, 157, 195

Author Index

Abram, J. 58, 225
Addley, E. 10, 225
Alvarez, A. 223, 225
American Psychiatric Association 225
Amez, S. 63, 225
Anzieu, D. 59, 225
Arnold, L. 23, 29, 35, 49, 71, 79, 80, 81,
   85, 90, 173, 197, 209, 210, 212,
   217, 218, 221, 225

Bailey, S. 228
Barton, L. 10, 225
Bell, D. 67, 68, 225
Beremudez, J.L. 198, 225
Bick, E. 59, 60, 97, 105, 106, 116, 125,
   129, 174, 193, 194, 225
Bion, W.R. 17, 61, 72, 83, 88, 128, 136,
   192, 193, 225
Bollas, C. 15, 69, 195, 225
Botero, H. 63, 225
Bourdieu. P. 120, 204, 225
Brentano 67
Breuer, J. 74, 227
Briggs, S. 41, 60, 174, 225
Broad, B. 18, 190, 230
Brown, I. 7
Buckroyd, J. 7, 102, 225, 226
Bullowa, M. 231
Burr, V. 188, 226

Carroll, R. 7, 219, 226
Casement, P. 69, 104, 226
Chasseguet-Smirgel, J. 68, 226
Cobb 67
Collins, D. 187–8, 209, 226
Cooper, M. 200, 229
Crossley, N. 69, 226
Crump, A. 7

Damasio, A. 198, 226
Davis, M. 232, 233

Daw, D. 155
Denzin, N.K. 202, 226
Dersen, J. 227
Diamond, N. 7, 199, 226
Dubinsky, A. 230
Dubinsky, H. 230

Edelman, G. 198, 226
Eliot, T.S. 14, 181
Elliott, A. 69, 226
Epston, D. 214, 232
Evans, C. 14, 228

Fanning, A. 7
Favazza, A. 9, 30, 70, 71, 72, 226
Feldman, M. 14, 226
Field, N. 172, 226
Field, T.M. 40, 226
Fitzsimmons, J. 7
Fonagy, P. 17, 124, 125, 170, 189, 213,
   226, 227
Foucault, M. 18, 227
Fox, N. 203, 227
Freud, S. 59, 74, 132, 199, 227
Frosh, S. 69, 226

Gardner, F. 15, 71, 79, 82, 95, 187, 219,
   223, 227
Garland, C. 17, 102, 122, 227
Giovacchini, P.L. 108, 109, 210, 227
Glaser, B.G. 24, 227
Greenspan, G. 14, 227

Harvey, D. 19, 227
Hazlehurst, M. 18, 231
Heidegger, M. 67, 69, 227
Heimann, P. 171, 227
Hope, N. 7
Hopkins, J. 40, 227
Husserl, E. 67

Janacek, G. 228
Joseph, B. 227

Kahan, J. 14, 229
Keene, J. 209, 228
Keil, F. 231
Keleman, S. 172, 228
Kertay, L. 203, 228
Klein, M. 46, 47, 48, 53, 71, 83, 132, 205, 217, 228
Kohut, H. 136, 228
Krystal, H. 49, 50, 86, 143, 228

Lacan, J. 69, 228
Lacey, J. 14, 228
Leask, P. 7
Lesser, R.C. 70, 228
Levinas, E. 73, 228
Likierman, M. 7, 48, 104, 228
Loewenthal, D. 7, 70, 231
Ludington-Hoe, S. 40, 228

McDougall, J. 196, 228
Maffei, C. 227
Marsh, J. 7
Marshall, I. 200, 228
May, A. 7
Merleau-Ponty, M. 69, 228
Miller, L. 42, 53, 160, 228
Minz, I. 196
Modell, A.H. 193, 229
Mollon, P. 136, 214, 229
Moran, D. 67, 229

Nguyen, N. 228

Ogden, T. 69, 125, 147, 170, 171, 229
Olds, D. 200, 229
Orbach, S. 75, 91, 92, 229

Pally, R. 198, 229
Parker, I. 70, 229
Pattison, E. 14, 229
Pembroke, L. 29, 71, 229
Pert, C. 17, 229
Phillips, Adam 18, 72, 189, 229
Phillips, Asha 7, 63, 229

Pines, D. 59, 229
Potter, J. 70, 229

Reid, S. 41, 230
Rhode, E. 128, 230
Rhode, M. 230
Richards, Barbara 215–16, 230
Richards, Barry 30, 185, 230
Richards, V. 7, 144, 230
Riviere, S. 203, 228
Rochat, P. 231
Rodman, F. 73, 230
Rosen, P. 14, 232
Rowling, J.K. 112, 230
Rustin, Margaret 14, 112, 113, 192, 203, 223, 228, 230
Rustin, Michael 7, 14, 41, 112, 113, 192, 203, 223, 228, 230
Ryan, J. 7
Ryle, A. 220, 230

Samuel, S. 14, 227
Sartre, J-P. 68
Satyshur, R. 228
Saunders, L. 18, 190, 230
Schafer, R. 70, 92, 155, 156, 204, 230
Schore, A. 17, 41, 50, 198, 199, 200, 230, 231
Scott, A. 62, 231
Seigal, C. 7
Sewell, K. 7
Shepherd, R. 232, 233
Shipton, G. 229
Shuttleworth, J. 53, 160, 228
Sifneos, P.E. 67, 231
Sinason, V. 231
Sokolowski, R. 68, 231
Sorenson, P. 65, 231
Spitz, R. 40, 86, 231
Stein, M. 18, 190, 191, 231
Stern, D.N. 46, 48, 69, 134, 231
Strauss, A. 24, 227
Strong, M. 72, 231
Sufian, J. 7, 18, 231
Sulloway, F.J. 199, 231

Swift, L. 228
Swinth, J. 228

Tantam, D. 220, 231
Target, M. 124, 125, 227
Taylor, M. 70, 231
Trevarthen, C. 48, 69, 231
Turp, M. 18, 19, 21, 36, 37, 40, 42, 60,
    86, 90, 102, 120, 121, 156, 157,
    172, 184, 195, 196, 200, 203, 205,
    215, 231, 232
Tustin, F. 223, 232

Walsh, B. 14, 232
Welldon, E.V. 14, 92, 187, 188, 232
White, M. 214, 232
Whittaker, J. 220, 231
Wilde, O. 203, 204
Wilson, R. 196, 231
Winnicott, C. 232, 233
Winnicott, D.W. 16, 19, 22, 39, 49, 53, 56,
    58, 59, 61, 65, 72, 73, 91, 92, 94,
    102, 119, 132, 135, 136, 144, 145,
    147, 155, 157, 159, 160, 167, 174,
    232, 184, 188, 193, 195, 196, 197,
    200, 201, 202, 233
Wise, M. 14, 71, 233

Yin, R. 70, 233

Zalidis, S. 108, 109, 233
Zohar, D. 200, 228